Frommer's®

Maui

METRIC CONVERSIONS

TEMPERATURE

110°F	
100°F	40°C
90°F	
80°F	30°C
70°F	
60°F	20°C
50°F	10°C
40°F	
32°F	0°C
20°F	
10°F	-10°C
0°F	-18°C
-10°F	
-20°F	-30°C

To convert F to C:
subtract 32 and multiply
by 5/9 (.555)

To convert C to F:
multiply by 1.8
and add 32

32°F = 0°C

DISTANCE

To convert	multiply by
inches to centimeters	2.54
centimeters to inches	.39
feet to meters	.30
meters to feet	3.28
yards to meters	.91
meters to yards	1.09
miles to kilometers	1.61
kilometers to miles	.62

1 mi = 1.6 km	1 km = .62 km
1 ft = .30 m	1 m = 3.3 ft

LIQUID VOLUME

To convert	multiply by
U.S. gallons to liters	3.8
Liters to U.S. gallons	.26
U.S. gallons to imperial gallons	.83
Imperial gallons to U.S. gallons	1.20
Imperial gallons to liters	4.55
Liters to imperial gallons	.22

1 liter = .26 U.S. gallon
1 U.S. gallon = 3.8 liter

WEIGHT

To convert	multiply by
Ounces to grams	28.35
Grams to ounces	.035
Pounds to kilograms	.45
Kilograms to pounds	2.20

1 ounce = 28 gr	1 gr = .04 ounce
1 lb = .4555 kg	1 kg = 2.2 lb

ISBN 0-7645-9884-8

5 1 0 9 9

9 780764 598845

Frommer's®

PORTABLE
Maui

4th Edition

by Jeanette Foster

Here's what critics say about Frommer's:

"Amazingly easy to use. Very portable, very complete."
—*Booklist*

"Detailed, accurate, and easy-to-read information for all price ranges."
—*Glamour Magazine*

WILEY

Wiley Publishing, Inc.

Published by:

WILEY PUBLISHING, INC.
111 River St.
Hoboken, NJ 07030-5774

ISBN-13: 978-0-7645-9884-5
ISBN-10: 0-7645-9884-8

Editor: Christine Ryan
Production Editor: Eric T. Schroeder
Photo Editor: Richard Fox
Cartographer: Tim Lohnes
Production by Wiley Indianapolis Composition Services

For information on our other products and services or to obtain technical
support, please contact our Customer Care Department within the U.S. at
800/762-2974, outside the U.S. at 317/572-3993 or fax 317/572-4002.

Wiley also publishes its books in a variety of electronic formats. Some con-
tent that appears in print may not be available in electronic formats.

Manufactured in the United States of America

5   4   3   2   1

Contents

List of Maps

ABOUT THE AUTHOR

A resident of the Big Island, **Jeanette Foster** has skied the slopes of Mauna Kea—during a Fourth of July ski meet, no less—and gone scuba diving with manta rays off the Kona Coast. A prolific writer widely published in travel, sports, and adventure magazines, she's also a contributing editor to *Hawaii* magazine and the editor of *Zagat's Survey to Hawaii's Top Restaurants*. In addition to this guide, Jeanette is the author of *Frommer's Hawaii, Frommer's Maui, Frommer's Honolulu, Waikiki & Oahu, Frommer's Hawaii with Kids,* and *Frommer's Hawaii from $80 a Day.*

AN INVITATION TO THE READER

In researching this book, we discovered many wonderful places—hotels, restaurants, shops, and more. We're sure you'll find others. Please tell us about them, so we can share the information with your fellow travelers in upcoming editions. If you were disappointed with a recommendation, we'd love to know that, too. Please write to:

Frommer's Portable Maui, 4th Edition

Wiley Publishing, Inc. • 111 River St. • Hoboken, NJ 07030-5774

AN ADDITIONAL NOTE

Please be advised that travel information is subject to change at any time—and this is especially true of prices. We therefore suggest that you write or call ahead for confirmation when making your travel plans. The authors, editors, and publisher cannot be held responsible for the experiences of readers while traveling. Your safety is important to us, however, so we encourage you to stay alert and be aware of your surroundings. Keep a close eye on cameras, purses, and wallets, all favorite targets of thieves and pickpockets.

FROMMER'S STAR RATINGS, ICONS & ABBREVIATIONS

Every hotel, restaurant, and attraction listing in this guide has been ranked for quality, value, service, amenities, and special features using a **star-rating system.** In country, state, and regional guides, we also rate towns and regions to help you narrow down your choices and budget your time accordingly. Hotels and restaurants are rated on a scale of zero (recommended) to three stars (exceptional). Attractions, shopping, nightlife, towns, and regions are rated according to the following scale: zero stars (recommended), one star (highly recommended), two stars (very highly recommended), and three stars (must-see).

In addition to the star-rating system, we also use **seven feature icons** that point you to the great deals, in-the-know advice, and unique experiences that separate travelers from tourists. Throughout the book, look for:

Finds	Special finds—those places only insiders know about
Fun Fact	Fun facts—details that make travelers more informed and their trips more fun
Kids	Best bets for kids—advice for the whole family
Moments	Special moments—those experiences that memories are made of
Overrated	Places or experiences not worth your time or money
Tips	Insider tips— great ways to save time and money
Value	Great values—where to get the best deals

The following **abbreviations** are used for credit cards:

AE	American Express	DISC	Discover	V	Visa
DC	Diners Club	MC	MasterCard		

FROMMERS.COM

Now that you have the guidebook to a great trip, visit our website at **www.frommers.com** for travel information on more than 3,000 destinations. With features updated regularly, we give you instant access to the most current trip-planning information available. At Frommers.com, you'll also find the best prices on airfares, accommodations, and car rentals—and you can even book travel online through our travel booking partners. At Frommers.com, you'll also find the following:

- Online updates to our most popular guidebooks
- Vacation sweepstakes and contest giveaways
- Newsletter highlighting the hottest travel trends
- Online travel message boards with featured travel discussions

Maui, the Valley Isle

Maui, also called the Valley Isle, is just a small dot in the vast Pacific Ocean, but it has the potential to offer visitors unforgettable experiences: floating weightless through rainbows of tropical fish, standing atop a 10,000-foot volcano watching the sun come up, listening to the raindrops in a bamboo forest.

Whether you want to experience the "real" Hawaii, go on a heart-pounding adventure, or simply relax on the beach, this book is designed to help you create the vacation of your dreams.

In the pages that follow, we've compiled everything you need to know to plan your ideal trip to Maui: information on airlines, seasons, a calendar of events, how to make camping reservations, and much more.

1 The Island in Brief

CENTRAL MAUI

Maui's main airport lies in this flat, often windy corridor between Maui's two volcanoes, and this is where the majority of the island's population lives. You'll find good shopping and dining bargains here but very little in the way of accommodations.

KAHULUI This is "Dream City," home to thousands of former sugar-cane workers who dreamed of owning their own homes away from the plantations. A couple of small hotels located just 2 miles from the airport are convenient for 1-night stays if you have a late arrival or early departure, but this is not a place to spend your vacation.

WAILUKU With its faded wooden storefronts, old plantation homes, and shops straight out of the 1940s, Wailuku is like a time capsule. Although most people race through on their way to see the natural beauty of **Iao Valley** ⍟, this quaint little town is worth a brief visit, if only to see a real place where real people actually appear to be working at something other than a suntan. Beaches surrounding Wailuku are not great for swimming, but the old town has a spectacular view of Haleakala, a couple of hostels and an excellent

Maui

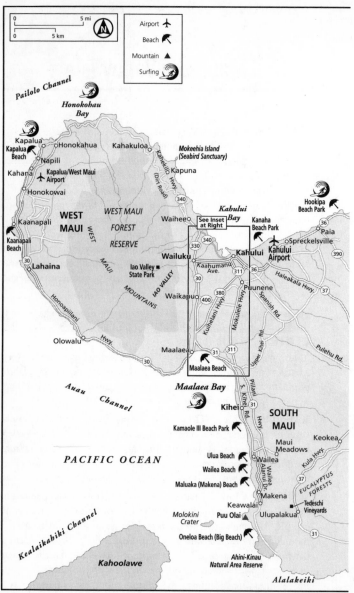

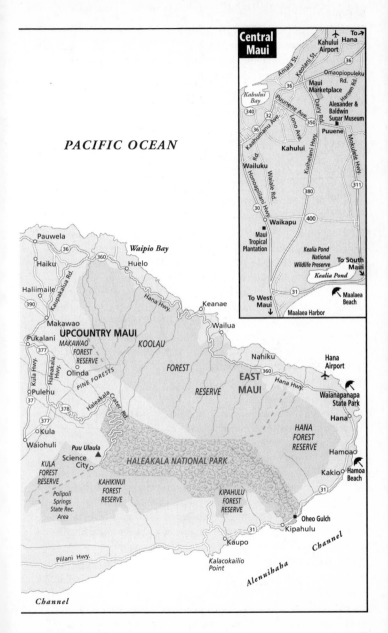

PACIFIC OCEAN

Central Maui

Kahului Airport

To Hana

Amala St.
Keolani St.
36
Omaopiopuleku Rd.
Maui Marketplace
Puunene Ave.
Dairy Rd.
Hansen Rd.
Kahului Bay
340
32
36
Alexander & Baldwin Sugar Museum
350
Puuene
Kaahumanu Ave.
Lono Ave.
Kuihelani Hwy.
Mokulele Hwy.
Kahului
Wailuku
Waiale Rd.
311
Honoapiilani Hwy.
30
380
Waikapu
400
Maui Tropical Plantation
Kealia Pond National Wildlife Preserve
To South Maui
Kealia Pond
To West Maui
31
Maalaea Beach
Maalaea Harbor

Pauwela
36
Waipio Bay
Haiku
360
Huelo
Haliimaile
390
Kaupakalua Rd.
Hana Hwy.
Keanae
Makawao
UPCOUNTRY MAUI
KOOLAU
Wailua
Pukalani
377
MAKAWAO FOREST RESERVE
FOREST
Nahiku
360
Hana Airport
Kula Hwy.
Haleakala Hwy.
Olinda
PINE FORESTS
RESERVE
EAST MAUI
Hana Hwy.
Waianapanapa State Park
Pulehu
37
Haleakala Crater Rd.
Hana
378
HANA FOREST RESERVE
377
Kula
Puu Ulaula
Science City
HALEAKALA NATIONAL PARK
Hamoao
Waiohuli
KULA FOREST RESERVE
KAHIKINUI FOREST RESERVE
Kakio
Hamoa Beach
Polipoli Springs State Rec. Area
KIPAHULU FOREST RESERVE
31
Piilani Hwy.
Oheo Gulch
Kipahulu
Kaupo
Kalacokailio Point
31
Alenuihaha
Channel
Channel

3

historic B&B, great budget restaurants, a tofu factory, some interesting bungalow architecture, a Frank Lloyd Wright building on the outskirts of town, and the always-endearing Bailey House Museum.

WEST MAUI

This is the fabled Maui you see on postcards. Jagged peaks, green valleys, a wilderness full of native species—the majestic West Maui Mountains are the epitome of earthly paradise. The beaches here are some of the islands' best. And it's no secret: This stretch of coastline along Maui's "forehead," from Kapalua to the historic port of Lahaina, is the island's most bustling resort area. Expect a few mainland-style traffic jams.

Starting at the southern end of West Maui and moving northward, the coastal communities are as listed below.

LAHAINA 🏝 This old whaling seaport teems with restaurants, T-shirt shops, and a gallery on nearly every block, but there's still lots of real history to be found amid the tourist development. The town is a great base for visitors: A few old hotels (like the newly restored 1901 Pioneer Inn on the harbor), quaint B&Bs, and a handful of oceanfront condos offer a variety of choices, most within walking distance to the beach as well as town. This is the place to stay if you want to be in the center of things—oodles of restaurants, shops, and nightlife—but note that the town is rather congested and doesn't have enough parking.

KAANAPALI 🏝🏝 Farther north along the West Maui coast is Hawaii's first master-planned resort. Pricey midrise hotels, which line nearly 3 miles of lovely gold-sand beach, are linked by a landscaped parkway and separated by a jungle of plants. Golf greens wrap around the slope between beachfront and hillside properties. **Whalers Village** (a seaside mall with such fancy names as Tiffany and Louis Vuitton, plus the best little whale museum in Hawaii) and other restaurants are easy to reach on foot along the waterfront walkway or via resort shuttle, which also serves the small West Maui airport just to the north. Shuttles also go to Lahaina, 3 miles to the south, for shopping, dining, entertainment, and boat tours. Kaanapali is popular with convention groups and families.

FROM HONOKOWAI TO NAPILI In the building binge of the 1970s, condominiums sprouted along this gorgeous coastline like mushrooms after a rain. Today, these older oceanside units offer excellent bargains. The great location—along sandy beaches, within minutes of both the Kapalua and the Kaanapali resort areas, and close to the goings-on in Lahaina town—makes this area a great place to stay for value-conscious travelers. It feels more peaceful and residential than either Kaanapali or Lahaina.

In **Honokowai** and **Mahinahina,** you'll find mostly older units that tend to be cheaper; there's not much shopping here aside from convenience stores, but you'll have easy access to the shops and restaurants of Kaanapali.

Kahana is a little more upscale than Honokowai and Mahinahina. Most of the condos here are big high-rise types, built more recently than those immediately to the south. You'll find a nice selection of shops and restaurants in the area, and Kapalua–West Maui Airport is nearby.

Napili is a much-sought-after area for condo seekers: It's quiet; has great beaches, restaurants, and shops; and is close to Kapalua. Units are generally more expensive here (although we've found a few hidden gems at affordable prices; see the Napili Bay entry on p. 52).

KAPALUA ✿   North beyond Kaanapali and the shopping centers of Napili and Kahana, the road starts to climb, and the vista opens up to fields of silver-green pineapple and manicured golf fairways. Turn down the country lane of Pacific pines toward the sea, and you could only be in Kapalua. It's the very exclusive domain of two gracious and expensive hotels, set on one of Hawaii's best gold-sand beaches, next to two bays that are marine-life preserves (with fabulous surfing in winter).

Even if you don't stay here, you're welcome to come and enjoy Kapalua. Both of the fancy hotels provide public parking and beach access. The resort champions innovative environmental programs; it also has an art school, a golf school, three golf courses, historic features, a collection of swanky condos and homes, and wide-open spaces that include a rainforest preserve—all open to the general public. Kapalua is a great place to stay put. However, if you plan to "tour" Maui, know that it's a long drive from here to get to many of the island's highlights.

SOUTH MAUI

This is the hottest, sunniest, driest coastline on Maui, and the most popular one for sun worshipers—Arizona by the sea. Rain rarely falls, and temperatures stick around 85°F (29°C) year-round. On former scrubland from Maalaea to Makena are now four distinct areas—Maalaea, Kihei, Wailea, and Makena—and a surprising amount of traffic.

MAALAEA   If the western part of Maui is a head, Maalaea is just under the chin. This oceanfront village centers on the small boat harbor (with a general store, a couple of restaurants, and a huge new mall) and the **Maui Ocean Center** ⊛, an aquarium/ocean complex. This quaint region offers several condominium units to choose among, but visitors staying here should be aware that it is almost always very windy.

KIHEI   Kihei is less a proper town than a nearly continuous series of condos and minimalls lining South Kihei Road. This is Maui's best vacation bargain: Budget travelers flock to the eight sandy beaches along this scalloped, condo-packed, 7-mile stretch of coast. Kihei is neither charming nor quaint, but it does offer sunshine, affordability, and convenience. If you want latte in the morning, fine beaches in the afternoon, and Hawaii Regional Cuisine in the evening, all at budget prices, head to Kihei.

WAILEA ⊛   Only 2½ decades ago, this was wall-to-wall scrub kiawe trees, but now Wailea is a manicured oasis of multimillion-dollar resort hotels strung along 2 miles of palm-fringed gold coast. Today you'll find warm, clear water full of tropical fish; year-round sunshine and clear blue skies; and hedonistic pleasure palaces on 1,500 acres of black-lava shore. Amazing what a billion dollars can do.

This is the playground of the stretch-limo set. The planned resort development has a shopping village, three prized golf courses of its own and three more in close range, and a tennis complex. A growing number of large homes sprawls over the upper hillside (some offering excellent bed-and-breakfast units at reasonable prices). The resorts along this fantasy coast are spectacular, to say the least.

Appealing natural features include the coastal trail, a 3-mile round-trip path along the oceanfront with pleasing views everywhere you look. The trail's south end borders an extensive garden of native coastal plants, as well as ancient lava-rock house ruins juxtaposed with elegant oceanfront condos. But the chief attractions, of course, are those five outstanding beaches (the best is Wailea).

MAKENA ⊛   After passing through well-groomed Wailea, suddenly the road enters raw wilderness. Although beautiful, Makena is an end-of-the-road kind of place: It's a long drive from here to anywhere on Maui, so if you want to tour a lot of the island, you might want to book somewhere else. But if you crave a quiet, relaxing respite, where the biggest trip of the day is from your bed to the pristine beach, Makena is your place.

Beyond Makena you'll discover Haleakala's last lava flow, which ran to the sea in 1790; the bay named for French explorer La Perouse; and a chunky lava trail known as the King's Highway, which leads around Maui's empty south shore past ruins and fish camps. Puu Olai stands like Maui's Diamond Head on the shore, where a sunken crater shelters tropical fish and empty golden-sand beaches stand at the end of dirt roads.

UPCOUNTRY MAUI

After a few days at the beach, you'll probably take notice of the 10,000-foot mountain in the middle of Maui. The slopes of Haleakala ("House of the Sun") are home to cowboys, farmers, and other country people. They're all up here enjoying the crisp air, emerald pastures, eucalyptus, and flower farms of this tropical Olympus; there's even a misty California redwood grove. Houses old and new are strung along a road that runs from Makawao, an old *paniolo*-turned–New Age village, to Kula, where the road leads up to the crater and **Haleakala National Park** ☆☆☆. The rumpled, two-lane blacktop of Highway 37 narrows on the other side of Tedeschi Winery, where wine grapes and wild elk flourish on the Ulupalakua Ranch, the biggest on Maui. A stay upcountry is usually affordable, a chance to commune with nature, and a nice contrast to the sizzling beaches and busy resorts below.

MAKAWAO ☆ Until recently, this small, two-street upcountry town consisted of little more than a post office, gas station, feed store, bakery, and restaurant/bar serving the cowboys and farmers living in the surrounding community; the hitching posts outside storefronts were really used to tie up horses. As the population of Maui started expanding in the 1970s, a health-food store popped up, followed by boutiques, a chiropractic clinic, and a host of health-conscious restaurants. The result is an eclectic amalgam of old *paniolo* Hawaii and the baby-boomer trends of transplanted mainlanders. **Hui No'eau Visual Arts Center,** Hawaii's premier arts collective, is definitely worth a peek. The only accommodations here are reasonably priced bed-and-breakfasts, perfect for those who enjoy great views and don't mind slightly chilly nights.

KULA ☆ A feeling of pastoral remoteness prevails in this upcountry community of old flower farms; humble cottages; and new suburban ranch houses with million-dollar views that take in the ocean, isthmus, West Maui Mountains, Lanai, and Kahoolawe off in the distance. At night, the lights run along the gold coast like a string of pearls, from Maalaea to Puu Olai. Kula sits at a cool 3,000 feet, just below the cloud line, and from here, a winding road snakes its way up to Haleakala National Park. Everyone here grows something—Maui onions; carnations; orchids; and proteas, those strange-looking blossoms that look like *Star Trek* props. The local B&Bs cater to guests seeking cool tropical nights, panoramic views, and a rural upland escape. Here, you'll find the true peace and quiet that only rural farming country can offer—yet you're still just 30 to 40 minutes away from the beach and an hour's drive from Lahaina.

EAST MAUI

THE ROAD TO HANA ★★   When old sugar towns die, they usually fade away in rust and red dirt. Not **Paia.** The tangle of electrical, phone, and cable wires hanging overhead symbolizes the town's ability to adapt to the times; it may look messy, but it works. Here, trendy restaurants, eclectic boutiques, and high-tech windsurf shops stand next door to the ma-and-pa grocery, fish market, and storefronts that have been serving customers since the plantation days. Hippies took over in the 1970s; although their macrobiotic restaurants and old-style artists' co-op have made way for Hawaii Regional Cuisine and galleries featuring the works of renowned international artists, Paia still manages to maintain a pleasant vibe of hippiedom. The town's main attraction, though, is **Hookipa Beach Park,** where the wind that roars through the isthmus of Maui brings windsurfers from around the world, who come to fly over the waves on gossamer wings linked to surfboards.

Ten minutes down the road from Paia and up the hill from the Hana Highway—the connector road to the entire east side of Maui—sits **Haiku.** Once a pineapple-plantation village, complete with cannery (today a shopping complex), Haiku offers vacation rentals and B&Bs in a quiet, pastoral setting: the perfect base for those who want to get off the beaten path and experience a quieter side of Maui but don't want to feel too removed (the beach is only 10 min. away).

About 15 to 20 minutes past Haiku is the largely unknown community of **Huelo.** Every day, thousands of cars whiz by on the road to Hana. But if you take the time to stop, you'll discover a hidden Hawaii, where Mother Nature is still sensual and wild, where ocean waves pummel soaring lava cliffs, and where serenity prevails. Huelo is not for everyone, but if you want the magic of a place still largely untouched by "progress," check into a B&B or vacation rental here.

HANA ★★   Set between an emerald rainforest and the blue Pacific is a village probably best defined by what it lacks: golf courses, shopping malls, and McDonald's. Except for two gas stations and a bank with an ATM, you'll find little of what passes for progress here. Instead, you'll discover fragrant tropical flowers, the sweet taste of backyard bananas and papayas, and the easy calm and unabashed small-town aloha spirit of old Hawaii. What saved "Heavenly" Hana from the inevitable march of progress? The 52-mile **Hana Highway,** which winds around 600 curves and crosses more than 50 one-lane bridges on its way from Kahului. You can go to Hana for the day—it's a 3-hour drive (and a half century away)—but 3 days are better. The tiny town has one hotel, a handful of great B&Bs, and some spectacular vacation rentals (where else can you stay in a tropical cabin in a rainforest?).

2 Visitor Information

For advance information on traveling in Maui, contact the **Maui Visitors Bureau,** 1727 Wili Pa Loop, Wailuku, Maui, HI 96793 (© **800/525-MAUI** or 808/244-3530; fax 808/244-1337; www.visit maui.com).

The **Kaanapali Beach Resort Association** is at 2530 Kekaa Dr., Suite 1-B, Lahaina, HI 96761 (© **800/245-9229** or 808/661-3271; fax 808/661-9431; www.maui.net/~kbra).

The state agency responsible for tourism is the **Hawaii Visitors and Convention Bureau (HVCB),** Suite 801, Waikiki Business Plaza, 2270 Kalakaua Ave., Honolulu, HI 96815 (© **800/GO-HAWAII** or 808/923-1811; www.gohawaii.com).

If you want information about working and living in Maui, contact **Maui Chamber of Commerce,** 250 Alamaha St., Unit N-16A, Kahului, HI 96732 (© **808/871-7711;** www.mauichamber.com).

INFORMATION ON MAUI'S PARKS

NATIONAL PARKS   Both Maui and Molokai have one national park each: **Haleakala National Park,** P.O. Box 369, Makawao, HI 96768 (© **808/572-4400;** www.nps.gov/hale); and **Kalaupapa National Historical Park,** P.O. Box 2222, Kalaupapa, HI 96742 (© **808/567-6802;** www.nps.gov/kala). For more information, see "Hiking" in chapter 5.

STATE PARKS   To find out more about state parks on Maui and Molokai, contact the **Hawaii State Department of Land and Natural Resources,** 54 S. High St., Wailuku, HI 96793 (© **808/984-8109;** www.hawaii.gov), which provides information on hiking and camping, and will send you free topographic trail maps on request.

3 Money

ATMs

Hawaii pioneered the use of **ATMs** more than 2 decades ago, and now they're everywhere. You'll find them at most banks, in supermarkets, at Long's Drugs, and in most resorts and shopping centers. **Cirrus** (© 800/424-7787; www.mastercard.com) and **PLUS** (© 800/843-7587; www.visa.com) are the two most popular networks; check the back of your ATM card to see which network your bank belongs to (most banks belong to both these days).

TRAVELER'S CHECKS

Traveler's checks are something of an anachronism from the days before the ATM made cash accessible at any time. Traveler's checks used to be the only sound alternative to traveling with dangerously large amounts of cash. They were as reliable as currency but, unlike cash, could be replaced if lost or stolen.

These days, traveler's checks are less necessary because most cities have 24-hour ATMs that allow you to withdraw small amounts of cash as needed. However, keep in mind that you will likely be charged an ATM withdrawal fee if the bank is not your own, so if you're withdrawing money every day, you might be better off with traveler's checks—provided that you don't mind showing identification every time you want to cash one.

You can get traveler's checks at almost any bank. **American Express** offers denominations of $20, $50, $100, $500, and (for cardholders only) $1,000. You'll pay a service charge ranging from 1% to 4%. You can also get American Express traveler's checks over the phone by calling © 800/221-7282; Amex gold- and platinum-card holders who use this number are exempt from the 1% fee.

Visa offers traveler's checks at Citibank locations nationwide, as well as at several other banks. The service charge ranges between 1.5% and 2%; checks come in denominations of $20, $50, $100, $500, and $1,000. Call © 800/732-1322 for information. AAA members can obtain Visa checks for a $9.95 fee (for checks up to $1,500) at most AAA offices or by calling © 866/339-3378. **MasterCard** also offers traveler's checks. Call © 800/223-9920 for a location near you.

If you choose to carry traveler's checks, be sure to keep a record of their serial numbers separate from your checks in the event that they are stolen or lost. You'll get a refund faster if you know the numbers.

CREDIT CARDS

Credit cards are accepted all over the island. They're a safe way to carry money, and they provide a convenient record of all your expenses. You can also withdraw cash advances from your credit cards at banks or ATMs, provided you know your PIN. If you don't know yours, call the number on the back of your credit card and ask the bank to send it to you. It usually takes 5 to 7 business days, though some banks will provide the number over the phone if you tell them your mother's maiden name or some other personal information. Still, be sure to keep some cash on hand for that rare occasion when a restaurant or small shop doesn't take plastic.

4 When to Go

Most visitors don't come to Maui when the weather's best in the islands; rather, they come when it's at its worst everywhere else. Thus, the **high season**—when prices are up and resorts are booked to capacity—generally runs from mid-December through March or mid-April. The last 2 weeks of December in particular are the prime time for travel to Maui; if you're planning a holiday trip, make your reservations as early as possible; count on holiday crowds; and expect to pay top dollar for accommodations, car rentals, and airfare. Whale-watching season begins in January and continues through the rest of winter, sometimes lasting into May.

The **off seasons,** when the best bargain rates are available, are spring (from mid-Apr to mid-June) and fall (from Sept to mid-Dec)—a paradox, because these are the best seasons in terms of reliably great weather. If you're looking to save money, or if you just want to avoid the crowds, this is the time to visit. Hotel rates tend to be significantly lower during these off seasons. Airfares also tend to be lower—again, sometimes substantially—and good packages and special deals are often available.

Note: If you plan to come to Maui between the last week in April and mid-May, be sure to book your accommodations, interisland air reservations, and car rental in advance. In Japan, the last week of April is called **Golden Week,** because three Japanese holidays take place one after the other; the islands are especially busy with Japanese tourists during this time.

Due to the large number of families traveling in **summer** (June–Aug), you won't get the fantastic bargains of spring and fall. However, you'll still do much better on packages, airfare, and accommodations than you will in the winter months.

THE WEATHER

Because Maui lies at the edge of the tropical zone, it technically has only two seasons, both of them warm. The dry season corresponds to summer, and the rainy season generally runs during the winter from November to March. It rains every day somewhere in the islands at any time of the year, but the rainy season can cause "gray" weather and spoil your tanning opportunities. Fortunately, it seldom rains for more than 3 days straight, and rainy days often just consist of a mix of clouds and sun, with very brief showers.

The **year-round temperature** usually varies no more than 15°F (9°C), but it depends on where you are. Maui is like a ship in that it has leeward and windward sides. The **leeward** sides (the west and south) are usually hot and dry, whereas the **windward** sides (east and north) are generally cooler and moist. If you want arid, sunbaked, desertlike weather, go leeward. If you want lush, often wet, junglelike weather, go windward. Your best bets for total year-round sun are the Kihei-Wailea and Lahaina-Kapalua coasts.

Maui is also full of **microclimates,** thanks to its interior valleys, coastal plains, and mountain peaks. If you travel into the mountains, it can change from summer to winter in a matter of hours, because it's cooler the higher up you go. In other words, if the weather doesn't suit you, go to the other side of the island—or head into the hills.

HOLIDAYS

When Hawaii observes holidays, especially those over a long weekend, travel among the islands increases, interisland airline seats are fully booked, rental cars are at a premium, and hotels and restaurants are busier than usual.

Federal, state, and county government offices are closed on all federal holidays: January 1 (New Year's Day), third Monday in January (Martin Luther King Jr. Day), third Monday in February (Presidents' Day), last Monday in May (Memorial Day), July 4 (Independence Day), first Monday in September (Labor Day), second Monday in October (Columbus Day), November 11 (Veterans' Day), fourth Thursday in November (Thanksgiving Day), and December 25 (Christmas).

State and county offices also are closed on local holidays, including Prince Kuhio Day (Mar 26), honoring the birthday of Hawaii's first delegate to the U.S. Congress; King Kamehameha Day (June 11), a statewide holiday commemorating Kamehameha the Great, who united the islands and ruled from 1795 to 1819;

and Admission Day (3rd Fri in Aug), which honors Hawaii's admission as the 50th state in the United States on August 21, 1959.

MAUI CALENDAR OF EVENTS

As with any schedule of upcoming events, the following information is subject to change; always confirm the details before you plan your schedule around an event. For a complete and up-to-date list of events throughout Maui, Molokai, and Lanai, point your browser to **www.visitmaui.com** or **www. calendarmaui.com**.

January

PGA Kapalua Mercedes Championship, Kapalua Resort. Top PGA golfers compete for $1 million. Call ℂ **808/669-2440** or visit www.kapaluamaui.com. Early January.

Chinese New Year, Lahaina. Lahaina town rolls out the red carpet for this important event with a traditional lion dance at the historic Wo Hing Temple on Front Street, accompanied by fireworks, food booths, and a host of activities. Call ℂ **888/310-1117** or 808/667-9175. Also on Market Street in Wailuku; call ℂ **808/270-7414.** January or February.

Hula Bowl Football All-Star Classic, War Memorial Stadium. An annual all-star football classic featuring America's top college players. Call ℂ **808/874-9500** or visit www.hulabowlmaui.com; ticket orders are processed beginning April 1 for the next year's game.

February

Whale Day Celebration, Kalama Park, Kihei. A daylong celebration in the park with a parade of whales, entertainment, a crafts fair, games, and food. Call ℂ **808/249-8811** or visit www.visitmaui.com. Mid-February.

March

Ocean Arts Festival, Lahaina. The entire town of Lahaina celebrates the annual migration of Pacific humpback whales with an Ocean Arts Festival in Banyan Tree Park. Artists display their best ocean-themed art for sale, and Hawaiian musicians and hula troupes entertain. Enjoy marine-related activities, games, and a Creature Feature touch-pool exhibit for children. Call ℂ **888/310-1117** or 808/667-9194, or visit www.visitlahaina.com. Mid-March.

Run to the Sun, Paia to Haleakala. The world's top ultramarathoners make the journey from sea level to the top of 10,000-foot Haleakala, some 37 miles. Call ℂ **808/891-2516** or visit www.virr.com. Late March.

East Maui Taro Festival, Hana. Here's your chance to taste taro in many different forms, from poi to chips. Also on hand are Hawaiian exhibits, demonstrations, and food booths. Call © **808/248-8972** or visit www.calendarmaui.com. Generally the end of March or early April.

April

Buddha Day, Lahaina Jodo Mission, Lahaina. Each year this historic mission holds a flower-festival pageant honoring the birth of Buddha. Call © **808/661-4303** or visit www.calendarmaui.com. First Saturday in April.

Annual Ritz-Carlton Kapalua Celebration of the Arts, Ritz-Carlton Kapalua. Contemporary and traditional artists give free hands-on lessons. Call © **808/669-6200** or visit www.celebration ofthearts.org. The 4-day festival begins the Thursday before Easter.

That Ulupalakua Thing! Maui County Agricultural Trade Show and Sampling, Ulupalakua Ranch and Tedeschi Winery, Ulupalakua. The name may be long and cumbersome, but this event is hot, hot, hot. It features local-product exhibits, food booths, and live entertainment. Call © **808/878-2839** or visit www.ulupalakuathing.com. Late April.

May

Outrigger Canoe Season, all islands. From May to September nearly every weekend, canoe paddlers across the state participate in outrigger canoe races. Call © **808/261-6615** or visit www.y2k anu.com for this year's schedule of events.

Annual Lei Day Celebration, Fairmont Kea Lani, Wailea. May Day is Lei Day in Hawaii, celebrated with lei-making contests, pageantry, arts and crafts, and concerts throughout the islands. Call © **808/875-4100** or visit www.visitmaui.com. May 1.

International Festival of Canoes, West Maui. Celebration of the Pacific islands' seafaring heritage. Events include canoe paddling and sailing regattas, a luau feast, cultural arts demonstrations, canoe-building exhibits, and music. Call © **888/310-1117** or visit www.calendarmaui.com. Mid- to late May.

June

King Kamehameha Celebration, statewide. It's a state holiday with a massive floral parade, *hoolaulea* (party), and much more. Call © **888/310-1117** or 808/667-9194, or visit www.visitlahaina. com for Maui events. Early June.

Maui Film Festival, Wailea Resort. Five days and nights of screenings of premieres and special films, along with traditional Hawaiian storytelling, chants, hula, and contemporary music. Call ℂ **808/579-9996** or visit mauifilmfestival.com. The second or third week in June.

Hawaiian Slack-Key Guitar Festival, Maui Arts and Cultural Center, Kahului. Great music performed by the best musicians in Hawaii. It's 5 hours long and absolutely free. Call ℂ **808/239-4336** or visit www.hawaiianslackkeyguitarfestivals.com. Late June.

July

Makawao Parade and Rodeo, Makawao, Maui. The annual parade and rodeo event have been taking place in this upcountry cowboy town for generations. Call ℂ **800/525-MAUI** or 808/572-9565. Early July.

Kapalua Wine and Food Festival, Kapalua. Famous wine and food experts and oenophiles gather at the Ritz-Carlton and Kapalua Bay hotels for formal tastings, panel discussions, and samplings of new releases. Call ℂ **800/KAPALUA** or visit www.kapaluaresort.com.

August

Maui Onion Festival, Whalers Village, Kaanapali, Maui. Everything you ever wanted to know about the sweetest onions in the world. Food, entertainment, tasting, and the Maui Onion Cook-Off. Call ℂ **808/661-4567** or visit www.whalersvillage.com. Early August 5 and 6.

Hawaii State Windsurf Championship, Kanaha Beach Park, Kahului. Top windsurfers compete. Call ℂ **808/877-2111.** August 5, 2006.

September

Aloha Festivals, various locations. Parades and other events celebrate Hawaiian culture. Call ℂ **800/852-7690** or 808/545-1771, or visit www.alohafestivals.com for a schedule of events.

A Taste of Lahaina, Lahaina Civic Center, Maui. Some 30,000 people show up to sample 40 signature entrees of Maui's premier chefs during this weekend festival, which includes cooking demonstrations, wine tastings, and live entertainment. The event begins Friday night with Maui Chefs Present, a themed dinner/cocktail party featuring about a dozen of Maui's best chefs. Call ℂ **888/310-1117** or 808/667-9194, or visit www.visit lahaina.com. Early September.

Maui Marathon, Kahului to Kaanapali, Maui. Runners line up at the Maui Mall before daybreak and head off for Kaanapali. Call ℂ **808/871-6441** or visit www.virr.com. Mid-September.

Maui County Fair, War Memorial Complex, Wailuku. The oldest county fair in Hawaii features a parade, amusement rides, live entertainment, and exhibits. Call ℂ **800/525-MAUI** or 808/244-3530, or visit www.calendarmaui.com. Late September or early October.

October

Aloha Classic World Wavesailing Championship, Hookipa Beach, Maui. The top windsurfers in the world gather for this final event in the Pro Boardsailing World Tour. If you're on Maui, don't miss it—it's spectacular to watch. Call ℂ **808/575-9151.** Depending on the waves and the wind, the championship could be held in October or November.

Halloween in Lahaina, Maui. There are Carnival in Rio, Mardi Gras in New Orleans, and Halloween in Lahaina. Come to this giant costume party (some 20,000 people show up) on the streets of Lahaina; Front Street is closed off for the party. Call ℂ **888/310-1117** or 808/667-9194, or visit www.visitlahaina.com. October 31.

November

Hawaii International Film Festival, various locations on Maui. A cinema festival with a cross-cultural spin, featuring filmmakers from Asia, the Pacific Islands, and the United States. Call ℂ **800/752-8193** or 808/528-FILM, or visit www.hiff.org. Mid-November.

Maui Invitational Basketball Tournament, Lahaina Civic Center, Maui. Top college teams vie in this annual preseason tournament. Call ℂ **312/755-3504.** Usually held around Thanksgiving.

December

Hui Noeau Christmas House, Makawao. The festivities in the beautifully decorated Hui mansion include shopping, workshops and art demonstrations, children's activities and visits with Santa, holiday music, fresh-baked goods, and local foods. Call ℂ **808/572-6560** or visit www. huinoeau.com. Late November and early December.

Festival of Lights, island-wide. Festivities include parades and tree-lighting ceremonies. Call ℂ **808/667-9175** on Maui or 808/567-6361 on Molokai. Early December.

First Light, Maui Arts and Cultural Center, Maui. The Academy of Motion Pictures holds major screenings of top films. Not to be missed. Call ✆ **808/579-9996** or visit www.mauifilmfestival.com. Late December.

5 Travel Insurance

Check your existing insurance policies and credit-card coverage before you buy travel insurance. You may already be covered for lost luggage, canceled tickets, or medical expenses. The cost of travel insurance varies widely, depending on the cost and length of your trip, your age and health, and the type of trip you're taking.

TRIP-CANCELLATION INSURANCE   Trip-cancellation insurance helps you get your money back if you have to back out of a trip, if you have to go home early, or if your travel supplier goes bankrupt. Allowed reasons for cancellation can range from sickness to natural disasters to the State Department declaring your destination unsafe for travel. Insurance policy details vary, so read the fine print—and especially make sure that your airline or cruise line is on the list of carriers covered in case of bankruptcy. For more information, contact one of the following recommended insurers: **Access America** (✆ 800/284-8300; www.accessamerica.com); **Travel Guard International** (✆ 800/826-1300; www.travelguard.com); **Travel Insured International** (✆ 800/243-3174; www.travel insured.com); or **Travelex Insurance Services** (✆ 800/228-9792; www.travelex-insurance.com).

MEDICAL INSURANCE   Most health insurance policies cover you if you get sick away from home—but check, particularly if you're insured by an HMO. If you require additional medical insurance, try **MEDEX Assistance** (✆ **410/453-6300;** www.medexassist.com) or **Travel Assistance International** (✆ **800/821-2828;** www.travel assistance.com); for general information on services, call the company's Worldwide Assistance Services, Inc., at ✆ **800/777-8710.**

6 Specialized Travel Resources

FOR TRAVELERS WITH DISABILITIES

Travelers with disabilities are made to feel very welcome in Maui. Hotels are usually equipped with wheelchair-accessible rooms, and tour companies provide many special services. The **Hawaii Center for Independent Living,** 414 Kauwili St., Suite 102, Honolulu, HI

96817 (© **808/522-5400;** fax 808/586-8129; www.hawaii.gov/health; cpdppp@aloha.net), can provide information and send you a copy of the *Aloha Guide to Accessibility* ($15).

The only travel agency in Hawaii specializing in needs for travelers with disabilities is **Access Aloha Travel** (© **800/480-1143;** wwwaccessalohatravel.com), which can book anything, including rental vans, accommodations, tours, cruises, airfare, and just about anything else you can think of.

The following travel agencies don't specialize in Hawaiian travel, but they offer customized tours and itineraries for travelers with disabilities. **Flying Wheels Travel** (© **507/451-5005;** www.flying wheelstravel.com) offers escorted tours and cruises that emphasize sports and private tours in minivans with lifts. **Access-Able Travel Source** (© **303/232-2979;** www.access-able.com) offers extensive access information and advice for traveling around the world with disabilities. **Accessible Journeys** (© **800/846-4537** or 610/521-0339; www.disabilitytravel.com) caters specifically to slow walkers and wheelchair travelers and to their families and friends.

For travelers with disabilities who wish to do their own driving, hand-controlled cars can be rented from **Avis** (© **800/331-1212;** www.avis.com) and **Hertz** (© **800/654-3131;** www.hertz.com). The number of hand-controlled cars in Hawaii is limited, so be sure to book well in advance. Maui recognizes other states' windshield placards indicating that the driver of the car is disabled, so be sure to bring yours with you.

Vision-impaired travelers who use a Seeing Eye dog need to present documentation that the dog is a trained Seeing Eye dog and has had rabies shots. For more information, contact the **Animal Quarantine Facility** (© **808/483-7171;** www.hawaii.gov).

FOR GAY & LESBIAN TRAVELERS

Known for its acceptance of all groups, Hawaii welcomes gays and lesbians just as it does anybody else. For the latest information on the gay-marriage issue, contact the **Hawaii Marriage Project** (© **808/532-9000**).

Pacific Ocean Holidays, P.O. Box 88245, Honolulu, HI 96830 (© **800/735-6600** or 808/923-2400; www.gayhawaii. com), offers vacation packages that feature gay-owned and gay-friendly lodgings. It also publishes the *Pocket Guide to Hawaii: A Guide for Gay Visitors & Kamaaina,* a list of gay-owned and gay-friendly businesses throughout the islands. Send $5 for a copy (mail order only; no phone orders, please), or access the online version on the website.

The International Gay and Lesbian Travel Association (IGLTA) (© 800/448-8550 or 954/776-2626; www.iglta.org) is the trade association for the gay and lesbian travel industry and offers an online directory of gay- and lesbian-friendly travel businesses; go to its website and click Members.

Out and About (© 800/929-2268 or 415/486-2591; www.out andabout.com) offers a monthly newsletter packed with good information on the global gay and lesbian scene. Its website features links to gay and lesbian tour operators and other gay-themed travel links, plus extensive online travel information to subscribers only. Out and About's guidebooks are available at most major bookstores and through www.adlbooks.com.

FOR SENIORS

Discounts for seniors are available at almost all of Maui's major attractions and occasionally at hotels and restaurants. Always inquire when making hotel reservations and especially when you're buying your airline ticket; most major domestic airlines offer senior discounts.

Members of **AARP** (© 800/424-3410 or 202/434-2277; www. aarp.org) are usually eligible for such discounts. AARP also puts together organized-tour packages at moderate rates.

Some great, low-cost trips to Hawaii are offered to people 55 and older through **Elderhostel,** 75 Federal St., Boston, MA 02110 (© 617/426-8056; www.elderhostel.org), a nonprofit group that arranges travel and study programs around the world. You can obtain a complete catalog of offerings by writing to Elderhostel, P.O. Box 1959, Wakefield, MA 01880-5959.

If you're planning to visit Haleakala National Park, you can save sightseeing dollars if you're 62 or older by picking up a **Golden Age Passport** from any national park, recreation area, or monument. This lifetime pass has a one-time fee of $10 and provides free admission to all of the parks in the system, plus a 50% savings on camping and recreation fees. You can pick one up at any park entrance. Be sure to have proof of your age with you.

FOR FAMILIES

Maui is paradise for children: beaches to frolic on, water to splash in, unusual sights to see, and a host of new foods to taste.

The larger hotels and resorts have supervised programs for children and can refer you to qualified babysitters. You can also contact **People Attentive to Children** (PATCH; ✆ 808/242-9232; www. patch-hi.org), which will refer you to individuals who have taken their training courses on child care.

Baby's Away (✆ **800/942-9030** or 808/875-9093; www.babys away.com) rents cribs, strollers, highchairs, playpens, infant seats, and the like to make your baby's vacation (and yours) much more enjoyable.

Remember that Maui's sun is probably much stronger than what you're used to at home, so it's important to protect your kids, and keep infants out of the sun altogether.

Recommended family travel Internet sites include **Family Travel Forum** (www.familytravelforum.com), a comprehensive site that offers customized trip planning; **Family Travel Network** (www.familytravelnetwork.com), an award-winning site that offers travel features, deals, and tips; **Traveling Internationally with Your Kids** (www.travelwithyourkids.com), a comprehensive site offering sound advice for long-distance and international travel with children; and **Family Travel Files** (www.thefamilytravelfiles.com), which offers an online magazine and a directory of off-the-beaten-path tours and tour operators for families.

Also look for the just-released, first edition of *Frommer's Hawaii with Kids* (Wiley Publishing, Inc.).

7 Getting There

If possible, fly directly to Maui; doing so can save you a 2-hour layover in Honolulu and another plane ride. If you're headed for Molokai or Lanai, you'll have to connect through Honolulu.

If you think of the island of Maui as the shape of a head and shoulders of a person, you'll probably arrive on its neck, at **Kahului Airport.**

At press time, six airlines fly directly from the U.S. mainland to Kahului: **United Airlines** (✆ 800/241-6522; www.ual.com) offers daily nonstop flights from San Francisco and Los Angeles; **Aloha Airlines** (✆ 800/367-5250; www.alohaair.com) has nonstop service from Sacramento, Oakland, Orange County, and San Diego, all in California. **Hawaiian Airlines** (✆ 800/367-5320; www.hawaiian air.com) has direct flights from Portland and Seattle; **American Airlines** (✆ 800/433-7300; www.aa.com) flies direct from Los Angeles and San Jose; **Delta Airlines** (✆ 800/221-1212; www.delta.com)

Tips **Agricultural Restrictions**

You cannot bring fresh fruits and vegetables into Hawaii, even if you're coming from the U.S. mainland and have no need to clear Customs.

---

offers direct flights from San Francisco and Los Angeles; and **American Trans Air** (© 800/435-9282; www.ata.com) has direct flights from Los Angeles, San Francisco, and Phoenix.

The other carriers—including **Continental** (© 800/525-0280; www.continental.com) and **Northwest Airlines** (© 800/225-2525; www.nwa.com)—fly to Honolulu, where you'll have to pick up an interisland flight to Maui. (The airlines listed in the paragraph above also offer many more flights to Honolulu from additional cities on the mainland.) Both **Aloha Airlines** and **Hawaiian Airlines** offer jet service from Honolulu. See "Interisland Flights" later in this chapter.

For information on airlines serving Hawaii from places other than the U.S. mainland, see chapter 2.

LANDING AT KAHULUI AIRPORT

If there's a long wait at baggage claim, step over to the state-operated **Visitor Information Center,** where you can pick up brochures and the latest issue of *This Week Maui,* which features great regional maps of the islands, and ask about island activities. After collecting your bags from the poky, automated carousels, step out, take a deep breath, proceed to the curbside rental-car pickup area, and wait for the appropriate rental-agency shuttle van to take you a half mile away to the rental-car checkout desk. (All major rental companies have branches at Kahului; see "Getting Around" later in this chapter.)

If you're not renting a car, the cheapest way to get to your hotel is **SpeediShuttle** (© **808/875-8070;** www.speedishuttle.com), which can take you between Kahului Airport and all the major resorts between 5am and 11pm daily. Rates vary, but figure on $30 for one to Wailea (one-way), $41 for one to Kaanapali (one-way), and $57 one-way to Kapalua. Be sure to call before your flight to arrange pickup.

You'll see taxis outside the airport terminal, but note that they are quite expensive; expect to spend around $60 to $75 for a ride from Kahului to Kaanapali and $50 from the airport to Wailea.

If possible, avoid landing on Maui between 3pm and 6pm, when the working stiffs on Maui are "pau work" (finished with work) and a major traffic jam occurs at the first intersection.

AVOIDING KAHULUI   If you're planning to stay at any of the hotels in Kapalua or at the Kaanapali resorts, you might consider flying **Island Air** (© **800/323-3345;** www.islandair.com) from Honolulu to **Kapalua–West Maui Airport.** From this airport, it's only a 10- to 15-minute drive to most hotels in West Maui, as opposed to an hour from Kahului. **Pacific Wings** (© **888/873-0877** or 808/575-4546; fax 808/873-7920; www.pacificwings.com) flies eight-passenger, twin-engine Cessna 402C aircraft into tiny **Hana Airport** and also flies into Kahului.

INTERISLAND FLIGHTS

Don't expect to jump a ferry between any of the Hawaiian islands. Today everyone island-hops by plane. Since September 11, 2001, the two interisland carriers have cut way, way, way back on the number of interisland flights. The airlines warn you to show up at least 90 minutes before your flight, and believe me, with all the security inspections, you will need all 90 minutes to catch your flight. Also, be sure to book your interisland connection from Honolulu to Maui in advance.

Aloha Airlines (© **800/367-5250** or 808/244-9071; www.aloha air.com) is the state's largest provider of interisland air transport service. It offers 15 regularly scheduled daily jet flights a day from Honolulu to Maui on its all-jet fleet of Boeing 737 aircraft. Aloha's sibling company, **Island Air** (© **800/323-3345** or 808/484-2222; www.islandair.com), operates deHavilland DASH-8 and DASH-6 turboprop aircraft and serves Hawaii's small interisland airports on Maui, Molokai, and Lanai, with flights connecting them to Oahu.

Hawaiian Airlines (© **800/367-5320** or 808/871-6132; www. hawaiianair.com) is Hawaii's other interisland airline featuring jet planes.

Kahului-based **Pacific Wings** (© **888/873-0877** or 808/575-4546; www.pacificwings.com) flies eight-passenger, twin-engine Cessna 402C aircraft. It currently offers flights between Kahului and Hana, Molokai, Lanai, and Honolulu.

Just as we went to press, a new start-up airline was announced, which, if it can raise enough capital and get the necessary FAA certification, plans to be in operation in 2006 with flights from Honolulu to Maui. **FlyHawaii Airlines** was still in the planning stages but proposes to use three 68-seat ATR-72 turboprop aircraft. For more information, call © **808/599-5588** or visit www.flyhi.com.

8 Money-Saving Package Deals

Booking an all-inclusive travel package that includes some combination of airfare, accommodations, rental car, meals, airport and baggage transfers, and sightseeing can be the most cost-effective way to travel to Maui.

Package tours are not the same as escorted tours. They are simply a way to buy airfare and accommodations (and sometimes extras like sightseeing tours and rental cars) at the same time. When you're visiting Hawaii, a package can be a smart way to go. That's because packages are sold in bulk to tour operators, which then resell them to the public at a cost that drastically undercuts standard rates.

Packages, however, vary widely. Some offer a better class of hotels than others. Some offer the same hotels for lower prices. With some packagers, your choice of accommodations and travel days may be limited. Which package is right for you depends entirely on what you want.

Start out by **reading this guide.** Do a little homework, and read up on Maui so that you can be a smart consumer. Compare the rack rates that we've published to the discounted rates being offered by the packagers to see what kinds of deals they're offering. If you're being offered a stay in a hotel we haven't recommended, do more research to learn about it, especially if it isn't a reliable franchise. It's not a deal if you end up at a dump.

Be sure to **read the fine print.** Make sure you know *exactly* what's included in the price you're being quoted and what's not. Are hotel taxes and airport transfers included, or will you have to pay extra? Before you commit to a package, make sure you know how much flexibility you have. Some packagers require ironclad commitments, while others will go with the flow, charging only minimal fees for changes or cancellations.

The best place to start looking for a package deal is in the travel section of your local Sunday newspaper. Also check the ads in the

---

Tips Package-Buying Tip

For one-stop shopping on the Web, go to **Pleasant Hawaiian Holidays** (*©* **800/2-HAWAII** or 800/242-9244; www.pleasant holidays.com), by far the biggest and most comprehensive packager to Hawaii; it offers an extensive, high-quality collection of 50 condos and hotels in every price range.

Tips   **Hawaii on the Web**

Below are some of the best Hawaii-specific websites for planning your trip:

- **Maui Visitors Bureau** (www.visitmaui.com)
- **Planet Hawaii** (www.planet-hawaii.com)
- **Maui Island Currents** (www.islandcurrents.com)
- **Maui Net** (www.maui.net)
- **The Hawaiian Language Website** (www.geocities.com/ ~olelo)

back of such national travel magazines as *Arthur Frommer's Budget Travel* and *Travel Holiday.* **Liberty Travel** (ⓒ **888/271-1584;** www. libertytravel.com), for instance, one of the biggest packagers in the Northeast, usually boasts a full-page ad in Sunday papers. **American Express Travel** (ⓒ **800/AXP-6898;** www.americanexpress. com/travel) can also book you a well-priced Hawaiian vacation; it also advertises in many Sunday travel sections.

Excellent deals can be found at **More Hawaii for Less** (ⓒ **800/ 967-6687;** www.hawaii4less.com), a California-based company that specializes in air–condominium packages at unbelievable prices.

Other reliable packagers include the airlines themselves, which often package their flights with accommodations. Among the airlines offering good-value package deals to Hawaii are **American Airlines FlyAway Vacations** (ⓒ 800/321-2121; www.aa.com), **Continental Airlines Vacations** (ⓒ 800/634-5555 or 800/301-3800; www.coolvacations.com), **Delta Dream Vacations** (ⓒ 800 /872-7786; www.deltavacations.com), and **United Vacations** (ⓒ 800/328-6877; www.unitedvacations.com). If you're traveling to the islands from Canada, ask your travel agent about package deals through **Air Canada Vacations** (ⓒ 800/776-3000; www.air canada.ca).

9 Getting Around

The only way to really see Maui is by rental car. There's no real island-wide public transit.

Maui has only a handful of major roads: One follows the coast-line around the two volcanoes that form the island, Haleakala and Puu Kukui; one goes up to Haleakala's summit; one goes to Hana; one goes to Wailea; and one goes to Lahaina. It sounds simple, right? Well, it isn't, because the names of the few roads change en route. Also, you should expect to encounter a traffic jam or two in the major resort areas.

The best and most detailed road maps are published by *This Week Magazine,* a free visitor publication available on Maui. Most rental-car maps are pretty good, too.

CAR RENTALS

Maui has one of the least expensive car-rental rates in the country. Cars are usually plentiful on Maui except on holiday weekends, which in Hawaii also means King Kamehameha Day, Prince Kuhio Day, and Admission Day (see "When to Go" earlier in this chapter).

All the major car-rental agencies have offices on Maui, usually at both Kahului and West Maui airports. They include **Alamo** (© 800/327-9633; www.goalamo.com), **Avis** (© 800/321-3712; www.avis.com), **Budget** (© 800/572-0700; www.budget.com), **Dollar** (© 800/800-4000; www.dollarcar.com), **Hertz** (© 800/654-3011; www.hertz.com), and **National** (© 800/227-7368; www.nationalcar.com).

There are also a few frugal car-rental agencies offering older cars at discount prices. **Word of Mouth Rent-a-Used-Car** ⚘, in Kahului

---

Tips Traffic Advisory

The road from central Maui to Kihei and Wailea, **Mokulele Highway (Hwy. 311),** is a dangerous strip that's often the scene of head-on crashes involving intoxicated and speeding drivers; be careful. Also be alert on the **Honoapiilani Highway (Hwy. 30)** en route to Lahaina, because drivers who spot whales in the channel between Maui and Lanai often slam on the brakes and cause major tie-ups and accidents.

There are 29 emergency call boxes on the island's busiest highways and remote areas, including along the Hana and Haleakala highways and on the north end of the island in the remote community of Kahakuloa.

Another traffic note: Buckle up your seat belt; Hawaii has stiff fines for noncompliance.

(© 800/533-5929 or 808/877-2436; www.mauirentacar.com), offers an older, four-door compact without air-conditioning for $120 a week, plus tax; with air-conditioning, it's $140 a week, plus tax. **Maui Cruisers,** in Wailuku (© 877/749-7889 or 808/249-2319; www.maui cruisers.net), with free airport pickup and return, rents used Nissan Sentras and Toyota Tercels, 8 to 12 years old but in good running condition, for $31 a day or $154 a week (including tax and insurance).

To rent a car in Hawaii, you must be at least 25 years old and have a valid driver's license and a credit card.

INSURANCE   Hawaii is a no-fault state, which means that if you don't have collision-damage insurance, you are required to pay for all damages before you leave the state, whether or not the accident was your fault. Your personal car insurance back home may provide rental-car coverage; read your policy or call your insurer before you leave home. Bring your insurance identification card if you decline the optional insurance, which usually costs $12 to $20 a day. Obtain the name of your company's local claim representative before you go. Some credit-card companies also provide collision-damage insurance for their customers; check with yours before you rent.

OTHER TRANSPORTATION OPTIONS

TAXIS   For island-wide 24-hour service, call **Alii Cab Co.** (© 808/661-3688 or 808/667-2605). You can also try **Kihei Taxi** (© 808/879-3000), **Wailea Taxi** (© 808/874-5000), or **Maui Central Cab** (© 808/244-7278) if you need a ride.

SHUTTLES   **SpeediShuttle** (© **808/875-8070;** www.speedi shuttle.com) can take you between Kahului Airport and all the major resorts from 5am to 11pm daily (for details, see "Landing at Kahului Airport" under "Getting There," earlier in this chapter).

Holo Ka'a Public Transit (© **808/879-2828;** www.akina tours.com) is a public/private partnership that has convenient, economical, and air-conditioned shuttle buses. The costs range from free shuttle vans within the resort areas, like Wailea, to just $1 for the bus from Kaanapali to Lahaina.

FAST FACTS: Maui

American Express For 24-hour traveler's check refunds and purchase information, call ℂ 800/221-7282. Local offices are located in South Maui at the **Grand Wailea Resort** (ℂ 808/875-4526) and the **Westin Maui** at Kaanapali Beach (ℂ 808/661-7155).

Dentists Emergency dental care is available at **Kihei Dental Center,** 1847 S. Kihei Rd., Kihei (ℂ 808/874-8401), or in Lahaina at the **Aloha Lahaina Dentists,** 134 Luakini St. (in the Maui Medical Group Building), Lahaina (ℂ 808/661-4005).

Doctors No appointment is necessary at **West Maui Healthcare Center,** Whalers Village, 2435 Kaanapali Pkwy., Suite H-7 (near Leilani's Restaurant), Kaanapali (ℂ 808/667-9721), which is open 365 days a year nightly until 10pm. In Kihei call **Urgent Care,** 1325 S. Kihei Rd., Suite 103 (at Lipoa St., across from Star Market; ℂ 808/879-7781), open daily from 6am to midnight; doctors are on call 24 hours a day.

Emergencies Dial ℂ 911 for the police, an ambulance, and the fire department. District stations are located in Lahaina (ℂ 808/661-4441) and in Hana (ℂ 808/248-8311). For the **Poison Control Center,** call ℂ 800/362-3585.

Hospitals For medical attention, go to **Maui Memorial Hospital,** in Central Maui at 221 Mahalani, Wailuku (ℂ 808/244-9056), or East Maui's **Hana Medical Center,** on Hana Highway (ℂ 808/248-8924).

Post Offices To find the nearest post office, call ℂ 800/ASK-USPS. In Lahaina, there are branches at the Lahaina Civic Center, 1760 Honoapiilani Hwy.; in Kahului, there's a branch at 138 S. Puunene Ave.; and in Kihei, there's one at 1254 S. Kihei Rd.

Weather For the current weather, call ℂ 808/871-5111; for recreational activities, call ℂ 808/871-5054; for Haleakala National Park weather, call ℂ 808/871-5111; for marine weather and surf and wave conditions, call ℂ 808/877-3477.

2

For International Visitors

Whether it's your first visit or your 10th, a trip to the United States may require additional planning. The pervasiveness of American culture around the world may make the United States feel like familiar territory to foreign visitors, but leaving your own country for the States—especially the unique island of Maui—still requires some arrangements before you leave home. This chapter will provide you with essential information, helpful tips, and advice for the more common problems that some visitors encounter.

1 Preparing for Your Trip
ENTRY REQUIREMENTS
Check at any U.S. embassy or consulate for current information and requirements. You can also obtain a visa application and other information online at the **U.S. State Department**'s website at **http://travel.state.gov**.

VISAS The U.S. State Department has a **Visa Waiver Program** allowing citizens of certain countries to enter the United States without a visa for stays of up to 90 days. At press time these included Andorra, Australia, Austria, Belgium, Brunei, Denmark, Finland, France, Germany, Iceland, Ireland, Italy, Japan, Liechtenstein, Luxembourg, Monaco, the Netherlands, New Zealand, Norway, Portugal, San Marino, Singapore, Slovenia, Spain, Sweden, Switzerland, the United Kingdom, and Uruguay. Citizens of these countries need only a valid passport and a round-trip air or cruise ticket in their possession upon arrival. If they first enter the United States, they may also visit Mexico, Canada, Bermuda, and/or the Caribbean islands and return to the United States without a visa. Further information is available from any U.S. embassy or consulate. Canadian citizens may enter the United States without visas; they need only proof of residence.

Citizens of all other countries must have (1) a valid passport that expires at least 6 months later than the scheduled end of their visit to the United States and (2) a tourist visa, which may be obtained without charge from any U.S. consulate.

To obtain a visa, the traveler must submit a completed application form (either in person or by mail) with a 1½-inch-square photo and must demonstrate binding ties to a residence abroad. Usually you can obtain a visa at once or within 24 hours, but it may take longer during the summer rush from June through August. If you cannot go in person, contact the nearest U.S. embassy or consulate for directions on applying by mail. Your travel agent or airline office may also be able to provide you with visa applications and instructions. The U.S. consulate or embassy that issues your visa will determine whether you will be issued a multiple- or single-entry visa and any restrictions regarding the length of your stay.

MEDICAL REQUIREMENTS   Unless you're arriving from an area known to be suffering from an epidemic (particularly cholera or yellow fever), inoculations or vaccinations are not required for entry into the United States. If you have a medical condition that requires **syringe-administered medications,** carry a valid signed prescription from your physician—the Federal Aviation Administration (FAA) no longer allows airline passengers to pack syringes in their carry-on baggage without documented proof of medical need. If you have a disease that requires treatment with **narcotics,** you should also carry documented proof with you—smuggling narcotics aboard a plane is a serious offense that carries severe penalties in the U.S.

For **HIV-positive visitors,** requirements for entering the United States are somewhat vague and change frequently. According to the latest publication of *HIV and Immigrants: A Manual for AIDS Service Providers,* the Immigration and Naturalization Service (INS) doesn't require a medical exam for entry into the United States, but INS officials may stop individuals because they look sick or because they are carrying AIDS/HIV medicine. For up-to-the-minute information, contact **AIDSinfo** (© **800/448-0440,** or 301/519-6616 outside the U.S.; www.aidsinfo.nih.gov) or the **Gay Men's Health Crisis** (© **212/367-1000;** www.gmhc.org).

DRIVER'S LICENSES   Foreign driver's licenses are mostly recognized in the United States, although you may want to get an international driver's license if your home license is not written in English.

PASSPORT INFORMATION

Safeguard your passport in an inconspicuous, inaccessible place like a money belt. Make a copy of the critical pages, including the passport number, and store it in a safe place, separate from the passport itself. If you lose your passport, visit the nearest consulate of your native country as soon as possible for a replacement. Passport applications are downloadable from the Internet sites listed below.

Note that the International Civil Aviation Organization (ICAO) has recommended a policy requiring that *every* individual who travels by air have his or her own passport. In response, many countries are now requiring that children must be issued their own passport to travel internationally, where before those under 16 or so may have been allowed to travel on a parent or guardian's passport.

CUSTOMS
WHAT YOU CAN BRING IN
Every visitor more than 21 years of age may bring in, free of duty, the following: (1) 1 liter of wine or hard liquor; (2) 200 cigarettes, 100 cigars (but not from Cuba), or 3 pounds of smoking tobacco; and (3) $100 worth of gifts. These exemptions are offered to travelers who spend at least 72 hours in the United States and who have not claimed them within the preceding 6 months. It is altogether forbidden to bring into the country foodstuffs (particularly fruit, cooked meats, and canned goods) and plants (vegetables, seeds, tropical plants, and the like). Foreign tourists may bring in or take out up to $10,000 in U.S. or foreign currency with no formalities; larger sums must be declared to U.S. Customs on entering or leaving, which includes filing form CM 4790. For more specific information regarding U.S. Customs and Border Protection, contact your nearest U.S. embassy or consulate, or the **U.S. Customs** office (© **202/927-1770;** www.customs.ustreas.gov).

WHAT YOU CAN TAKE HOME
Rules governing what you can bring back duty-free vary from country to country and are subject to change, but they're generally posted on the Internet. **U.K. citizens** should contact HM Customs & Excise at © **0845/010-9000** (from outside the U.K., 020/8929-0152) or consult its website at www.hmce.gov.uk.

For a clear summary of **Canadian** rules, request the booklet *I Declare,* issued by the **Canada Customs and Revenue Agency** (© **800/461-9999** in Canada or 204/983-3500; www.ccra-adrc. gc.ca). A helpful brochure available from **Australian** consulates or Customs offices is *Know Before You Go.* For more information, call the **Australian Customs Service** at © **1300/363-263** or log on to www.customs.gov.au. **New Zealand** citizens should request the pamphlet *New Zealand Customs Guide for Travellers, Notice No. 4* from **New Zealand Customs,** The Customhouse, 17–21 Whitmore St., Box 2218, Wellington (🕿 **0800/428-786** or 04/473-6099; www.customs.govt.nz).

HEALTH INSURANCE

Although it's not required of travelers, health insurance is highly recommended. Unlike many European countries, the United States does not usually offer free or low-cost medical care to its citizens or visitors. Doctors and hospitals are expensive and in most cases will require advance payment or proof of coverage before they render their services. Policies can cover everything from the loss or theft of your baggage and trip cancellation to the guarantee of bail in case you're arrested. Good policies will also cover the costs of an accident, repatriation, or death. Packages such as **Europ Assistance's "Worldwide Healthcare Plan"** are sold by European automobile clubs and travel agencies at attractive rates. **Worldwide Assistance Services,** Inc. (🕿 **800/821-2828;** www.worldwideassistance.com), is the agent for Europ Assistance in the United States.

MONEY

CURRENCY   The most common **bills** are the $1 (colloquially, a "buck"), $5, $10, and $20 denominations. There are also $2 bills (seldom encountered), $50 bills, and $100 bills (the last two are usually not welcome as payment for small purchases). Note that redesigned bills were introduced in the last few years, but the old-style bills are still legal tender.

There are seven denominations of coins: 1¢ (1 cent, or a penny); 5¢ (5 cents, or a nickel); 10¢ (10 cents, or a dime); 25¢ (25 cents, or a quarter); 50¢ (50 cents, or a half dollar); the new gold "Sacagawea" coin, worth $1; and, prized by collectors, the rare, older silver dollar.

EXCHANGING CURRENCY   To exchange foreign currency on Maui, you'll need to go to a bank (call first to see if currency exchange is available) or use your hotel. There also are currency services at **Honolulu International Airport.**

CREDIT CARDS   Credit cards are widely used in Hawaii. You can save yourself trouble by using plastic rather than cash or traveler's checks in most hotels, restaurants, retail stores, and a growing number of food and liquor stores. You must have a credit card to rent a car in Hawaii.

2 Getting to & Around the United States

The only airline with direct flights from foreign cities to Maui is **Air Canada** (© 800/776-3000; www.aircanada.ca). Because of Maui's short runway, most international visitors will have to fly to Honolulu first to clear Customs and then get an interisland flight to Maui.

Airlines serving Hawaii from places other than the U.S. mainland include **Air Canada** (© 800/776-3000; www.aircanada.ca); **Air New Zealand** (© 0800/737-000 in Auckland, 64-3/379-5200 in Christchurch, or 800/926-7255 in the U.S.; www.airnewzealand. com), which flies between Auckland and Hawaii; **Qantas** (© 008/ 177-767 in Australia or 800/227-4500 in the U.S.; www.qantas. com.au), which flies between Sydney and Honolulu; **Japan Air Lines** (© 03/5489-1111 in Tokyo or 800/525-3663 in the U.S.; www.japanair.com); **All Nippon Airways (ANA)** (© 03/5489-1212 in Tokyo or 800/235-9262 in the U.S.; www.fly-ana.com); **China Airlines** (© 02/715-1212 in Taipei or 800/227-5118 in the U.S.; www.china-airlines.com); **Air Pacific,** serving Fiji, Australia, New Zealand, and the South Pacific (© 800/227-4446; www.air pacific.com); **Korean Airlines** (© 02/656-2000 in Seoul, 800/223-1155 on the East Coast, 800/421-8200 on the West Coast, or 800/438-5000 from Hawaii; www.koreanair.com); and **Philippine Airlines** (© 631/816-6691 in Manila or 800/435-9725 in the U.S.; www.philippineair.com).

Locally, **Hawaiian Airlines** (© **800/367-5320;** www.hawaiian air.com) flies nonstop to Sydney, Tahiti, and American Samoa. If you're traveling in the United States beyond Hawaii, some large American airlines—such as **American, Delta, Northwest, TWA,** and **United**—offer travelers on transatlantic or transpacific flights special discount tickets under the name **Visit USA,** allowing travel between any U.S. destinations at reduced rates. These tickets must be purchased before you leave your foreign point of departure. This system is the best, easiest, and fastest way to see the United States at low cost. You should obtain information well in advance from your travel agent or the office of the airline concerned.

Visitors arriving by air should cultivate patience and resignation before setting foot on U.S. soil. Getting through immigration control may take as long as 2 hours on some days, especially summer weekends. Add the time it takes to clear Customs, and you'll see that you should make a very generous allowance for delay in planning connections between international and domestic flights—an average of 2 to 3 hours at least.

After you have cleared Customs in Honolulu, hop a short, 20-minute interisland flight to Maui. For further information about travel to Hawaii, see "Getting There" and "Getting Around" in chapter 1.

FAST FACTS: For International Visitors

Automobile Organizations Auto clubs will supply maps, suggested routes, guidebooks, accident and bail-bond insurance, and emergency road service. The major auto club in the United States, with 955 offices nationwide, is the **American Automobile Association (AAA,** often called "Triple A"); however, there are no offices on Maui, Molokai, or Lanai. Members of some foreign auto clubs have reciprocal arrangements with AAA and enjoy its services at no charge. If you belong to an auto club, inquire about AAA reciprocity before you leave. AAA can also provide you with an **International Driving Permit** validating your foreign license. You may be able to join AAA even if you are not a member of a reciprocal club. To inquire, call ℂ **800/736-2886** or visit www.aaa.com.

Some car-rental agencies now provide automobile-club–type services, so inquire about their availability when you rent your car.

Climate See "When to Go" in chapter 1.

Electricity Hawaii, like the U.S. mainland and Canada, uses 110–120 volts (60 cycles), compared to the 220–240 volts (50 cycles) used in most of Europe and in other areas of the world, including Australia and New Zealand. Small appliances of non-American manufacture, such as hair dryers or shavers, will require a plug adapter with two flat, parallel pins; larger ones will require a 100-volt transformer.

Embassies & Consulates All embassies are in Washington, D.C. Some countries have consulates general in major U.S. cities, and most have a mission to the United Nations in New York City. If your country isn't listed below, call for directory information in Washington, D.C. (ℂ **202/555-1212**), or visit **www.embassy.org/embassies**.

The embassy of **Australia** is at 1601 Massachusetts Ave. NW, Washington, DC 20036 (ℂ **202/797-3000;** www.austemb.org).

There is also an Australian consulate in Hawaii at 1000 Bishop St., Penthouse Suite, Honolulu, HI 96813 (© 808/524-5050).

The embassy of **Canada** is at 501 Pennsylvania Ave. NW, Washington, DC 20001 (© **202/682-1740;** www.canadian embassy.org). Canadian consulates are also at 1251 Ave. of the Americas, New York, NY 10020 (© 212/596-1628), and at 550 South Hope St., Ninth Floor, Los Angeles, CA 90071 (© 213/ 346-2700).

The embassy of **Japan** is at 2520 Massachusetts Ave. NW, Washington, DC 20008 (© **202/238-6700;** www.embjapan.org). The consulate general of Japan is located at 1742 Nuuanu Ave., Honolulu, HI 96817 (© 808/543-3111).

The embassy of **New Zealand** is at 37 Observatory Circle NW, Washington, DC 20008 (© **202/328-4800;** www.nzemb. org). The only New Zealand consulate in the United States is at 780 Third Ave., New York, NY 10017 (© 202/328-4800).

The embassy of the **Republic of Ireland** is at 2234 Massachusetts Ave. NW, Washington, DC 20008 (© **202/462-3939;** www.irelandemb.org). There's a consulate office in San Francisco at 44 Montgomery St., Suite 3830, San Francisco, CA 94104 (© 415/392-4214).

The embassy of the **United Kingdom** is at 3100 Massachusetts Ave. NW, Washington, DC 20008 (© **202/588-6640;** www.fco.gov.uk/directory). British consulates are at 845 Third Ave., New York, NY 10022 (© 212/745-0200), and 11766 Wilshire Blvd., Suite 400, Los Angeles, CA 90025 (© 310/477-3322).

Emergencies Call © **911** to report a fire, call the police, or get an ambulance.

Gasoline (Petrol) One U.S. gallon equals 3.8 liters, and 1.2 U.S. gallons equals 1 Imperial gallon. You'll notice there are several grades (and price levels) of gasoline available at most gas stations. You'll also notice that their names change from company to company. The ones with the highest octane are the most expensive, but most rental cars take the least expensive "regular" gas, with an octane rating of 87.

Safety Although tourist areas are generally safe, visitors should always stay alert. It's wise to ask the island tourist office if you're in doubt about which neighborhoods are safe. Avoid deserted areas, especially at night. Generally speaking, you can feel safe in areas where there are many people and open establishments.

Taxes The United States has no VAT (value-added tax) or other indirect taxes at a national level. Every state, and every city in it, has the right to levy its own local tax on all purchases, including hotel and restaurant checks, airline tickets, and so on. In Hawaii, sales tax is 4%; there's also a 7.25% hotel-room tax and a small excise tax, so the total tax on your hotel bill will be 11.42%.

Telephone & Fax The telephone system in the United States is run by private corporations, so rates, particularly for long-distance service and operator-assisted calls, can vary widely—especially on calls made from public telephones. Local calls—that is, calls to other locations on the island you're on—made from public phones in Hawaii cost 50¢.

Generally, hotel surcharges on long-distance and local calls are astronomical. You are usually better off using a **public pay telephone,** which you will find clearly marked in most public buildings and private establishments as well as on the street. Many convenience stores and newsstands sell **prepaid calling cards** in denominations up to $50.

Most **long-distance** and **international calls** can be dialed directly from any phone. **For calls within the United States and to Canada,** dial 1 followed by the area code and the seven-digit number. **For other international calls,** dial 011 followed by the country code, city code, and the telephone number of the person you are calling. Some country and city codes are as follows: **Australia** 61, Melbourne 3, Sydney 2; **Ireland** 353, Dublin 1; **New Zealand** 64, Auckland 9, Wellington 4; **United Kingdom** 44, Belfast 232, Birmingham 21, Glasgow 41, London 71 or 81.

If you're calling the **United States from another country,** the country code is 01.

In Hawaii, interisland phone calls are considered long-distance and are often as costly as calling the U.S. mainland. The international country code for Hawaii is 1, just as it is for the rest of the United States and Canada.

For **reversed-charge** or **collect calls** and for **person-to-person calls,** dial 0 (zero, not the letter O), followed by the area code and number you want; an operator will then come on the line, and you should specify that you are calling collect, person-to-person, or both. If your operator-assisted call is international, ask for the overseas operator.

Note that all phone numbers with the area code 800, 888, 866, and 877 are toll-free. However, calls to numbers in area codes 700 and 900 (chat lines, "dating" services, and so on) can be very expensive—usually a charge of 95¢ to $3 or more per minute.

For **local directory assistance** ("information"), dial 411. For **long-distance information,** dial 1, then the appropriate area code and 555-1212; for **directory assistance for another island,** dial 1, then 808, then 555-1212.

Fax facilities are widely available and can be found in most hotels and many other establishments. Try **The UPS Store, FedEx Kinko's** (check the local Yellow Pages), or any photo-copying shop.

Telephone Directories There are two kinds of telephone directories in the United States. The general directory, the so-called White Pages, lists private and business subscribers in alphabetical order. The inside front cover lists the emergency numbers for police, fire, and ambulance, along with other vital numbers. The first few pages include a guide to long-distance and international calling, complete with country codes and area codes.

The second directory, printed on yellow paper (hence its name, Yellow Pages), lists all local services, businesses, and industries by type of activity, with an index at the front.

Time Hawaii Standard Time is in effect year-round. Hawaii is 2 hours behind Pacific Standard Time and 5 hours behind Eastern Standard Time. In other words, when it's noon in Hawaii, it's 2pm in California and 5pm in New York during standard time on the mainland. There's no daylight saving time here, so when daylight saving time is in effect on the mainland, Hawaii is 3 hours behind the West Coast and 6 hours behind the East Coast.

Hawaii is east of the international date line, putting it in the same day as the U.S. mainland and Canada.

Tipping It's part of the American way of life to tip. Many service employees receive little direct salary and must depend on tips for their income. The following are some general rules:

In **hotels,** tip bellhops at least $1 per piece of luggage ($2-$3 if you have a lot of luggage), and tip the housekeeping staff $1 per person, per day. Tip the doorman or concierge only if he or she has provided you with some specific service (for example, calling a cab for you or obtaining difficult-to-get theater tickets). Tip the valet-parking attendant $1 to $2 every time you get your car.

In **restaurants, bars,** and **nightclubs,** tip service staff 15% to 20% of the check, tip bartenders 10% to 15%, and tip valet-parking attendants $1 to $2 per vehicle. Tip the doorman only if he or she has provided you with some specific service (such as calling a cab for you). Tipping is not expected in cafeterias and fast-food restaurants.

Tip **cab drivers** 15% of the fare.

As for **other service personnel,** tip skycaps at airports at least $1 per piece ($2-$3 if you have a lot of luggage), and tip hairdressers and barbers 15% to 20%. Tipping ushers at theaters is not expected.

Where to Stay

Maui has accommodations to fit every taste and budget, from luxury oceanfront suites and historic bed-and-breakfasts to reasonably priced condos that will sleep a family of four.

The high season, during which rooms are always booked and rates are at the top end, runs from mid-December to March. A second high season, when rates are high but reservations are somewhat easier to get, is summer (late June to early Sept). The off seasons, with fewer tourists and cheaper rates, are April to early June and late September to mid-December.

Remember to add Hawaii's 11.42% accommodations tax to your final bill. Parking is free unless otherwise noted.

Important note: Before you book, be sure to read "The Island in Brief" in chapter 1, which will help you choose your ideal location.

1 Central Maui

KAHULUI

If you're arriving late at night or you have an early-morning flight out, the best choice near Kahului Airport is the **Maui Beach Hotel,** 170 Kaahumanu Ave. (© **888/649-3222** or 808/877-0051; fax 808/871-5797; http://castleresorts.com/MBH). The nondescript, motel-like rooms start at $120 ($105 if you book on the Internet) and include free airport shuttle service (6am–9pm only).

WAILUKU

Old Wailuku Inn at Ulupono 🐟🐟 *(finds*   This 1924 former plantation manager's home, lovingly restored by innkeepers Janice and Thomas Fairbanks, offers a genuine old Hawaii experience. The theme is Hawaii of the 1920s and 1930s. The spacious rooms are gorgeously outfitted with exotic ohia-wood floors, high ceilings, and traditional Hawaiian quilts. Some of the mammoth bathrooms have claw-foot tubs; others have Jacuzzis. The "Vagabond House" is a modern three-room complex in the inn's lavishly landscaped back yard. The rooms are decorated in island-designer Sig Zane's floral prints, with rare framed prints of indigenous Hawaiian flowers plus modern amenities such as an ultraluxurious multihead shower. A full gourmet breakfast is served on the enclosed back lanai. You'll feel right at home lounging on the generous-size living-room sofa or watching the world go by from an old wicker chair on the lanai.

2199 Kahookele St. (at High St., across from the Wailuku School), Wailuku, HI 96732. © 800/305-4899 or 808/244-5897. Fax 808/242-9600. www.mauiinn.com. 10 units. $125–$180 double. Rates include full breakfast. Extra person $20. 2-night minimum. MC, V. **Amenities:** Jacuzzi; laundry service; dry cleaning. *In room:* A/C, TV/VCR, dataport, coffeemaker, DSL.

2 West Maui

LAHAINA
VERY EXPENSIVE

Puunoa Beach Estates (Kids) If money is no problem and you are taking a family to Maui, consider these 10 gorgeous town houses in an exclusive 3-acre enclave on a white-sand beach. The individually owned and decorated units (1,700 sq. ft. and larger), all with private beachfront lanais, boast hardwood floors, marble bathrooms, and the most up-to-date kitchens. Prices are high, but the amenity list has everything you should want for a first-class vacation rental in a dream location. It's within walking distance of the center of Lahaina, but the residential location makes you feel miles away.

45 Kai Pali Place, Lahaina, HI 96761. Managed by Classic Resorts. © 800/642-6284 or 808/661-3339. Fax 808/667-1145. www.puunoabeachestates.com. 10 units. $650 2-bedroom (4 people); $875 3-bedroom with loft (8 people). 3-night minimum. AE, MC, V. **Amenities:** Outdoor pool; whirlpool; sauna; fitness center; concierge; dry-cleaning service; barbecues; daily maid service; free Internet access; complimentary snorkeling equipment, newspaper, video library, fax service. *In room:* A/C, TV/VCR, dataport, full kitchen, fridge, coffeemaker, hair dryer, iron, safe, master bedroom with whirlpool, washer and dryer.

Nickel-&-Dime Charges at High-Priced Hotels

Several upscale resorts in Hawaii have begun charging a so-called "resort fee." This daily fee (generally $15 a day) is added on to your bill for such "complimentary" items as a daily newspaper, local phone calls, use of the fitness facilities, and so on. Amenities that the resort has been happily providing its guests for years are now tacked on to your bill under the guise of a "fee." In other words, this is a sneaky way to increase the prices further without telling you.

MODERATE

Best Western Pioneer Inn This two-story, plantation-style structure has big verandas that overlook the streets of Lahaina and the harbor. Rooms feature vintage bathrooms and new curtains and carpets. The quietest rooms face either the garden courtyard or the square-block-size banyan tree next door. I recommend room no. 31, over the banyan court, with a view of the ocean and the harbor. If you want to watch all the Front Street action, book no. 49 or 36.

658 Wharf St. (in front of Lahaina Pier), Lahaina, HI 96761. ℂ **800/457-5457** or 808/661-3636. Fax 808/667-5708. www.pioneerinnmaui.com. 34 units. $145–$180 double. Extra person $15 (12 or older). AE, DC, DISC, MC, V. **Amenities:** Restaurant (good for breakfast); bar with live music; outdoor pool; big shopping arcade; laundry service. *In room:* A/C, TV, fridge, coffeemaker, hair dryer, iron.

House of Fountains Bed & Breakfast *Finds* This 7,000-square-foot contemporary home, in a quiet residential subdivision at the north end of town, is popular with visitors from around the world. The oversize rooms are fresh and quiet, with white ceramic-tile floors, handmade koa furniture, Hawaiian quilt bedspreads, and a Hawaiiana theme. In 2002, hostess Daniela Atay won the prestigious "Most Hawaiian Accommodation" award from the Hawaii Visitors and Convention Bureau. The four downstairs rooms all open onto flower-filled private patios. Guests share the fully equipped guest kitchen and barbecue area. The nearest beach is about a 5-minute drive away, and tennis courts are nearby. Around the pool are a Hawaiian hale, an imu pit, and an area that's perfect for Hawaiian weddings (arrangements available).

1579 Lokia St. (off Fleming Rd., north of Lahaina town), Lahaina, HI 96761. ℂ **800/ 789-6865** or 808/667-2121. Fax 808/667-2120. www.alohahouse.com. 6 units (shower only). $105–$160 double (2 people per room). Rates include full breakfast. AE, MC, V (additional 5% charge if using credit card). From Hwy. 30, take the Fleming Rd. exit; turn left on Ainakea; after 2 blocks, turn right on Malanai St.; go 3 blocks and turn left onto Lokia St. **Amenities:** Outdoor pool; Jacuzzi; washer/dryers. *In room:* A/C, TV/VCR, fridge, hair dryer, phone.

Lahaina Inn *(symbol)* If you like old hotels that have genuine historic touches, you'll love this place. As in many old hotels, some of these Victorian antique–stuffed rooms are small; if that's a problem for you, ask for a larger unit. All come with private bathrooms and lanais. The best room in the house is no. 7, which overlooks the beach, the town, and the island of Lanai; you can watch the action below or close the door and ignore it. There's an excellent, though unaffiliated, restaurant in the same building (David Paul's Lahaina Grill, p. 81), with a bar downstairs.

Lahaina & Kaanapali Accommodations & Attractions

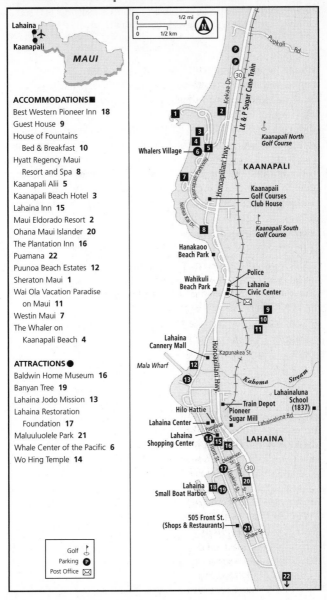

MAUI

Lahaina
Kaanapali

ACCOMMODATIONS ■

Best Western Pioneer Inn **18**
Guest House **9**
House of Fountains
  Bed & Breakfast **10**
Hyatt Regency Maui
  Resort and Spa **8**
Kaanapali Alii **5**
Kaanapali Beach Hotel **3**
Lahaina Inn **15**
Maui Eldorado Resort **2**
Ohana Maui Islander **20**
The Plantation Inn **16**
Puamana **22**
Puunoa Beach Estates **12**
Sheraton Maui **1**
Wai Ola Vacation Paradise
  on Maui **11**
Westin Maui **7**
The Whaler on
  Kaanapali Beach **4**

ATTRACTIONS ●

Baldwin Home Museum **16**
Banyan Tree **19**
Lahaina Jodo Mission **13**
Lahaina Restoration
  Foundation **17**
Maluuluolele Park **21**
Whale Center of the Pacific **6**
Wo Hing Temple **14**

Golf
Parking **P**
Post Office ✉

0   1/2 mi
0   1/2 km

Puokoli Rd.

LK & P Sugar Cane Train

Kekaa Dr.

Honoapiilani Hwy.

Kaanapali Parkway

Nohea Kai Dr.

Whalers Village

KAANAPALI

Kaanapali North
Golf Course

Kaanapaii
Golf Courses
Club House

Kaanapali South
Golf Course

Hanakaoo
Beach Park

Wahikuli
Beach Park

Police
Lahaina
Civic Center

Lahaina
Cannery Mall

Mala Wharf

Kapunakea St.

Kahoma Stream

Lahainaluna
School
(1837)

Train Depot
Pioneer
Sugar Mill

Hilo Hattie
Lahaina Center
Lahaina
Shopping Center

Lahainaluna Rd.

Papalaua

Front St.

LAHAINA

Dickenson St.

Wainee St.

Luakini St.

Lahaina
Small Boat Harbor

Prison St.

505 Front St.
(Shops & Restaurants)

Shaw St.

41

127 Lahainaluna Rd. (near Front St.), Lahaina, HI 96761. ℂ **800/669-3444** or 808/ 661-0577. Fax 808/667-9480. www.lahainainn.com. 12 units (most with shower only). $125–$175 double. AE, MC, V. Next-door parking $7/day. **Amenities:** Bar; concierge; activities desk. In room: A/C, hair dryer, iron.

Ohana Maui Islander 🐟 *Value*

This wooden complex's units, especially those with kitchenettes, offer great value. The larger ones work well for families on a budget. The property sits on a quiet side street within walking distance of restaurants, shops, attractions, and the beach (just 3 blocks away). All of the good-size rooms, decorated in tropical-island style, are comfortable and quiet. The entire complex is spread across 10 landscaped acres and includes a sun deck, a barbecue, and a picnic area. The aloha-friendly staff will take the time to answer all of your questions. *Budget tip:* When booking, ask about "SimpleSaver Rates"; you can save a bundle off the rack rates.

660 Wainee St. (between Dickenson and Prison sts.), Lahaina, HI 96761. ℂ **800/ 462-6262** or 808/667-9766. Fax 808/661-3733. www.ohanahotels.com. 360 units. $159 double; $179 studio with kitchenette; $209 1-bedroom with kitchen (sleeps up to 4); $299 2-bedroom with kitchen (sleeps 6). Extra rollaway bed $18, cribs free. AE, DC, DISC, MC, V. Parking $5. **Amenities:** Outdoor pool; tennis courts (lit for night play until 10pm); activities desk; coin-op washer/dryers. In room: A/C, TV, kitchenette (in some units), fridge, coffeemaker, hair dryer, iron, safe.

The Plantation Inn 🐟🐟 *Finds*

This charming Victorian-style inn, located a couple of blocks from the water, looks like it's been here 100 years or more, but it's actually of 1990s vintage—an artful deception. The rooms are romantic to the max, tastefully done with period furniture, hardwood floors, stained glass, and ceiling fans. There are four-poster canopy beds in some rooms, brass beds in others. All units are soundproof and come with a private lanai; the suites have kitchenettes. The rooms wrap around the large pool and deck. Also on the property is Gerard's, an outstanding French restaurant (hotel guests get a discount on dinner; p. 82). Breakfast is served around the pool and in the elegant pavilion lounge.

174 Lahainaluna Rd. (between Wainee and Luakini sts., 1 block from Hwy. 30), Lahaina, HI 96761. ℂ **800/433-6815** or 808/667-9225. Fax 808/667-9293. www. theplantationinn.com. 19 units (some with shower only). $160–$265 double. (Check the Internet for great package deals.) Rates include full breakfast. Extra person $25. AE, DC, DISC, MC, V. **Amenities:** Acclaimed restaurant and bar; large outdoor pool; Jacuzzi; concierge; activities desk; coin-op washer/dryers. In room: A/C, TV/VCR, kitchenette (in suites), fridge, hair dryer, iron, safe.

Puamana

These 28 acres of town houses set right on the water are ideal for those who want to be able to retreat from the crowds and into the serene quiet of an elegant neighborhood. Each unit is a privately owned individual home, with no neighbors above or below. Most are exquisitely decorated, and all come with full kitchen, lanai, barbecue, and at least two bathrooms. The clubhouse has an ocean-front lanai, library, card room, sauna, table-tennis tables, and office. I've found the best rates by booking through Klahani Travel (contact information below), but its office is not on-site, which has caused some problems with guests getting assistance. If you'd rather book directly with the Puamana association office, contact Puamana Community Association, 34 Puailima Place, Lahaina, HI 96761 (© **808/ 661-3423;** fax 808/667-0398; info@Puamana.info).

1565 Kuuipo St. (at the extreme southern end of Lahaina, ½ mile from downtown). Reservations: c/o Klahani Travel, Lahaina Cannery Mall, 1221 Honoapiilani Hwy., Lahaina, HI 96761. © **800/669-6284** or 808/667-2712. Fax 808/661-5875. www.klahani.com. 40 units. $125–$200 1-bedroom unit; $150–$275 2-bedroom; $300–$500 3-bedroom. 3-night minimum. AE, DC, DISC, MC, V. **Amenities:** 3 pools (1 for adults only); tennis court; Jacuzzi; game room; activities desk; on-site laundry. *In room:* TV, kitchen, fridge, coffeemaker, hair dryer, iron, washer/dryer (in some units).

Wai Ola Vacation Paradise on Maui ⌘   Just 2 blocks from the beach, in a quiet, residential development behind a tall concrete wall, lies this lovely retreat, with shade trees, sitting areas, gardens, a pool, and a range of accommodations (a small studio, a couple of suites inside the home, a separate honeymoon cottage, a one-bedroom apartment, or the entire 5,000-sq.-ft. house). Every unit has a welcome fruit basket when you arrive, plus coffee beans for the coffeemaker. You'll also find a deck, barbecue facilities, and an outdoor wet bar on the property. There's a great beach just a 3-minute drive away, and tennis courts are nearby.

1565 Kuuipo St. (P.O. Box 12580), Lahaina, HI 96761. © **800/492-4652** or 808/ 661-7901. Fax 808/661-1119. www.waiola.com. 5 units. Double rates $95 studio; $135 suite; $150 1-bedroom apt; $175 honeymoon cottage; entire house $725–$900. Extra person $15. AE, DISC, MC, V. **Amenities:** Outdoor pool; Jacuzzi; complimentary use of watersports equipment; free high-speed Internet; free self-service washer/dryers. *In room:* A/C, TV/DVD/VCR, dataport, kitchenette, fridge, coffeemaker, hair dryer, iron.

INEXPENSIVE

Guest House ⌘⌘ *Finds*   This is one of Lahaina's great bed-and-breakfast deals: a charming house with more amenities than the expensive Kaanapali hotels just down the road. The roomy home features parquet floors and floor-to-ceiling windows; the large swimming pool is surrounded by a deck and comfortable lounge chairs. Every guest room has a quiet lanai and a romantic hot tub. Guests share the kitchen and computers with high-speed Internet access. The Guest House also operates Trinity Tours and offers discounts on car rentals and many island activities. Tennis courts are nearby, and the nearest beach is about a block away. Scuba divers are welcome here and are provided with places to store their gear.

1620 Ainakea Rd. (off Fleming Rd., north of Lahaina town), Lahaina, HI 96761. ℂ 800/621-8942 or 808/661-8085. Fax 808/661-1896. www.mauiguest house.com. 4 units. $129 double; $115 single. Rates include full breakfast. MC, V. Take Fleming Rd. off Hwy. 30; turn left on Ainakea; it's 2 blocks down. **Amenities:** Huge outdoor pool; free watersports equipment; concierge; activities desk; car-rental desk; self-service washer/dryers. *In room:* A/C, TV/VCR/DVD, fridge, free high-speed wireless Internet, Jacuzzi.

KAANAPALI
VERY EXPENSIVE

Hyatt Regency Maui Resort and Spa ★★ (Kids) Spa goers will love this resort. Hawaii's first oceanfront spa, the Spa Moana, opened here in 2000 with some 9,000 square feet of facilities and a huge menu of massages, body treatments, and therapies. Book your treatment before you leave home—this place is popular.

The management has poured some $19 million in renovations into rooms in this fantasy resort. It certainly has lots of imaginative touches: a collection of exotic species (pink flamingos, unhappy-looking penguins, and an assortment of loud parrots and macaws in the lobby), nine waterfalls, and an eclectic Asian and Pacific art collection. The resort covers some 40 acres; even if you don't stay here, you might want to walk through the expansive tree-filled atrium and the parklike grounds. The ½-acre outdoor pool features a 150-foot lava tube slide and a cocktail bar under the falls. There's even a children-only pool with its own beach, tidal pools, and fountains, and a "Camp Hyatt" children's program.

The rooms, spread out among three towers, are pleasantly outfitted and have very comfortable separate sitting areas and private lanais with eye-popping views. The latest, most comfortable bedding is now standard in every room (including fluffy feather beds). The very romantic Swan Court (p. 88) is not to be missed for a special dinner.

200 Nohea Kai Dr., Lahaina, HI 96761. ℂ 800/233-1234 or 808/661-1234. Fax 808/667-4714. www.maui.hyatt.com. 806 units. $345–$660 double; $530–$695 Regency Club; from $850 suite. Resort fee $15. Extra person $35 ($50 in Regency Club rooms). Children 18 and under stay free in parent's room using existing bedding. Packages available. AE, DC, DISC, MC, V. Valet parking $10, free self-parking. **Amenities:** 5 restaurants; 2 bars; a ½-acre outdoor pool; 36-hole golf course; 6 tennis courts; health club with weight room; brand-new, state-of-the-art spa; Jacuzzi; watersports equipment rentals; bike rentals; Camp Hyatt kids' program, offering

supervised activities for 5- to 12-year-olds; game room; concierge; activities desk; car-rental desk; business center; big shopping arcade; salon; room service; in-room or spa massage; babysitting; coin-op washer/dryers; laundry service; dry cleaning; concierge-level rooms. *In room:* A/C, TV, dataport, minibar, fridge (on request), coffeemaker, hair dryer, iron, safe.

Kaanapali Alii *Kids* The height of luxury, these oceanfront condominium units sit on 8 landscaped acres right on Kaanapali Beach. Kaanapali Alii combines all the amenities of a luxury hotel with the convenience of a condominium to make a stay memorable. Each of the one-bedroom (1,500 sq. ft.) and two-bedroom (1,900 sq. ft.) units is impeccably decorated and comes with all the comforts of home (fully equipped kitchen, washer/dryer, lanai, two full bathrooms) and then some (room service and daily maid service). The beachside recreation area includes a swimming pool, plus a separate children's pool, whirlpool, gas barbecue grills and picnic areas, exercise rooms, saunas, and tennis courts. There's even a yoga class on Monday, Wednesday, and Friday on the lawn.

50 Nohea Kai Dr., Lahaina, HI 96761. © 800/642-6284 or 808/661-3330. Fax 808/667-1145. www.kaanapali-alii.com. 264 units. $360–$540 1-bedroom for 4; $490–$760 2-bedroom for 6. AE, DC, DISC, MC, V. **Amenities:** Poolside cafe; 2 outdoor pools; 36-hole golf course; 3 lighted tennis courts; fitness center; Jacuzzi; watersports equipment rentals; children's program; game room; concierge; activities desk; room service; in-room massage; babysitting; same-day dry cleaning. *In room:* A/C, TV, dataport, kitchen, fridge, coffeemaker, hair dryer, iron, safe, washer/dryers.

Sheraton Maui *Kids* Terrific facilities for families and fitness buffs and a premier beach location make this beautiful resort an all-around great place to stay. The grande dame of Kaanapali Beach is built into the side of a cliff on the white-sand cove next to Black Rock (a lava formation that rises 80 ft. above the beach), where there's excellent snorkeling. After its recent renovation, the resort is virtually new, with six buildings of six stories or less set in well-established tropical gardens. The new lagoonlike pool features lava-rock waterways, wooden bridges, and an open-air whirlpool. But not everything has changed, thankfully. Cliff divers still swan dive off the torch-lit lava-rock headland in a traditional sunset ceremony—a sight to see. And the views of Kaanapali Beach, with Lanai and Molokai in the distance, are some of the best around.

The new emphasis is on family appeal, with a class of rooms dedicated to those traveling with kids. Every unit is outfitted with amenities galore, right down to toothbrushes and toothpaste.

2605 Kaanapali Pkwy., Lahaina, HI 96761. © 800/782-9488 or 808/661-0031. Fax 808/661-0458. www.sheraton.com/maui. 510 units. $360–$680 double; from $800 suite. Extra person $55. Children 17 and under stay free in parent's room using existing bedding. Resort fee $14. AE, DC, DISC, MC, V. Valet parking $5. **Amenities:** 3 restaurants; 2 bars (1 poolside); lagoon-style pool; 36-hole golf course; 3 tennis courts; fitness center; boutique spa; Jacuzzi; watersports equipment rentals; children's program; concierge; activities desk; car-rental desk; business center; salon; room service; babysitting; same-day laundry service and dry cleaning; coin-op washer/dryers. *In room:* A/C, TV, dataport, fridge, coffeemaker, hair dryer, iron, safe.

Westin Maui *(R) (Kids)*   The 758-room Westin Maui recently built a $5 million spa and gym. To add further to the healthy environment, smoking is no longer allowed in guest rooms (it is allowed in some public areas). I love the fabulous custom-designed, pillow-top "heavenly beds," which come with a choice of five different pillows. Once you get up, head to the "aquatic playground"—an 87,000-square-foot pool area with five free-form heated pools joined by swim-through grottoes, waterfalls, and a 128-foot-long water slide. The fantasy theme extends from the estatelike grounds into the interior's public spaces, which are filled with the shrieks of tropical birds and the splash of waterfalls. The oversize architecture and $2 million art collection make a pleasing backdrop for all the action. Most of the rooms in the two 11-story towers overlook the aquatic playground and the ocean.

2365 Kaanapali Pkwy., Lahaina, HI 96761. *(©)* **888/625-4949** or 808/667-2525. Fax 808/661-5764. www.westinmaui.com. 758 units. $360–$700 double; from $1,000 suite. Extra person $60. Resort fee $18. AE, DC, DISC, MC, V. Valet parking $10. **Amenities:** 5 restaurants; 3 bars; 5 free-form outdoor pools; 36-hole golf course; tennis courts; health club and spa with aerobics, steam baths, sauna, massage, and body treatments; Jacuzzi; watersports equipment rentals; bike rental; children's program; game room; concierge; activities desk; car-rental desk; business center; shopping arcade; salon; room service; in-room and spa massage; babysitting; same-day laundry service and dry cleaning. *In room:* A/C, TV, dataport, minibar, fridge, coffeemaker, hair dryer, iron, safe.

EXPENSIVE

Maui Eldorado Resort *(R) (Kids)*   These spacious condominium units—each with full kitchen, washer/dryer, and daily maid service—feature views from every window. You'll find it hard to believe that this was one of Kaanapali's first properties in the late 1960s; this first-class choice still looks like new. The Outrigger chain has managed to keep prices down to reasonable levels, especially in spring and fall. This is a great choice for families, with big units, grassy areas that are perfect for running off excess energy, and a beachfront (with beach cabanas and a barbecue area) that's usually safe for swimming. Tennis courts are nearby.

2661 Kekaa Dr., Lahaina, HI 96761. © **800/688-7444** or 808/661-0021. Fax 808/667-7039. www.outrigger.com. 204 units. $205–$240 studio double; $255–$295 1-bedroom (rates for up to 4); $355–$480 2-bedroom (rates for up to 6). Numerous packages available, including 5th night free, rental-car packages, senior rates, and more. AE, DC, DISC, MC, V. **Amenities:** 3 outdoor pools; 36-hole golf course; concierge/activities desk; car-rental desk; some business services; washer/dryers. *In room:* A/C, TV, dataport, kitchen, fridge, coffeemaker, hair dryer, iron, safe, washer/dryer.

The Whaler on Kaanapali Beach ★★   In the heart of Kaana-
pali, right on the world-famous beach, lies this oasis of elegance, privacy, and luxury. The relaxing atmosphere strikes you as soon as you enter the open-air lobby, where light reflects off the dazzling koi in the meditative lily pond. No expense has been spared on these gorgeous accommodations; each unit has a full kitchen, washer/dryer, marble bathroom, 10-foot beamed ceilings, and blue-tiled lanai. Every unit boasts spectacular views of Kaanapali's gentle waves or the humpback peaks of the West Maui Mountains. Next door is Whalers Village, with numerous restaurants, bars, and shops. Kaanapali Golf Club's 36 holes are across the street.

2481 Kaanapali Pkwy. (next to Whalers Village), Lahaina, HI 96761. Aston Hotels © **800/922-7866** or 808/661-4861. Fax 808/661-8315. www.astonhotels.com. 360 units. High season $245–$290 studio double; $280–$500 1-bedroom (rate for up to 4 people); $470–$730 2-bedroom (up to 6). Off season $215–$260 studio; $280–$440 1-bedroom; $380–$600 2-bedroom. Check Internet for specials. Extra person $20. Parking $7/day. AE, DC, DISC, MC, V. **Amenities:** Outdoor pool; 5 tennis courts; refurbished fitness room; Hinamana Salon & Spa (which offers massage, pedicure, and manicures); Jacuzzi; concierge desk; activities desk; coin-op washer/dryers; dry cleaning; BBQ area. *In room:* A/C, TV/VHS/DVD, dataport, kitchen, fridge, coffeemaker, hair dryer, iron, safe, free dial-up Internet access (wireless access additional fee), washer/dryer.

MODERATE

Kaanapali Beach Hotel ★ *Value*   It's older and less high-tech
than its upscale neighbors, but the Kaanapali has an irresistible local style and a real Hawaiian warmth. Three low-rise wings, bordering a fabulous stretch of beach, are set around a wide, grassy lawn with coco palms and a whale-shaped pool. The spacious, spotless motel-like rooms are done in wicker and rattan, with Hawaiian-style bedspreads and lanais. The beachfront rooms are separated from the water only by a landscaped walking trail.

Old Hawaii values and customs are always close at hand, and the service is some of the friendliest around. Tiki torches, hula, and Hawaiian music create a festive atmosphere in the expansive open courtyard every night. As part of the hotel's extensive Hawaiiana program, you can learn to cut pineapple, weave lauhala, or dance the hula. There are also an arts-and-crafts fair 3 days a week and a Hawaiian library.

2525 Kaanapali Pkwy., Lahaina, HI 96761. © **800/262-8450** or 808/661-0011. Fax 808/667-5978. www.kbhmaui.com. 430 units. $169–$295 double; from $260 suite. Extra person $25. Car, golf, bed-and-breakfast, and romance packages available, as well as senior discounts. AE, DC, DISC, MC, V. Valet parking $8, self-parking $6. **Amenities:** 2 restaurants (plus a dinner show Tues–Sat); bar; outdoor pool; 36-hole golf course nearby; access to tennis courts; watersports equipment rentals; children's program; concierge/guest services; activities desk; convenience shops; salon; babysitting; coin-op washer/dryers. *In room:* A/C, TV, fridge, coffeemaker, iron, safe.

HONOKOWAI, KAHANA & NAPILI
EXPENSIVE
Napili Kai Beach Resort 🌟🌟 *Finds* The one- and two-story units with double-hipped Hawaii-style roofs face their very own gold-sand beach, which is safe for swimming. Many units have a view of the Pacific, with Molokai and Lanai in the distance. Those who prefer air-conditioning should book into the Honolua Building, where you'll get a fully air-conditioned room set back from the shore around a grassy, parklike lawn and pool. Most (but not all) units have a fully stocked kitchenette with full-size fridge, cooktop, microwave, toaster oven, washer/dryer, and coffeemaker; some have dishwashers as well. On-site pluses include daily maid service, shuffleboard courts, barbecue areas, complimentary coffee and tea, lei making, hula lessons, horticultural tours, and a free weekly mai tai party. There are three nearby championship golf courses and excellent tennis courts at next-door Kapalua Resort.

5900 Honoapiilani Rd. (at the extreme north end of Napili, next to Kapalua), Lahaina, HI 96761. © **800/367-5030** or 808/669-6271. Fax 808/669-0086. www.napilikai.com. 162 units. $200–$240 hotel room double; $250–$325 studio double (sleeps 3–4); $385–$405 1-bedroom suite (sleeps up to 5); $555–$700 2-bedroom (sleeps up to 7). Packages available. AE, DISC, MC, V. **Amenities:** Well-recommended restaurant; bar; 4 outdoor pools; 2 18-hole putting greens (with free golf putters for guest use); complimentary use of tennis racquets; good-size fitness room filled with the latest equipment; Jacuzzi; complimentary watersports equipment; free children's activities at Easter, June 15–Aug 31, and at Christmas; concierge; activities desk; babysitting; laundry service; dry cleaning; coin-op washer/dryers. *In room:* A/C (in most units), TV, kitchenette, fridge, coffeemaker, hair dryer, iron, safe.

MODERATE
Hale Kai 🌟 *Kids* This small, two-story condo complex is ideally located, right on the beach and next door to a county park, which is great for those traveling with kids. Shops, restaurants, and ocean activities are all within a 6-mile radius. The units are older but in excellent shape and come with well-equipped kitchens. Lots of

Where to Stay & Dine from Honokowai to Kapalua

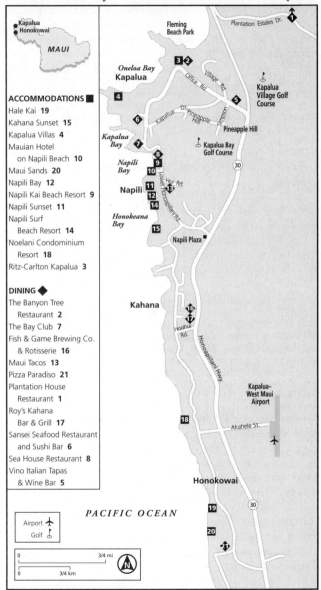

ACCOMMODATIONS ■

Hale Kai **19**

Kahana Sunset **15**

Kapalua Villas **4**

Mauian Hotel
on Napili Beach **10**

Maui Sands **20**

Napili Bay **12**

Napili Kai Beach Resort **9**

Napili Sunset **11**

Napili Surf
Beach Resort **14**

Noelani Condominium
Resort **18**

Ritz-Carlton Kapalua **3**

DINING ◆

The Banyon Tree
Restaurant **2**

The Bay Club **7**

Fish & Game Brewing Co.
& Rotisserie **16**

Maui Tacos **13**

Pizza Paradiso **21**

Plantation House
Restaurant **1**

Roy's Kahana
Bar & Grill **17**

Sansei Seafood Restaurant
and Sushi Bar **6**

Sea House Restaurant **8**

Vino Italian Tapas
& Wine Bar **5**

guests clamor for the oceanfront pool units, but I find the park-view units cooler, and they still have ocean views (upstairs units also have cathedral ceilings). This place fills up fast, so book early; repeat guests make up most of the clientele.

3691 Lower Honoapiilani Rd. (in Honokowai), Lahaina, HI 96761. ℂ **800/446-7307** or 808/669-6333. Fax 808/669-7474. www.halekai.com. 25 units. $115–$130 1-bedroom double; $150–$170 2-bedroom (rates for up to 4); $225 3-bedroom (up to 6). Extra person $15. 5-night minimum. MC, V. **Amenities:** Outdoor pool; concierge; car-rental desk; coin-op washer/dryers. *In room:* TV/VCR, kitchen, fridge, coffeemaker, hair dryer, iron.

Kahana Sunset 𝒜𝒜 *Kids*   Lying in the crook of a sharp horseshoe curve on Lower Honoapiilani Road is this series of wooden condo units, stair-stepping down the side of a hill to a postcard-perfect white-sand beach. In the midst of the buildings sits a grassy lawn with a small pool and Jacuzzi; down by the sandy beach are gazebos and picnic areas. The units feature full kitchens (complete with dishwashers), washer/dryers, large lanais with terrific views, and sleeper sofas. This is a great complex for families: The beach is safe for swimming, the grassy area is away from traffic, and the units are roomy.

4909 Lower Honoapiilani Hwy. (at the northern end of Kahana, almost in Napili). Rentals c/o Premier Properties, P.O. Box 10219, Lahaina, HI 96761. ℂ **800/669-1488** or 808/669-8011 or c/o Sullivan Properties, ℂ **800/326-9874** or 808/669-0423. Fax 808/669-9170. www.kahanasunset.com. 79 units. $135–$265 1-bedroom (sleeps up to 4); $150–$410 2-bedroom (sleeps 6). AE, MC, V. From Hwy. 30, turn *makai* (toward the ocean) at the Napili Plaza (Napilihau St.), then left on Lower Honoapiilani Rd. **Amenities:** 2 outdoor pools (1 just for children); concierge; barbecue area. *In room:* TV/VCR/DVD, kitchen, coffeemaker, iron, safe (in some units), washer/dryer.

Mauian Hotel on Napili Beach 𝒜   The Mauian is perched above a beautiful ½-mile-long white-sand beach with great swimming and snorkeling; there's a pool with chaise longues, umbrellas, and tables on the sun deck, and the verdant grounds are bursting with tropical color. The rooms feature hardwood floors, Indonesian-style furniture, and big lanais with great views. Thoughtful little touches include fresh flowers, plus chilled champagne for guests celebrating a special occasion. There are no phones or TVs in the rooms, but the large *ohana* (family) room does have a TV with a VCR and an extensive library for those who can't bear the solitude. There's complimentary coffee, and phones and fax service are available in the business center. Great restaurants are just a 5-minute walk away, and Kapalua Resort is up the street. The nightly sunsets off the beach are spectacular.

5441 Lower Honoapiilani Rd. (in Napili), Lahaina, HI 96761. ✆ **800/367-5034** or 808/669-6205. Fax 808/669-0129. www.mauian.com. 44 units. $150–$195 double (sleeps up to 4). Rates include continental breakfast. Extra person $10. Children under 5 stay free in parent's room. AE, DISC, MC, V. **Amenities:** Outdoor pool; golf course nearby; tennis courts nearby; activities desk; barbecues; coin-op washer/dryer; shuffleboard court. *In room:* Kitchen, fridge, coffeemaker, no phone.

Maui Sands   The Maui Sands was built back when property wasn't as expensive and developers took the extra time and money to surround their condos with lush landscaping. It's hard to get a unit with a bad view: All face either the ocean (with views of Lanai and Molokai) or tropical gardens blooming with brilliant heliconia, flowering hibiscus, and sweet-smelling ginger. Each roomy unit has a big lanai and a full kitchen. With two big bedrooms, plus space in the living room for a fifth person (or even a sixth), the larger units are good deals for families. There's a narrow beach out front.

Maui Resort Management, 3600 Lower Honoapiilani Rd. (in Honokowai), Lahaina, HI 96761. ✆ **800/367-5037** or 808/669-1902. Fax 808/669-8790. www.maui getaway.com. 76 units. $105–$155 1-bedroom (sleeps up to 3); $180–$220 2-bedroom (sleeps 5). Extra person $10. 7-night minimum. MC, V. **Amenities:** Outdoor pool; coin-op washer/dryer. *In room:* A/C, TV, kitchen, fridge, coffeemaker.

Napili Surf Beach Resort ⭐ *Finds*   This well-maintained, superbly landscaped condo complex has a great location on Napili Beach. Facilities include two pools, three shuffleboard courts, and three gas barbecue grills. The well-furnished units (all with full kitchens) were renovated in 2004 with new carpet, new beds, and some units even have all-new kitchens. Free daily maid service, a rarity in condo properties, keeps the units clean. Management encourages socializing: In addition to weekly mai tai parties and coffee socials, the resort hosts annual shuffleboard and golf tournaments, as well as get-togethers on July 4th, Thanksgiving, Christmas, and New Year's.

50 Napili Place (off Lower Honoapiilani Rd., in Napili), Lahaina, HI 96761. ✆ **800/ 541-0638** or 808/669-8002. Fax 808/669-8004. www.napilisurf.com. 53 units (some with shower only). $140–$200 studio (sleeps up to 3); $215–$290 1-bedroom (sleeps up to 4). Extra person $15. No credit cards. **Amenities:** 2 outdoor pools; shuffleboard; barbecue grills; coin-op washer/dryers. *In room:* TV/VCR, full kitchen, fridge, coffeemaker, iron, safe.

Noelani Condominium Resort ⭐⭐ *Kids*   This oceanfront condo is a great value, whether you stay in a studio or a three-bedroom unit. Everything is first class, from the furnishings to the oceanfront location. Though it's on the water, there's no sandy beach here (despite the photos posted on their website)—but next door is a sandy cove at the county park. There's good snorkeling off the cove, which is frequented by spinner dolphins and turtles in summer and humpback whales in winter. All units feature complete kitchens, entertainment centers, and spectacular views (all except the studio units also have their own washer/dryers and dishwashers). My favorites are in the Anthurium Building, where the condos have oceanfront lanais just 20 feet from the water. The deluxe studios in the Orchid Building have great ocean views for just $119. Guests are invited to a continental breakfast orientation on their first day and mai tai parties at night. There are also barbecue grills for guests' use.

4095 Lower Honoapiilani Rd. (in Kahana), Lahaina, HI 96761. ✆ **800/367-6030** or 808/669-8374. Fax 808/669-7904. www.noelani-condo-resort.com. 50 units. $107–$150 studio double; $157–$180 1-bedroom (sleeps up to 4); $237–$257 2-bedroom (sleeps up to 6); $297–$317 3-bedroom (sleeps up to 8). Rates include continental breakfast on 1st morning. Extra person $10. Children under 18 stay free in parent's room. Packages for honeymooners, seniors, and AAA members available. 3-night minimum. AE, MC, V. **Amenities:** 2 freshwater swimming pools (1 heated for night swimming); access to nearby health club; oceanfront Jacuzzi; concierge; activities desk; car-rental desk; coin-op washer/dryers. *In room:* TV/VCR, kitchen, fridge, coffeemaker, hair dryer, iron, safe, washer/dryer (in larger units).

INEXPENSIVE

Napili Bay ☆ *Finds*   One of Maui's best secret bargains is this small, two-story complex right on Napili's beautiful ½-mile white-sand beach. It's perfect for a romantic getaway: The atmosphere is comfortable and relaxing, the ocean lulls you to sleep at night, and birdsong wakes you in the morning. The beach here is one of the best on the coast, with great swimming and snorkeling. The studio apartments are definitely small, but they pack in everything you should need to feel at home, from a full kitchen to a comfortable queen-size bed, and a roomy lanai that's great for watching the sun set over the Pacific. There's no air-conditioning, but louvered windows and ceiling fans keep the units fairly cool during the day. There are lots of restaurants and a convenience store within walking distance, and you're about 10 to 15 minutes away from Lahaina and some great golf courses.

33 Hui Dr. (off Lower Honoapiilani Hwy., in Napili), c/o Aloha Condos Hawaii, P.O. Box 396681, Keauhou, Hi 96740. ✆ **877/782-5642.** www.alohacondos.com. 33 units. $95–$225 studio for 2. 5-night minimum. MC, V. **Amenities:** Coin-op washer/dryers. *In room:* TV, kitchen, fridge, coffeemaker.

Napili Sunset *Value*   Housed in three buildings (two on the ocean and one across the street), these clean, older, well-maintained units offer good value. At first glance the plain two-story structures don't look like much, but the location, the bargain prices, and the friendly staff are the real hidden treasures here. In addition to daily maid service, the units all have full kitchens (with dishwashers), ceiling fans (no air-conditioning), sofa beds, small dining rooms, and small bedrooms. The beach—one of Maui's best—can get a little crowded because the public beach access is through this property. The studio units are all located in the building off the beach and a few steps up a slight hill; they're a good size, with a full kitchen and either a sofa bed or a Murphy bed, and they overlook the small pool and garden. The one- and two-bedroom units are all on the beach (the downstairs units have lanais that lead right to the sand). The staff makes sure each unit has the basics—paper towels, dishwasher soap, coffee filters, condiments—to get your stay off to a good start. There are restaurants within walking distance.

46 Hui Rd. (in Napili), Lahaina, HI 96761. (℃ **800/447-9229** or 808/669-8083. Fax 808/669-2730. www.napilisunset.com. 42 units. High season $120 studio double; $245 1-bedroom double; $340 2-bedroom (sleeps up to 4). Off season $105 studio; $225 1-bedroom; $290 2-bedroom. Extra person $12. Children under 3 stay free in parent's room. 3-night minimum. MC, V. **Amenities:** Small outdoor pool; coin-op washer/dryers (free detergent supplied). *In room:* TV, kitchen, fridge, coffeemaker.

KAPALUA

If you're interested in a luxurious condo or town house, consider **Kapalua Villas** (℃ **800/545-0018** or 808/669-8088; www.kapalua villas.com). The palatial units dotting the oceanfront cliffs and fairways of this idyllic coast are a (relative) bargain, especially if you're traveling with a group. The one-bedroom condos go for $209 to $369, two bedrooms for $309 to $579, three bedrooms for $435 to $585. Package deals (which include golf, tennis, honeymoon amenities, and car) can save you even more money.

Ritz-Carlton Kapalua 𝒜𝒜 *(Kids)*   Hospitality, the hallmark of Ritz-Carltons around the world, was not up to the usual standard when I last visited the Ritz in Kapalua. First, we were not taken to our room by the bell staff, and the front desk gave us the wrong directions on how to get to our room. The next morning, the service in the breakfast dining room was nonexistent. Guests had to hunt down the coffeepot and serve themselves.

I hope management can correct these flaws, because this Ritz is a complete universe, one of those resorts where you can happily sit by the ocean with a book for 2 whole weeks and never leave the grounds. It rises proudly on a knoll, in a singularly spectacular setting between the rainforest and the sea.

The style is fancy plantation, elegant but not imposing. The public spaces are open, airy, and graceful. Rooms are up to the usual Ritz standard, outfitted with marble bathrooms, private lanais, and in-room fax capability. If you can afford it, stay on the **Club Floor** 🏵🏵🏵—it offers the best amenities in the state, including French-roast coffee in the morning, a buffet at lunch, cookies in the afternoon, and pupus and drinks at sunset. The Ritz Kids program offers a variety of educational activities and sports.

The excellent The Banyan Tree Restaurant (p. 92) has a new chef, and the relaxing spa has just undergone extensive renovation. The resort's Hawaiian cultural program is one of Maui's best, with twice weekly movies and "talk story," along with other events.

1 Ritz-Carlton Dr., Kapalua, HI 96761. ℂ 800/262-8440 or 808/669-6200. Fax 808/669-1566. www.ritzcarlton.com. 548 units. $365–$675 double; from $405 suite; from $900 Club Floor suites. Extra person $50 ($100 in Club Floor rooms). Resort fee $15. Wedding/honeymoon, golf, and other packages available. AE, DC, DISC, MC, V. Valet parking $15; free self-parking. **Amenities:** 4 restaurants; 4 bars (including 1 serving drinks and light fare next to the beach); outdoor pool; access to the Kapalua Resort's 3 championship golf courses (each with its own pro shop) and its deluxe tennis complex; fitness room; spa; 2 outdoor hot tubs; watersports equipment rentals; bike rentals; children's program; game room; concierge; activities desk; car-rental desk; business center; shopping arcade; salon; room service; in-room and spa massage; babysitting; same-day laundry and dry cleaning; concierge-level rooms (some of Hawaii's best, with top-drawer service and amenities). *In room:* A/C, TV, dataport, minibar, coffeemaker, hair dryer, iron, safe, high-speed Internet access.

3 South Maui

MAALAEA

I recommend two booking agencies that rent a host of condominiums and unique vacation homes in the Kihei/Wailea/Maalaea area: **Kihei Maui Vacation** (ℂ **800/541-6284** or 808/879-7581; www.kmvmaui.com) and **Condominium Rentals Hawaii** (ℂ **800/367-5242** or 808/879-2778; www.crhmaui.com).

KIHEI
EXPENSIVE

Maalaea Surf Resort 🏵   This is the place for people who want a quiet, relaxing vacation on a well-landscaped property, with a beautiful white-sand beach right outside. Located at the quiet end of Kihei Road, this two-story complex sprawls across 5 acres of lush tropical gardens. The luxury town houses all have ocean views, big kitchens (with dishwashers), cable TV, and VCRs. Amenities include maid service (Mon–Sat), shuffleboard, barbecue grills, and discounts on tee times at nearby golf courses. Restaurants and shops are within a 5-minute drive.

Where to Stay & Dine in South Maui

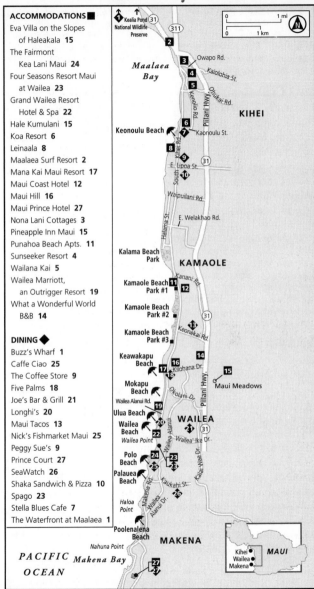

ACCOMMODATIONS ■

Eva Villa on the Slopes
of Haleakala **15**

The Fairmont
Kea Lani Maui **24**

Four Seasons Resort Maui
at Wailea **23**

Grand Wailea Resort
Hotel & Spa **22**

Hale Kumulani **15**

Koa Resort **6**

Leinaala **8**

Maalaea Surf Resort **2**

Mana Kai Maui Resort **17**

Maui Coast Hotel **12**

Maui Hill **16**

Maui Prince Hotel **27**

Nona Lani Cottages **3**

Pineapple Inn Maui **15**

Punahoa Beach Apts. **11**

Sunseeker Resort **4**

Wailana Kai **5**

Wailea Marriott,
an Outrigger Resort **19**

What a Wonderful World
B&B **14**

DINING ◆

Buzz's Wharf **1**

Caffe Ciao **25**

The Coffee Store **9**

Five Palms **18**

Joe's Bar & Grill **21**

Longhi's **20**

Maui Tacos **13**

Nick's Fishmarket Maui **25**

Peggy Sue's **9**

Prince Court **27**

SeaWatch **26**

Shaka Sandwich & Pizza **10**

Spago **23**

Stella Blues Cafe **7**

The Waterfront at Maalaea **1**

Kealia Pond
National Wildlife
Preserve

Maalaea Bay

Owapo Rd.

Kaiolohia St.

Kenolio Rd.

Ohukai Rd.

Piilani Hwy.

KIHEI

Keonoulu Beach

Kaonoulu St.

South Kihei Rd.

E. Lipoa St.

Waipuilani Rd.

Halama St.

E. Welakhao Rd.

Kalama Beach
Park

KAMAOLE

Kamaole Beach
Park #1

Kanani Rd.

Kamaole Beach
Park #2

Kamaole Beach
Park #3

Keonekai Rd.

Keawakapu
Beach

Kilohana Dr.

Piilani Hwy.

Maui Meadows

Mokapu
Beach

Wailea Alanui Rd.

Okolani Dr.

Ulua Beach

WAILEA

Wailea
Beach

Wailea Alanui

Wailea Point

Wailea 'Ike Dr.

Polo
Beach

Kaukahi St.

Palauea
Beach

Makena Rd.

Wailea Alanui Dr.

Kaulana Beach Dr.

Haloa
Point

Poolenalena
Beach

MAKENA

Nahuna Point

*PACIFIC
OCEAN*

Makena Bay

Kihei
Wailea
Makena

MAUI

12 S. Kihei Rd. (at S. Kihei Rd. and Hwy. 350), Kihei, HI 96753. ⓒ **800/423-7953** or 808/879-1267. Fax 808/874-2884. www.maalaeasurfresort.com. 34 units. $250–$285 1-bedroom unit (sleeps up to 4 people); $330–$390 2-bedroom (sleeps up to 6). MC, V. **Amenities:** 2 outdoor pools; 2 tennis courts; concierge; activities desk; car-rental desk; coin-op washer/dryers. *In room:* A/C, TV/VCR/DVD, kitchen, fridge, coffeemaker, hair dryer, iron, safe.

Maui Coast Hotel 🎣🎣 This place stands out as one of the only moderately priced hotels in Kihei (which is largely full of affordable condo complexes rather than traditional hotels or resorts). Ask about the room/car packages: The Maui Coast's Extra Value package gives you a rental car for just a few dollars more than the regular room rate. It's a great location, about a block from Kamaole Beach Park I, with plenty of bars, restaurants, and shopping within walking distance and a golf course nearby. The rooms offer extras such as sitting areas, whirlpool tubs, ceiling fans, and private lanais.

2259 S. Kihei Rd. (1 block from Kamaole Beach Park I), Kihei, HI 96753. ⓒ **800/895-6284** or 808/874-6284. Fax 808/875-4731. www.mauicoasthotel.com. 265 units. $195 double; $225 suite; $255 1-bedroom (sleeps up to 4). Children 17 and under stay free in parent's room using existing bedding. Rollaway bed $20. Packages including rental car available. AE, DC, DISC, MC, V. **Amenities:** Restaurant; pool bar with nightly entertainment; outdoor pool (plus children's wading pool); 2 night-lit tennis courts; fitness room; concierge; activities desk; room service; laundry service; dry cleaning; free use of self-serve washer/dryers. *In room:* A/C, TV, fridge, coffeemaker, hair dryer, iron, safe.

Maui Hill 🎣 If you can't decide between the privacy of a condo and the conveniences of a hotel, try this place. Managed by the respected Aston chain, Maui Hill gives you the best of both worlds. Located on a hill above the heat of Kihei town, this large, Spanish-style resort (with stucco buildings, red-tile roofs, and arched entries) combines all the amenities and activities of a hotel—pool, hot tub, tennis courts, Hawaiiana classes, maid service, and more—with large luxury condos that have full kitchens and plenty of privacy. Nearly all units have ocean views, dishwashers, washer/dryers, queen-size sofa beds, and big lanais. Beaches, restaurants, and shops are within easy walking distance, and a golf course is nearby. Management goes out of its way to make sure your stay is perfect.

2881 S. Kihei Rd. (across from Kamaole Park III, between Keonekai St. and Kilohana Dr.), Kihei, HI 96753. ⓒ **800/92-ASTON** or 808/879-6321. Fax 808/879-8945. www.aston-hotels.com. 140 units. High season $215–$310 1-bedroom apt; $265–$350 2-bedroom; $305–$390 3-bedroom. AE, DC, DISC, MC, V. **Amenities:** Outdoor pool; putting green; tennis courts; Jacuzzi; concierge; activities desk; car-rental desk; laundry service; dry cleaning; barbecue grills; coin-op washer/dryers. *In room:* A/C, TV/VCR, kitchen, fridge, coffeemaker, hair dryer, iron, safe, washer/dryer.

MODERATE

Eva Villa on the Slopes of Haleakala ⚐⚐ (Finds) This three-
unit bed-and-breakfast is located on ½ acre of lushly landscaped property at the top of the Maui Meadows subdivision. From the rooftop lanai, guests have a spectacular view of the sunset. From the continental breakfast stocked in each roomy unit's kitchen (fresh island fruit, juice, bread, muffins, jam, and coffee/tea) to the decor of the suites to the heated pool, Jacuzzi, and individual barbecue facilities, this is a great place to stay. The location couldn't be better—just a few minutes' drive to Kihei's sunny beaches, golf courses, tennis, and shopping, and restaurants in Kihei and Wailea. The cottage has a living room, full kitchen, and separate bedroom; the poolside studio is a one-room unit with a huge kitchen; and the poolside suite has two bedrooms and a kitchenette.

815 Kumulani Dr., Kihei, HI 96753. © 800/824-6409 or 808/874-6407. Fax 808/874-6407. www.mauibnb.com. 3 units. $125–$145. Extra person $15. No credit cards. **Amenities:** Heated outdoor pool; Jacuzzi; individual barbecue facilities. *In room:* TV/VCR, kitchen or kitchenette, coffeemaker, fridge, washer/dryer in cottage.

Leinaala ⚐ (Value) From Kihei Road, you can't see Leinaala amid
the jumble of buildings, but this oceanfront boutique condo offers excellent accommodations at 1980s prices. The building is set back from the water, with a county park—an oasis of green grass and tennis courts—in between. A golf course lies nearby. The units are compact but filled with everything you need: a full kitchen, sofa bed, and oceanview lanai. (Hideaway beds are available if you need one.)

998 S. Kihei Rd., Kihei, HI 96753. © 800/822-4409 or 808/879-2235. Fax 808/874-6144. www.mauicondo.com. 24 units. $145 1-bedroom double; $190 2-bedroom (sleeps up to 4). 4-night minimum. No credit cards. **Amenities:** Outdoor pool; coin-op washer/dryers. *In room:* A/C, TV, kitchen, fridge, coffeemaker.

Mana Kai Maui Resort ⚐ (Kids) This eight-story complex, situ-
ated on a beautiful white-sand cove, is an unusual combination of hotel and condominium. The hotel rooms, which account for half of the total number of units, are small but nicely furnished. The condo units are great for families and feature full kitchens and open living rooms with sliding-glass doors that lead to small lanais overlooking the sandy beach and ocean. Some units are beginning to show their age (the building is more than 30 years old), but they're all clean and comfortable. One of the best snorkeling beaches on the coast is just steps away; a golf course and tennis courts are nearby.

2960 S. Kihei Rd. (between Kilohana and Keonekai roads, at the Wailea end of Kihei), Kihei, HI 96753. © 800/367-5242 or 808/879-2778. Fax 808/879-7825. www.crhmaui.com. 105 units. $130 hotel room double; $180–$255 1-bedroom (sleeps up to 4); $230–$310 2-bedroom (up to 6). AE, MC, V. **Amenities:** Restaurant (Five Palms, p. 94); bar; outdoor pool; concierge; coin-op washer/dryers. *In room:* A/C (in hotel rooms only), TV, kitchen (in condo units), fridge, coffeemaker, safe.

Punahoa Beach Apartments 𝕲 *Value*   Book this place! I can't put it any more simply than that. The location—on a quiet side street with ocean frontage—is fabulous. A grassy lawn rolls about 50 feet down to the beach, where there are great snorkeling just offshore and a popular surfing spot next door; shopping and restaurants are all within walking distance. All of the beautifully decorated units in this small, four-story building have fully equipped kitchens and lanais with great ocean views. Rooms go quickly in winter, so reserve early.

2142 Iliili Rd. (off S. Kihei Rd., 300 ft. from Kamaole Beach I), Kihei, HI 96753. ℂ 800/564-4380 or 808/879-2720. Fax 808/875-9147. www.punahoabeach.com. 13 units. High season $130 studio double; $185–$198 1-bedroom double; $220 2-bedroom double. Off season $94 studio; $130–$145 1-bedroom; $160 2-bedroom. Extra person $15. 5-night minimum. AE, MC, V. **Amenities:** Coin-op washer/dryer. *In room:* TV, kitchen, fridge, coffeemaker, iron.

Sunseeker Resort *Finds*   This former budget property, located just across the street from a terrific white-sand beach, has a new management team that has spiffed up the studio and one-bedroom units with custom furniture and added air-conditioning and other amenities such as high-speed Internet access and concierge services. Studios offer terrific wallet-pleasing prices. The one-bedrooms, which have a pull-out sofa in the living room and new appliances in the kitchen, are a good deal in the off season at $160 but definitely not a deal during the high season at $200. All units have private lanais with ocean views.

551 S. Kihei Rd., P.O. Box 276, Kihei, HI 96753. ℂ **800/532-MAUI** or 808/879-1261. Fax 808/874-3877. www.mauisunseeker.com. 4 units. $85–$125 studio; $160–$200 1-bedroom. 3-night minimum. Extra person $15. AE, DISC, MC, V. **Amenities:** Hot tub; concierge; same-day laundry service; coin-op washer/dryer; gas barbecue. *In room:* A/C, TV/VCR, full kitchen (in 1-bedroom) or kitchenette (studio), coffeemaker, hair dryer, high-speed Internet.

INEXPENSIVE

Hale Kumulani 𝕲 *Kids* *Finds*   At the top of Maui Meadows subdivision, about a 5-minute drive to the beach, lies this ½-acre property, surrounded by a 40,000-acre wilderness area with two units. The first is a darling one-room cottage with full kitchen, wood flooring, high beam ceilings, living-room area (with full-size guest sofa/futon), large deck, and outdoor shower. Underneath the main house, but with a private entrance, is the waterfall suite. It has a kitchenette and a giant outdoor patio with an overhang that provides shade. Both units have access to the organic vegetable garden, numerous fruit trees, and beach equipment. Hosts Ron and Merry have a full-size crib, stroller, and junior beds available for kids.

874 Kumulani Dr., Maui Meadows, Kihei, HI 96753. ℂ 808/891-0425. Fax 808/ 891-0269. www.cottagemaui.com. 2 units. $125 double suite; $145 cottage double. 4-night minimum. MC, V. **Amenities:** 6 championship golf courses within 5 miles; aquatic center with 3 pools nearby (a 7-min. drive). *In room:* TV/VCR, kitchen (in cottage), kitchenette (in suite), fridge, coffeemaker, hair dryer, iron, washer/dryer.

Koa Resort 🐧 *(Kids)*   Located just across the street from the ocean, Koa Resort consists of five two-story wooden buildings on more than 5½ acres of landscaped grounds. The spacious, privately owned one-, two-, and three-bedroom units are decorated with care and come fully equipped, right down to dishwashers in the kitchens. Families should enjoy the tennis courts, pool, and putting green. The larger condos have both showers and tubs; the smaller units have showers only. All feature large lanais, ceiling fans, and washer/dryers. For maximum peace and quiet, ask for a unit far from Kihei Road. Bars, restaurants, and a golf course are nearby.

811 S. Kihei Rd. (between Kulanihakoi St. and Namauu Place). c/o Bello Realty, P.O. Box 1776, Kihei, HI 96753. ℂ 800/541-3060 or 808/879-3328. Fax 808/875-1483. www.bellomaui.com. 54 units (some with shower only). High season $85–$110 1-bedroom; $100–$130 2-bedroom; $160–$180 2-bedroom. MC, V. **Amenities:** Outdoor pool; 18-hole putting green; 2 tennis courts; Jacuzzi. *In room:* TV, kitchen, fridge, coffeemaker, iron, safe, washer/dryer.

Nona Lani Cottages 🐧 *(Finds)*   Picture this: a grassy expanse dotted with eight cottages tucked among palm, fruit, and sweet-smelling flower trees, right across the street from a white-sand beach. This is one of the great hidden deals in Kihei. The cottages are tiny but contain everything you'll need: a small but complete kitchen, twin beds that double as couches in the living room, a separate bedroom with a queen-size bed, and a lanai with table and chairs.

If the cabins are booked, or if you want a bit more luxury, you might opt for one of the private guest rooms. These beautiful units feature plush carpet, koa bed frames, air-conditioning, lanais, and private entrances.

455 S. Kihei Rd. (just south of Hwy. 31), P.O. Box 655, Kihei, HI 96753. ℂ 800/ 733-2688 or 808/879-2497. www.nonalanicottages.com. 11 units. $75–$95 double; $90–$105 cottage. Extra person $12–$15. 3-night minimum for rooms, 4-night minimum for cottages. No credit cards. **Amenities:** Coin-op washer/dryers. *In room:* A/C, TV, kitchen (in cottages), fridge, coffeemaker, no phone.

Pineapple Inn Maui *(Finds)*   Opened at the end of 2004, this charming inn is an exquisite find, with terrific prices. Located in the residential Maui Meadows area, with panoramic ocean views, this two-story inn boasts gorgeous landscaping, with tropical flowers and plants and a lily pond in the front and a giant saltwater pool and Jacuzzi overlooking the ocean. Each of the rooms is soundproof and expertly decorated, with a small kitchenette stocked with juice, pastries, and drinks on your arrival. There's also an incredible view off your own private lanai. If you need more room, book the darling two-bedroom, one-bathroom cottage (wood floors, beautiful artwork) with a full kitchen (even a dishwasher), separate bedrooms, and a private lanai. The cottage is landscaped for maximum privacy.

3170 Akala Dr., Kihei, HI 96753 *(C)* **877/212-MAUI (6284)** or 808/298-4403. www. pineappleinnmaui.com. 4 units, 1 2-bedroom cottage. $99–$119 double; $165 cottage for 4. 3-night minimum for rooms, 6-night minimum for cottage. No credit cards. **Amenities:** Large saltwater pool; Jacuzzi; complimentary laundry facilities; barbecue area. *In room:* A/C,TV/VCR, kitchenette (in rooms), full kitchen (in cottage), fridge, coffeemaker, hair dryer, no phone in rooms, phone/answering machine in cottage, wireless Internet access.

Wailana Kai *(Value)*   Bello Realty has added this renovated, two-story, 10-unit, one- and two-bedroom apartment complex to its collection. As of this writing, one-bedroom units start at $85, but this is a deal that will not last long. Once they get a reputation, the prices most likely will go up. Located at the end of a cul-de-sac and just a 1-minute walk to the beach, the property was totally renovated in 2004 with two types of units: standard (perfectly acceptable, clean, with new paint, furniture, and more) and deluxe (the ones I recommend, for only a few dollars more). All units have full kitchens and soundproof concrete walls, and the second floor has ocean views.

34 Wailana Place. c/o Bello Realty, P.O. Box 1776, Kihei, HI 96753. *(C)* **800/541-3060** or 808/879-3328. Fax 808/875-1483. www.bellomaui.com. 10 units. $85–$100 1-bedroom; $110–$125 2-bedroom. MC, V. **Amenities:** Outdoor pool; barbecue area, coin-op washer/dryer. *In room:* TV/VCR, kitchen, fridge, coffeemaker, iron.

What a Wonderful World B&B *(Value)*   This impeccably done B&B has a great location and excellent rates. Hostess Eva Tantillo has not only a full-service travel agency, but also a master's degree—along with several years of experience—in hotel management. The result? One of Maui's finest bed-and-breakfasts, centrally located in Kihei (½ mile to Kamaole II Beach Park, 5 min. from Wailea golf courses, and convenient to shopping and restaurants). Choose one of four units: the master suite (with small fridge, coffeemaker, and barbecue grill on the lanai); studio apartment (with fully equipped kitchen); or two one-bedroom apartments (also with full kitchens). You're also welcome to use the communal barbecue. Eva serves a gourmet family-style breakfast (eggs Benedict, waffles, fruit blintzes, and more) on her lanai, which boasts views of white-sand beaches and the West Maui Mountains.

2828 Umalu Place (off Keonakai St., near Hwy. 31), Kihei, HI 96753. (✆ **800/943-5804** or 808/879-9103. Fax 808/874-9352. www.amauibedandbreakfast.com. 4 units. $75 double; $89 studio double; $99 1-bedroom apt. 5% discount for paying in cash. Rates include full breakfast. Children 11 and under stay free in parent's room. AE, MC, V. **Amenities:** Hot tub; laundry facilities. *In room:* TV, kitchenette, fridge, coffeemaker, hair dryer, iron.

WAILEA

For a complete selection of condo units throughout Wailea and Makena, contact **Destination Resorts Hawaii** (✆ **800/367-5246** or 808/879-1595; fax 808/874-3554; www.drhmaui.com). Its luxury units include studio doubles starting at $200, one-bedroom doubles from $205, two bedrooms from $245, and three bedrooms from $345. Children under 12 stay free; minimum stays vary by property.

VERY EXPENSIVE

The Fairmont Kea Lani Maui ★★★   This blinding-white complex of arches and turrets is the place to get your money's worth. For the price of a hotel room, you get an entire suite—plus a few extras. Each unit in this all-suite luxury hotel has a kitchenette, a living room with entertainment center and sofa bed, a marble wet bar, an oversize marble bathroom with separate shower big enough for a party, a spacious bedroom, and a large lanai that overlooks the pools, lawns, and white-sand beach.

A real plus is the small boutique spa offering the very latest in body work in intimate, relaxing surroundings. Even if you are not staying on the property, try this spa.

The villas are definitely out of a fantasy. The rich and famous stay in these 2,000-square-foot two- and three-bedroom beach bungalows, each with its own plunge pool and gourmet kitchen.

4100 Wailea Alanui Dr., Wailea, HI 96753. (✆ **800/659-4100** or 808/875-4100. Fax 808/875-1200. www.fairmont.com/kealani. 450 units. $345–$785 suite (sleeps up to 4); from $1,400 villa. AE, DC, DISC, MC, V. **Amenities:** 4 restaurants (including Nick's Fishmarket Maui, p. 98); 3 bars (with sunset cocktails and nightly entertainment at the Caffé Ciao restaurant, p. 98); 2 large swimming "lagoons" connected by a 140-ft. water slide and swim-up bar, plus an adult pool; use of Wailea Golf Club's 3 18-hole championship golf courses, as well as the nearby Makena and Elleair golf courses; use of Wailea Tennis Center's 11 courts (3 lit for night play, and a pro shop); fine 24-hr. fitness center; excellent full-service spa offering the latest in body treatments, facials, and massage; Jacuzzi; watersports equipment rentals; bike rentals; children's program; game room; concierge; activities desk; car-rental desk; business center; shopping arcade; salon; room service; in-room and spa massage; babysitting; same-day laundry service and dry cleaning. *In room:* A/C, TV, dataport, kitchenette, minibar, fridge, coffeemaker, hair dryer, iron, safe, high-speed Internet access (additional fee), microwave.

Four Seasons Resort Maui at Wailea 𝒜𝒜𝒜 *Kids*   If money's no object, this is the place to spend it. Although it sits on a glorious beach between two other hotels, The Four Seasons seems like it inhabits its own separate world, thanks to an open courtyard of pools and gardens. First-rate amenities include outstanding restaurants, an excellent spa, and a wonderful activities program for kids (complimentary, of course). In fact, this may be the most kid-friendly hotel on Maui, with cookies and milk on arrival, children's menus in all restaurants, and complimentary baby gear.

The spacious (about 600 sq. ft.) rooms feature furnished lanais (nearly all with ocean views) that are great for watching whales in winter and sunsets year-round. The grand bathrooms contain deep marble tubs, showers for two, and lighted French makeup mirrors.

Wolfgang Puck's Spago restaurant (p. 97) features a fusion of Hawaiian and California cuisine in a dreamy open-air setting. Ferraro's at Seaside restaurant offers a casual atmosphere overlooking the Pacific by day; by night, it features authentic Italian *cucina rustica* with great sunset views and a romantic atmosphere under the stars. The poolside Pacific Grill offers lavish breakfast buffets and dinners featuring Pacific Rim cuisine.

The ritzy neighborhood surrounding the hotel is home to great restaurants and shopping, the Wailea Tennis Center (known as Wimbledon West), and six golf courses—not to mention that great beach, with gentle waves and islands framing the view on either side.

3900 Wailea Alanui Dr., Wailea, HI 96753. © **800/334-MAUI (6284)** or 808/874-8000. Fax 808/874-2222. www.fourseasons.com/maui. 380 units. $365–$705 double; $815 Club Floor double; from $660 suite. Packages available. Extra person $100 ($170 in Club Floor rooms). Children under 18 stay free in parent's room. AE, DC, MC, V. **Amenities:** 3 restaurants (including Spago, p. 97); 3 bars (with nightly entertainment); 3 fabulous outdoor pools; putting green; use of Wailea Golf Club's 3 18-hole championship golf courses, as well as the nearby Makena and Elleair golf courses; 2 on-site tennis courts (lit for night play); use of Wailea Tennis Center's 11 courts (3 lit for night play, and a pro shop); health club featuring outdoor cardiovascular equipment (with individual TV/video players); excellent spa (offering a variety of treatments in the spa, in-room, and oceanside); 2 whirlpools (1 for adults only); beach pavilion with watersports gear rentals and 1 hr. free use of snorkel equipment; complimentary use of bicycles; fabulous year-round kids' program, plus a teen recreation center and a children's video library and toys; game room (with shuffleboard, pool tables, jukebox, big-screen TV, and video games); one of Maui's best concierge desks; activities desk; car-rental desk; business center; shopping arcade; salon; room service; in-room, spa, or oceanside massage; babysitting; same-day laundry service and dry cleaning; concierge-level rooms. *In room:* A/C, TV, dataport, minibar, fridge, coffeemaker, hair dryer, iron, safe, high-speed Internet (additional fee).

Grand Wailea Resort Hotel & Spa 🐼🐼   Here's where grand becomes grandiose. This monument to excess is extremely popular with families, incentive groups, and conventions. It has a Japanese restaurant decorated with real rocks hewn from the slopes of Mount Fuji; 10,000 tropical plants in the lobby; an intricate pool system with slides, waterfalls, rapids, and a water-powered elevator to take you up to the top; an elaborate spa; a restaurant in a man-made tide pool; a floating New England–style wedding chapel; and nothing but oceanview rooms, outfitted with every amenity you should need. And it's all crowned with a $30 million collection of original art. Though minimalists may be put off, there's no denying that the Grand Wailea is plush, professional, and pampering, with all the diversions you could imagine. Oh, and did I mention the fantastic beach out front?

3850 Wailea Alanui Dr., Wailea, HI 96753. ⓒ **800/888-6100** or 808/875-1234. Fax 808/874-2442. www.grandwailea.com. 780 units. $485–$905 double; from $1,700 suite. Concierge (Na Pua) tower from $875. Resort fee $18. Extra person $50 ($100 in Na Pua Tower). AE, DC, DISC, MC, V. **Amenities:** 6 restaurants; 7 bars (including a nightclub with laser-light shows and a hydraulic dance floor); 2,000-ft.-long Action Pool, featuring a swim/ride through mountains and grottoes; use of Wailea Golf Club's 3 18-hole championship golf courses, as well as the nearby Makena and Elleair golf courses; use of Wailea Tennis Center's 11 courts (3 lit for night play, and a pro shop); complete fitness center; Hawaii's largest spa, the 50,000-sq.-ft. Spa Grande, with a blend of European-, Eastern-, and Hawaiian-style techniques; Jacuzzi; watersports equipment rentals; complimentary dive and windsurf lessons; bike rentals; children's program; game room; concierge; activities desk; car-rental desk; business center; shopping arcade; salon; room service; in-room and spa massage; babysitting; same-day laundry service and dry cleaning; concierge-level rooms. *In room:* A/C, TV, dataport, kitchenette, minibar, fridge ($25 per stay fee), coffeemaker, hair dryer, iron, safe.

EXPENSIVE

Wailea Marriott, an Outrigger Resort 🐼🐼   This classic open-air, 1970s-style hotel in a tropical garden by the sea gives you a sense of what Maui was like before the big resort boom. It was the first resort built in Wailea (in 1976), and it remains the most Hawaiian of them all. Airy and comfortable, with touches of Hawaiian art throughout and a terrific aquarium that stretches forever behind the front desk, it just feels right.

The hotel manages to fit into its environment without overwhelming it. Eight buildings, all low rise except for an eight-story tower, are spread along 22 gracious acres of lawns and gardens spiked by coco palms, with lots of open space and a ½ mile of oceanfront property on a point between Wailea and Ulua beaches. The vast, parklike expanses are a luxury on this now-crowded coast.

In 2000, the resort went through a $25 million renovation that expanded the entrance into an open-air courtyard with a waterfall and carp pond, transformed the south pool into a water-activities area complete with two water slides, and refurbished and upgraded the guest rooms.

Recently, they have added the small Mandara Spa with a large list of treatments from relaxing massages to aroma wraps to rejuvenating facials in a very Zen atmosphere. The only critique I have is that they do not (at this time) have a shower facility, so if you aren't staying at the hotel, bring a washcloth to wipe down with afterward.

3700 Wailea Alanui Dr., Wailea, HI 96753. © **800/367-2960** or 808/879-1922. Fax 808/874-8331. www.marriotthawaii.com. 524 units. $355–$525 double; from $650 suite. Extra person $40. Packages available. AE, DC, DISC, MC, V. **Amenities:** 2 restaurants; 2 bars; 3 outdoor pools; use of Wailea Golf Club's 3 18-hole championship golf courses; use of Wailea Tennis Center's 11 courts (3 lit for night play, and a pro shop); fitness room; Mandara Spa; Jacuzzi; watersports equipment rentals; children's program (plus kids-only pool and recreation center); concierge; activities desk; business center; shopping arcade; salon; room service; in-room and spa massage; babysitting; same-day laundry service and dry cleaning; coin-op washer/dryers. *In room:* A/C, TV, dataport, fridge, coffeemaker, hair dryer, iron, safe.

MAKENA

Maui Prince Hotel ✯✯ If you're looking for a vacation in a beautiful, tranquil spot with a golden-sand beach, here's your place. But if you plan to tour Maui, you might try another hotel. The Maui Prince is at the end of the road, far, far away from anything else on the island, so sightseeing in other areas would require a lot of driving.

When you first see the stark-white hotel, it looks like a high-rise motel stuck in the woods—but only from the outside. Inside, you'll discover an atrium garden with a koi-filled waterfall stream; an ocean view from every room; and a simple, clutter-free decor. Rooms are small but come with private lanais with great views.

5400 Makena Alanui, Makena, HI 96753. © **800/321-6284** or 808/874-1111. Fax 808/879-8763. www.mauiprincehotel.com. 310 units. $335–$525 double; from

$700 suite. Extra person $40. Packages available. AE, DC, MC, V. **Amenities:** 4 restaurants (including the excellent Prince Court, p. 99); 2 bars with local Hawaiian music nightly; 2 outdoor pools (adults' and children's); 36 holes of golf (designed by Robert Trent Jones, Jr.); 6 Plexipave tennis courts (2 lit for night play); fitness room; Jacuzzi; watersports equipment rentals; children's program; concierge; activities desk; shopping arcade; salon; room service; in-room massage; babysitting; same-day laundry service and dry cleaning. *In room:* A/C, TV, dataport, fridge, hair dryer, iron, safe.

4 Upcountry Maui

MAKAWAO, OLINDA & HALIIMAILE

When you stay in the cooler upcountry climate of Makawao, Olinda, and Haliimaile, on the slopes of Maui's 10,000-foot Haleakala volcano, you'll be (relatively) close to Haleakala National Park. Makawao and Olinda are approximately 90 minutes from the entrance to the park at the 7,000-foot level (you still have 3,000 ft. and another 30–45 min. to get to the top). Haliimaile, which is about 10 to 15 minutes driving time from Makawao, adds time to your drive up to the summit. Accommodations in Kula are the only other options that will get you closer to the summit so you can make the sunrise.

EXPENSIVE

Aloha Cottage ★★ *Finds*   This could be one of the most romantic spots on Maui. Hidden in the secluded rolling hills of Olinda on a 5-acre parcel of manicured, landscaped tropical foliage are two separate cottages, both designed and decorated by the hosts, Ron and Ranjana Serle. The Thai Treehouse ($245 a night) resembles an upscale Thai home with high-beam, vaulted ceilings; teak floors; and a king-size cherrywood bed in the center of the room. The private deck and private soaking tub make this a very romantic lodging. As fabulous as the Thai Tree House is, the Bali Bungalow ($275) is even better. Up a private driveway through a bamboo archway, the Balinese cottage features an octagonal design with multifaceted skylights, a large marble shower built for two, hand-carved teak cabinets in the kitchen area, and Oriental carpets on the hardwood floors. Out on the private deck is a soaking tub for two. Ranjana can arrange weddings, prepare a private dinner, set up personal massages, and even organize a private yoga session for two.

1879 Olinda Rd., Makawao, HI 96765. © **888/328-3330** or 808/573-8555. Fax 808/573-2551. www.alohacottage.com. 2 cottages. $245–$275 double. 3-night minimum. MC, V. *In room:* TV/VCR/CD, kitchen, fridge, coffeemaker, hair dryer, iron, safe, private soaking tub.

MODERATE

Olinda Country Cottages & Inn ★★ *Finds*   This charming B&B is set on the slopes of Haleakala in the crisp, clean air of Olinda, on an 8½-acre farm dotted with protea plants and surrounded by 35,000 acres of ranch lands (with miles of great hiking trails). The 5,000-square-foot country home, outfitted with a professional eye to detail, has large windows with incredible panoramic views of all of Maui. Upstairs are two guest rooms with country furnishings, private full bathrooms, and separate entryways. Connected to the main house but with its own private entrance, the Pineapple Sweet has a full kitchen, an antiques-filled living room, and a marble-tiled full bathroom. A separate 1,000-square-foot cottage is the epitome of cozy country luxury, with a fireplace, a bedroom with queen-size bed, cushioned window seats (with great sunset views), and cathedral ceilings. The 950-square-foot Hidden Cottage (located in a truly secluded spot surrounded by protea flowers) features three decks, 8-foot French glass doors, a full kitchen, a washer/dryer, and a private tub for two on the deck.

Restaurants are a 15-minute drive away in Makawao, and beaches are another 15 minutes beyond that. Once ensconced, however, you may never want to leave this enchanting inn.

2660 Olinda Rd. (near the top of Olinda Rd., a 15-min. drive from Makawao), Makawao, HI 96768. ⓒ **800/932-3435** or 808/572-1453. Fax 808/573-5326. www.mauibnbcottages.com. 5 units. $140 double; $140 suite double; $195–$245 cottage for 2 (sleeps up to 5). Extra person $25. 2-night minimum for rooms and suite, 3-night minimum for cottages. No credit cards. *In room:* TV, kitchen (in cottages), fridge, coffeemaker, washer/dryer (cottages only).

INEXPENSIVE

Banyan Tree House ★ *Finds*   Huge monkeypod trees (complete with swing and hammock) extend their branches over this 2½-acre property like a giant green canopy. The restored 1920s plantation manager's house is decorated with Hawaiian furniture from the 1930s. The house can accommodate a big family or a group of friends; it has three spacious bedrooms with big, comfortable beds and three marble-tiled bathrooms. A fireplace stands at one end of the huge living room, a large lanai runs the entire length of the house, and the hardwood floors shine throughout. The four smaller guest cottages have been totally renovated and also feature hardwood floors and marble bathrooms.

New additions to this grand property include a full-size swimming pool and Jacuzzi. The quiet neighborhood and old Hawaii ambience give this place a comfortable, easygoing atmosphere.

Restaurants and shops are just minutes away in Makawao, and the beach is a 15-minute drive away—but this place is so relaxing that you may find yourself wanting to do nothing more than lie in the hammock and watch the clouds float by.

3265 Baldwin Ave. (next to Veteran's Cemetery, less than a mile below Makawao), Makawao, HI 96768. ℂ **808/572-9021**. Fax 808/573-5072. www.hawaii mauirentals.com. 1 house, 4 cottages. $85–$115 cottage for 2; $350 3-bedroom house (sleeps up to 9). Extra person $20. Children 12 and under stay for $10 in parent's room. 3-night minimum for house. No credit cards. **Amenities:** Outdoor pool; Jacuzzi; babysitting; small charge for self-serve washer/dryer. *In room:* Kitchen or kitchenette, fridge, coffeemaker.

Hale Ho'okipa Inn Makawao ✈ *Finds* Step back in time at this 1924 plantation-style home, rescued by owner Cherie Attix in 1996 and restored to its original charm (on the State and National Historic Registers). Cherie lovingly refurbished the old wooden floors, filled the rooms with furniture from the 1920s, and hung works by local artists on the walls. The result is a charming, serene place to stay, just a 5-minute walk from the shops and restaurants of Makawao, 15 minutes from beaches, and an hour's drive from the top of Haleakala. The guest rooms have separate outside entrances and private bathrooms. The house's front and back porches are both wonderful for sipping tea and watching the sunset. The Kona Wing is a two-bedroom suite with private bathroom and use of the kitchen. Cherie recently added a separate cottage next door with one bed and bathroom, plus a sleeping loft with a half bathroom upstairs for $145 double.

32 Pakani Place, Makawao, HI 96768. ℂ **877/572-6698** or 808/572-6698. Fax 808/573-2580. www.maui-bed-and-breakfast.com. 4 units (2 with shower only). $95–$125 double; $145–$165 suite with full kitchen. Cottage is $145 double. Rates include continental breakfast. Extra person $10. MC, V. From Haleakala Hwy., turn left on Makawao Ave., then turn right on the 5th street on the right off Makawao Ave. (Pakani Place); 2nd to the last house on the right (green house with white picket fence and water tower). *In room:* TV, hair dryer.

KULA

Lodgings in Kula are the closest options to the entrance of Haleakala National Park (about 60 min. away).

Kula Cottage ✈ *Finds* I can't imagine having a less-than-fantastic vacation here. Tucked away on a quiet street amid a large grove of blooming papaya and banana trees, Cecilia and Larry Gilbert's romantic honeymoon cottage is very private; it even has its own driveway and carport. The 700-square-foot cottage has a full kitchen (complete with dishwasher) and three huge closets that offer

enough storage space for you to move in permanently. An outside lanai has a big gas barbecue and an umbrella-covered table and chairs. Cecilia delivers a continental breakfast daily. Groceries and a small takeout lunch counter are within walking distance. It's a 30-minute drive to the beach.

40 Puakea Place (off Lower Kula Rd.), Kula, HI 96790. ℭ **808/878-2043** or 808/871-6230. Fax 808/871-9187. www.kulacottage.com. 1 cottage. $95 double. Rate includes continental breakfast. 2-night minimum. No credit cards. *In room:* TV, kitchen, fridge, coffeemaker, washer/dryer.

Kula Lynn Farm Bed & Bath 🐾 (Kids   The Coons, the same great family that runs Maui's best sailing adventure on the *Trilogy,* offer this spectacular 1,600-square-foot unit on the ground floor of a custom-built pole house. From its location on the slopes of Haleakala, the panoramic view—across Maui's central valley, with the islands of Lanai and Kahoolawe in the distance—is worth the price alone. Wall-to-wall windows and high ceilings add to the feeling of spaciousness throughout. The two bedrooms, two bathrooms, and two queen-size sofa beds in the living room make this the perfect place for a family. No expense has been spared in the European-style kitchen, with top appliances and Italian marble floors. This place should appeal to those who enjoy a quiet location and such activities as barbecuing on the lanai and watching the sun set.

P.O. Box 847, Kula, HI 96790. ℭ **800/874-2666,** ext. 211, or 808/878-6176. Fax 808/878-6320. captcoon@verizon.net. 1 unit. $119 double. 5-night minimum. Rate includes breakfast fixings. Extra person $20. No credit cards. *In room:* TV/VCR, kitchen, fridge, coffeemaker, iron.

Malu Manu 🐾🐾 (Finds   This is one of the most romantic places to stay on Maui, with a panoramic view of the entire island from the front door. Tucked into the side of Haleakala Volcano at 4,000 feet is this old Hawaiian estate with a single-room log cabin (built as a writer's retreat in the early 1900s) and a 30-year-old family home. The writer's cabin has a full kitchen, a fireplace, and antiques galore. The two-bedroom, 2½-bathroom home also has antiques, koa walls, and beautiful eucalyptus floors. It's an ideal retreat for a romantic couple, a family, or two couples traveling together. The 7-acre property is filled with native forest, organic gardens (help yourself to lemons, avocados, and whatever else is ripe), a paddle-tennis court, and a Japanese-style outdoor soaking tub. If you're a dog person, the resident golden retriever, Alohi, may come over and make your acquaintance. This is one of the closest accommodations to Haleakala; restaurants are about a 15-minute drive away.

446 Cooke Rd. (mailing address: P.O. Box 175, Kula, HI 96790). ✆ **888/878-6161** or 808/878-6111. www.mauisunrise.com. 2 units. $150 double in log cabin; $185 double in 2-bedroom house. Extra person $10. 3-night minimum. MC, V. **Amenities:** Hot tub; paddle-tennis court; in-room massage; laundry facilities. *In room:* Kitchen, fridge, coffeemaker, iron.

5 East Maui: On the Road to Hana

KUAU

The Inn at Mama's Fish House 𝒶𝒶 The fabulous location (nestled in a coconut grove on secluded Kuau Beach), duplex cottages with beautifully decorated interiors (island-style rattan furniture and works by Hawaiian artists), and extras like Weber gas barbecues, huge 27-inch TVs, and lots of beach toys make this place a gem for those seeking a centrally located vacation rental. Guests even get a discount on lunch or dinner at Mama's Fish House next door. The one-bedroom units are nestled in tropical jungle (red ginger surrounds the garden patio), and the two-bedroom units face the beach. Both have terra-cotta floors, complete kitchens (even dishwashers), sofa beds, and laundry facilities.

799 Poho Place (off the Hana Hwy. in Kuau), Paia, HI 96779. ✆ **800/860-HULA** or 808/579-9764. Fax 808/579-8594. www.mamasfishhouse.com. 9 units. $175 1-bedroom (sleeps up to 4); $475 2-bedroom (up to 6). 3-night minimum stay. AE, DC, DISC, MC, V. *In room:* A/C, TV/VCR, kitchen, fridge, coffeemaker, hair dryer, iron.

HAIKU

Maui Dream Cottages *Value* Essentially a vacation rental, this country estate is located atop a hill overlooking the ocean. The grounds are dotted with fruit trees (bananas, papayas, and avocados, all free for the picking), and the front lawn is comfortably equipped with a double hammock, chaise longues, and table and chairs. One cottage has two bedrooms, a full kitchen, a washer/dryer, and an entertainment center. The other is basically the same but with only one bedroom (plus a sofa bed in the living room). They're both very well maintained and comfortably outfitted with furniture that's attractive but casual. The Haiku location is quiet and restful, and offers the opportunity to see how real islanders live. However, you'll have to drive a good 20 to 25 minutes to restaurants in Makawao or Paia. Hookipa Beach is about a 20-minute drive, and Baldwin Beach (good swimming) is 25 minutes away.

265 W. Kuiaha Rd. (1 block from Pauwela Cafe), Haiku, HI 96708. ✆ **808/575-9079.** Fax 808/575-9477. www.mauidreamcottage.com. 2 cottages (with shower only). $80 for 2. 7-night minimum. MC, V. *In room:* TV, kitchen, fridge, coffeemaker, washer/dryer.

Pilialoha B&B Cottage ✪   The minute you arrive at this split-level country cottage, located on a large lot with half-century-old eucalyptus trees, you'll see owner Machiko Heyde's artistry at work. Just in front of the quaint cottage (which is great for couples but can sleep up to five) is a garden blooming with some 200 varieties of roses. You'll find more of Machiko's handiwork inside. There's a queen-size bed in the master bedroom, a twin bed in a small adjoining room, and a queen-size sofa bed in the living room. A large lanai extends from the master bedroom. There's a great movie collection for rainy days or cool country nights, as well as a garage. Machiko delivers breakfast daily; if you plan on an early-morning ride to the top of Haleakala, she'll make sure you go with a thermos of coffee and her homemade bread.

2512 Kaupakalua Rd. (½ mile from Kokomo intersection), Haiku, HI 96708. ✆ **808/572-1440.** Fax 808/572-4612. www.pilialoha.com. 1 cottage. $130 double. Rates include continental breakfast. Extra person $20. 3-night minimum. MC, V. **Amenities:** Complimentary use of beach paraphernalia (including snorkel equipment); complimentary use of washer/dryer. *In room:* TV, kitchenette, fridge, coffeemaker.

Wild Ginger Falls ✪✪ *Finds*   This cozy, romantic intimate cottage, hidden in Miliko Gulch, overlooks a stream with a waterfall, bamboo, sweet-smelling ginger, and banana trees. It's perfect for honeymooners, lovers, and fans of Hawaiiana art. The moment you step into this 400-square-foot, artistically decorated Hawaiian cottage (with additional 156-sq.-ft. screened deck), you will be delighted at the memorabilia (ukulele tile, canoe paddle, and the like) throughout. The cottage has a full kitchen with everything you need for cooking. The comfy queen-size bed opens to the living area. The screened porch has a table, chairs, and a couch, perfect for curling up with a good book. Outside there's a barbecue, plus plenty of beach toys to borrow. Your hosts are Bob, a ceramic artist (with his creations on display throughout the cottage), and his wife, Sunny, who manages Dolphin Galleries (where she buys artwork for the cottage).

355 Kaluanui Rd., Makawao, HI 96768. ✆/fax **808/573-1173.** www.wildginger falls.com. 1 unit. $125 double. 3-night minimum. No credit cards. *In room:* TV/VCR, kitchen, fridge, coffeemaker, hair dryer, iron, washer/dryer.

HUELO/WAILUA

Huelo Point Flower Farm ✪ *Finds*   Here's a little Eden by the sea on a spectacular, remote, 300-foot sea cliff near a waterfall stream. This estate overlooking Waipio Bay has two guest cottages, a guesthouse, and a main house available for rent. The studio-size Gazebo

Cottage has three glass walls that make the most of the cottage's oceanfront location, a koa-wood captain's bed, a TV, a stereo, a kitchenette, a private oceanside patio, a private hot tub, and a half bathroom with outdoor shower. The new 900-square-foot Carriage House apartment sleeps four and has glass walls facing the mountain and sea, plus a kitchen, a den, decks, and a loft bedroom. The two-bedroom main house contains an exercise room, a fireplace, a sunken Roman bath, cathedral ceilings, and other extras. On-site are a natural pool with a waterfall and an oceanfront hot tub. You're welcome to pick fruit, vegetables, and flowers from the extensive garden. Homemade scones, tree-ripened papayas, and fresh-roasted coffee start your day. The secluded location, off the crooked road to Hana, is just a half-hour from Kahului, or about 20 minutes from Paia's shops and restaurants.

Off Hana Hwy., between mile markers 3 and 4 (P.O. Box 791808, Paia, HI 96779). ⓒ 808/572-1850. www.mauiflowerfarm.com. 4 units. $160 cottage double; $190 carriage house double; $350 guesthouse double; $450 main house double (sleeps 8). Extra person $20–$35. 2-night minimum for smaller houses, 5-night minimum for main house. No credit cards. **Amenities:** Outdoor pool; 3 Jacuzzis; self-serve washer/dryer. *In room:* TV, kitchenette (in cottage), kitchen (in houses), fridge, coffeemaker, hair dryer.

Kailua Maui Gardens *(Finds* In the middle of nowhere lies this nearly 2-acre tropical botanical garden with four bungalows dotting the property. Just a couple of miles down the serpentine Hana Highway from Huelo, in the remote area of Kailua, is an unlikely place for accommodations (it's a 30-min. drive to the nearest beach and 1 hr. to Hana), but for those who want to get away from it all, this could be your place. The small cabanas range from one-room studios with a futon and full kitchen to compact accommodations with basic kitchenette amenities. They all face out into gorgeous gardens. In the midst of the botanical garden are a pool, with cabana and covered barbecue area, and a hot tub. The garden sits right on the Hana Highway, so ask for a unit away from the road. Unfortunately, they have a 2-night minimum. Even if you don't stay here, stop by and visit the garden; hosts Kirk and Shelley love to show people their piece of paradise.

Located between mile markers 5 and 6 on the Hana Hwy. (S.R. 1, Box 9, Haiku, HI 96708). ⓒ 808/572-9726. Fax 808/572-8845. www.kailuamauigardens.com. 5 units. $125–$160 double. 2-night minimum. Extra person $10. MC, V. **Amenities:** Outdoor pool; 2 hot tubs; laundry facilities. *In room:* TV/VCR, kitchen or kitchenette, fridge, coffeemaker, CD/stereo.

6 At the End of the Road in East Maui: Hana

To locate the following accommodations, see the "Hana" map on p. 151.

EXPENSIVE

Hotel Hana-Maui ✦✦✦ *(Kids)*   Picture Shangri-La, Hawaiian-style: 66 acres rolling down to the sea in a remote Hawaiian village, with a wellness center, two pools, and access to one of the best beaches in Hana. This is the atmosphere, the landscape, and the culture of old Hawaii set in 21st-century accommodations. Every unit is excellent, but my favorites are the Sea Ranch Cottages (especially units 215–218 for the best views of turtles frolicking in the ocean), where individual duplex bungalows look out over the craggy shoreline to the rolling surf. You step out of the oversize, open, airy units (with floor-to-ceiling sliding doors) onto a huge lanai with views that will stay with you long after your tan has faded. These comfy units have been totally redecorated with every amenity you can think of, and you won't be nickeled-and-dimed for things like coffee and water—everything they give you, from the homemade banana bread to the bottled water, is complimentary. Cathedral ceilings, a plush feather bed, a giant-size soaking tub, Hawaiian artwork, bamboo hardwood floors—this is luxury. The white-sand beach (just a 5-min. shuttle away), top-notch wellness center with some of the best massage therapists in Hawaii, and numerous activities (horseback riding, mountain biking, tennis, pitch-and-putt golf) all add up to make this one of the top resorts in the state. There's no TV in the rooms, but the Club Room has a giant-screen TV, plus a VCR and Internet access. I highly recommend this little slice of paradise.

P.O. Box 9, Hana, HI 96713. ℂ 800/321-HANA or 808/248-8211. Fax 808/248-7202. www.hotelhanamaui.com. 66 units. $395–$455 Bay Cottages double; $525–$895 Sea Ranch Cottages double; $1,295 2-bedroom suite for 4; 2-bedroom Plantation Guest House from $2,500. AE, DC, DISC, MC, V. **Amenities:** Restaurant (with Hawaiian entertainment twice a week); bar (entertainment 4 times a week); in-room dining; 2 outdoor pools; complimentary use of the 3-hole practice golf courses (clubs are complimentary); complimentary tennis courts; fitness center; full-service spa; game room; concierge; activities desk; car-rental desk; business center; small shopping arcade; salon; room service; babysitting; laundry service. *In room:* Dataport, kitchenette, fridge, coffeemaker, hair dryer, iron, safe.

MODERATE

Ekena ✦   Just one glance at the 360-degree view, and you can see why hosts Robin and Gaylord gave up their careers on the mainland

and moved here. This 8½-acre piece of paradise in rural Hana boasts ocean and rainforest views; the floor-to-ceiling glass doors in the spacious Hawaiian-style pole house bring the outside in. The elegant two-story home is exquisitely furnished, from the comfortable U-shaped couch that invites you to relax and take in the view to the top-of-the-line mattress on the king-size bed. The kitchen is fully equipped with every high-tech convenience you can imagine (guests have made complete holiday meals here). Only one floor (and one two-bedroom unit) is rented at any one time to ensure privacy. The grounds are impeccably groomed and dotted with tropical plants and fruit trees. Hiking trails into the rainforest start right on the property, and beaches and waterfalls are just minutes away. Robin places fresh flowers in every room and makes sure you're comfortable; after that, she's available to answer questions, but she also respects your privacy.

P.O. Box 728 (off Hana Hwy., above Hana Airport), Hana, HI 96713. ⓒ 808/248-7047. Fax 808/248-7853. www.ekenamaui.com. 2 units. $185 for 2; $250–$350 for 4. Extra person $25. 3-night minimum. No credit cards. **Amenities:** Complimentary use of washer/dryers. *In room:* TV/DVD/VCR, kitchen, fridge, coffeemaker, iron, stereo/CD player.

Hamoa Bay Bungalow ⓚ *Finds*

Down a country lane guarded by two Balinese statues stands a little bit of Indonesia in Hawaii: a carefully crafted bungalow and an Asian-inspired two-bedroom house overlooking Hamoa Bay. This enchanting retreat is just 2 miles beyond Hasegawa's general store on the way to Kipahulu. It sits on 4 verdant acres within walking distance of Hamoa Beach (which author James Michener considered one of the most beautiful in the Pacific). The 600-square-foot Balinese-style cottage is distinctly tropical, with giant elephant-bamboo furniture from Indonesia, batik prints, a king-size bed, a full kitchen, and a screened porch with hot tub and shower. Hidden from the cottage is a 1,300-square-foot home with a soaking tub and private outdoor stone shower. It offers an elephant-bamboo king-size bed in one room, a queen-size bed in another, a screened-in sleeping porch, a full kitchen, and wonderful ocean views.

P.O. Box 773, Hana, HI 96713. ⓒ 808/248-7884. Fax 808/248-7853. www.hamoa bay.com. 2 units. $195 cottage (sleeps only 2); $250 house for 2; $350 house for 4. 3-night minimum. No credit cards. **Amenities:** Hot tub; complimentary use of washer/dryers. *In room:* TV/DVD/VCR, kitchen, fridge, coffeemaker, iron, stereo/CD.

Hana Hale Malamalama *Finds*

Hana Hale Malamalama sits on a historic site with ancient fish ponds and a cave mentioned in ancient chants. Host John takes excellent care of the ponds (you're welcome to watch him feed the fish at 5pm daily) and is fiercely protective of the hidden cave ("It's not a tourist attraction, but a sacred spot"). There's access to a nearby rocky beach, which isn't good for swimming but makes a wonderful place to watch the sunset. All accommodations include fully equipped kitchens, bathrooms, bedrooms, living/dining areas, and private lanais. Next to the fish pond, the Royal Lodge, a 2,600-square-foot architectural masterpiece built entirely of Philippine mahogany, has large skylights the entire length of the house and can be rented as a house or two separate units. The oceanfront Bamboo Inn contains two units (a studio and a one- or two-bedroom unit). The cottages range from the separate two-level Tree House cottage (with Jacuzzi tub for two, a Balinese bamboo bed, small kitchen/living area, and deck upstairs) to the Pond Side Bungalow (with private outdoor Jacuzzi tub and shower).

P.O. Box 374, Hana, HI 96713. © 808/248-7718. www.hanahale.com. 7 units. $135–$285 double. Extra person $15. 2-night minimum. MC, V. **Amenities:** Jacuzzi. *In room:* TV/DVD, kitchen, fridge, coffeemaker, Jacuzzi (in all but 1 unit).

Hana Oceanfront 🌟🌟
Just across the street from Hamoa Bay, Hana's premier white-sand beach, lie these two plantation-style units, impeccably decorated in old Hawaii decor. My favorite unit is the romantic cottage, complete with a front porch where you can sit and watch the ocean; a separate bedroom (with a bamboo sleigh bed), plus a pullout sofa for extra guests; top-notch kitchen appliances; and comfy living room. The 1,000-square-foot vacation suite, located downstairs from hosts Dan and Sandi's home (but totally soundproof—you'll never hear them) has an elegant master bedroom with polished bamboo flooring, a spacious bathroom with custom hand-painted tile, and a fully appointed gourmet kitchen. Outside is a 320-square-foot lanai. The units sit on the road facing Hana's most popular beach, so there is traffic during the day. At night the traffic disappears, the stars come out, and the sound of the ocean soothes you to sleep.

P.O. Box 843, Hana, HI 96713. © 808/248-7558. Fax 808/248-8034. www.hana oceanfrontcottages.com. 2 units. $225–$250 double. 3-night minimum. MC, V. **Amenities:** Barbecue area. *In room:* TV/VCR/DVD, full gourmet kitchen, fridge, coffeemaker, hair dryer, iron, stereo/CD.

Heavenly Hana Inn 🌟🌟 (Finds)
This place on the Hana Highway, just a stone's throw from the center of Hana town, is a little bit of heaven, where no attention to detail has been spared. Each suite has a sitting room with futon and couch, polished hardwood floors, and

separate bedroom with a raised platform bed (with an excellent, firm mattress). The black-marble bathrooms have huge tubs. Flowers are everywhere, ceiling fans keep the rooms cool, and the delicious gourmet breakfast—worth splurging for—is served in a setting filled with art. The grounds are done in Japanese style with a bamboo fence, tiny bridges over a meandering stream, and Japanese gardens.

P.O. Box 790, Hana, HI 96713. ©/fax **808/248-8442**. www.heavenlyhanainn.com. 3 units. $200–$275 suite. Full gourmet breakfast available for $17 per person. 2-night minimum. AE, DISC, MC, V. No children under age 15 accepted. *In room:* TV, no phone.

INEXPENSIVE

Hana's Tradewinds Cottage *✿ Value*   Nestled among the ginger and heliconias on a 5-acre flower farm are two separate cottages, each with full kitchen, carport, barbecue, private hot tub, TV, ceiling fans, and sofa bed. The studio cottage sleeps up to four; a bamboo shoji blind separates the sleeping area (with queen-size bed) from the sofa bed in the living room. The Tradewinds cottage has two bedrooms (with a queen-size bed in one room and two twins in the other), one bathroom (shower only), and a huge front porch. The atmosphere is quiet and relaxing, and hostess Rebecca Buckley, who has been in business for a decade, welcomes families (she has two children, a cat, and a very sweet golden retriever). You can use the laundry facilities at no extra charge.

135 Alalele Place (the airport road), P.O. Box 385, Hana, HI 96713. © **800/327-8097** or 808/248-8980. Fax 808/248-7735. www.hanamaui.net. 2 cottages. $120 studio double; $145 2-bedroom double. Extra person $10. 2-night minimum. AE, DISC, MC, V. *In room:* TV, kitchen, fridge, coffeemaker, no phone.

Kulani's Hideaway in Hana, Maui *✿ Value*   On the road to Waianapanapa State Park is one of Hana's best deals—two one-bedroom units, each with pullout sofa beds in the living room, full kitchen, cable TV (a plus in Hana), and washer/dryer, within walking distance of a fabulous black-sand beach. Outside is a large lanai for watching the clouds go by, with a barbecue area and picnic table in the yard. Book early.

P.O. Box 483, Hana, HI 96713. ©/fax **808/248-8234** or 808/248-4815. kulanis@ maui.net. 2 units. $80 double. Extra person $15. **Amenities:** Complimentary coffee. *In room:* TV, kitchen, fridge, coffeemaker, washer/dryer, no phone.

Waianapanapa State Park Cabins *Value*   These 12 rustic cabins are the best lodging deal on Maui. Everyone knows it, too—so make your reservations early (up to 6 months in advance). The

cabins are warm and dry, and come complete with kitchen, living room, bedroom, and bathroom with hot shower; furnishings include bedding, linen, towels, dishes, and very basic cooking and eating utensils. Don't expect luxury—this is a step above camping, albeit in a beautiful tropical jungle setting. The key attraction at this 120-acre state beach park is the unusual horseshoe-shaped black-sand beach on Pailoa Bay, popular for shore fishing, snorkeling, and swimming. There's a caretaker on-site, along with restrooms, showers, picnic tables, shoreline hiking trails, and historic sites. But bring mosquito protection—this *is* the jungle, after all.

Off Hana Hwy., c/o State Parks Division, 54 S. High St., Room 101, Wailuku, HI 96793. ⓒ **808/984-8109.** 12 cabins. $45 for 4 (sleeps up to 6). Extra person $5. 5-night maximum. No credit cards. *In room:* Kitchen, fridge, coffeemaker, no phone.

4

Where to Dine

With soaring visitor statistics and a glamorous image, the Valley Isle is fertile ground for enterprising chefs, and consequently, dining on Maui has become a culinary treat able to hold its own against most major metropolitan areas.

Despite the recent changes and growth in Maui's dining scene, some things haven't changed: You can still dine well at Lahaina's open-air waterfront watering holes, where the view counts for 50% of the experience. There are still budget eateries, but not many; Maui's old-fashioned, multigenerational mom-and-pop diners are disappearing, clinging to the edge of existence in the older neighborhoods of central Maui, such as lovable Wailuku. Although you'll have to work harder to find them in the resort areas, you won't have to go far to find creative cuisine, pleasing style, and stellar dining experiences.

In the listings below, reservations are not necessary unless otherwise noted.

1 Central Maui

MODERATE

Class Act ✪ GLOBAL   Part of a program run by the distinguished Food Service Department of Maui Community College (soon to be housed in a new state-of-the-art, $15 million culinary facility), this restaurant has a following. Student chefs show their stuff with a flourish in their "classroom," where they pull out all the stops. Linen, china, servers in ties and white shirts, and a four-course lunch make this a unique value. The appetizer, soup, salad, and dessert are set, but you can choose between the regular entrees and a heart-healthy main course prepared in the culinary tradition of the week. The menu roams the globe with highlights of Italy, Mexico, Maui, Napa Valley, France, New Orleans, and other locales. The filet mignon of French week is popular, as are the New Orleans gumbo and Cajun shrimp, the sesame-crusted mahimahi on taro-leaf pasta, the polenta flan with eggplant, and the bean- and green-chile chilaquile. Tea and soft drinks are offered—and they can get pretty fancy, with fresh fruit and spritzers—but otherwise it's BYOB.

Maui Community College, 310 Kaahumanu Ave., Wailuku. (*C*) 808/984-3480. www.hawaii.edu/maui/mca. Reservations recommended. 4-course lunch $25. Menu and cuisine type change weekly. MC, V. Wed and Fri 11am–12:30pm. Closed May–Aug for summer vacation.

Mañana Garage (*Finds* LATIN AMERICAN Chef Tom Lelli, formerly of Haliimaile General Store, is serving up some incomparable fare at this central Maui hot spot. The industrial motif features table bases like hubcaps, a vertical garage door as a divider for private parties, blown-glass chandeliers, and gleaming chrome and cobalt walls with orange accents. The menu is brilliantly conceived and executed. Fried green tomatoes are done just right and served with slivered red onions. Three different kinds of ceviche perfectly balance flavors and textures: lime, cilantro, chile, coconut, and fresh fish. They even have barbecued ribs. Mañana Garage has introduced exciting new flavors to Maui's dining scene—if you are on this side of the island, don't miss this incredible experience.

33 Lono Ave., Kahului. (*C*) 808/873-0220. Reservations recommended. Lunch main courses $7–$13; dinner main courses $16–$29. AE, DISC, MC, V. Mon 11am–9pm; Wed–Sat 11am–10:30pm; Sun 5–9pm.

Marco's Grill & Deli ITALIAN Located in the thick of central Maui, where the roads to upcountry, west, and South Maui converge, Marco's is popular among area residents for its homemade Italian fare and friendly informality. Everything—from the meatballs, sausages, and burgers to the sauces, salad dressings, and raviolis—is made in-house. The 35 different choices of hot and cold sandwiches and entrees are served all day, and they include vodka rigatoni with imported prosciutto, *pasta e fagioli* (a house specialty: smoked ham hock simmered for hours in tomato sauce, with red and white beans), and simple pasta with marinara sauce. This is one of those comfortable neighborhood fixtures favored by all generations. The antipasto salad, vegetarian lasagna, and roasted peppers are taste treats, but the meatballs and Italian sausage are famous in central Maui. They also have a full bar.

Dairy Center, 395 Dairy Rd., Kahului. (*C*) 808/877-4446. Main courses $11–$27. AE, DC, DISC, MC, V. Daily 7:30am–10pm.

A Saigon Cafe (*Finds* VIETNAMESE Jennifer Nguyen has stuck to her guns and steadfastly refused to erect a sign, but diners find their way here anyway. That's how good the food is. Fans drive from all over the island for her crisped, spiced Dungeness crab; her steamed *opakapaka* with ginger and garlic; and her wok-cooked Vietnamese specials, tangy with spices, herbs, and lemon grass. There are a dozen different soups, cold and hot noodles (including the popular beef noodle soup called *pho*), and chicken and shrimp cooked in a clay pot. You can create your own Vietnamese "burritos" from a platter of tofu, noodles, and vegetables that you wrap in rice paper and dip in garlic sauce. Among my favorites are the shrimp lemon grass, savory and refreshing, and the tofu curry, swimming in herbs and vegetables straight from the garden. The Nhung Dam—a hearty spread of basil, cucumbers, mint, romaine, bean sprouts, pickled carrots, turnips, and vermicelli, wrapped in rice paper and dipped in a legendary sauce—is cooked at your table.

1792 Main St., Wailuku. (C) **808/243-9560.** Main courses $6.50–$17. DC, MC, V. Mon–Sat 10am–9:30pm; Sun 10am–8:30pm. Heading into Wailuku from Kahului, go over the bridge and take the 1st right onto Central Ave., then the 1st right on Nani St. At the next stop sign, look for the building with the neon sign that says OPEN.

INEXPENSIVE

The **Queen Kaahumanu Center,** at 275 Kaahumanu Ave. (5 min. from Kahului Airport on Hwy. 32), has a very popular food court. **Edo Japan** teppanyaki is a real find, its flat Benihana-like grill dispensing marvelous, flavorful mounds of grilled fresh vegetables and chicken teriyaki for $5.70. **Maui Mixed Plate** dishes out "local style" cuisine of meat with rice and macaroni salad in the $4.45-to-$7 range. **Yummy Korean B-B-Q** offers the assertive flavors of Korea ranging from $4.75 to $7.50; **Panda Express** serves tasty Chinese food; and **Sushi Go** is a great place for fast sushi. Outside the food court but still in the shopping center are **The Coffee Store** (p. 95); **Ruby's,** dishing out hamburgers, fries, and shakes; and **Starbucks.** There's also a branch of **Maui Tacos** (p. 91).

AK's Café (kids) (Value) HEALTHY/PLATE LUNCHES   Chef Elaine Rothermel has a winner with this tiny cafe in the industrial district of Wailuku. It may be slightly off the tourist path, but it is well worth the effort to find this delicious eatery, with creative cuisine coming out of the kitchen; most dishes are healthy, and a few dishes are for those who just want to enjoy good food (forget about the calories). Prices are so eye-poppingly cheap, you might find yourself wandering back here during your vacation. Lunches feature everything from grilled chicken, garlic-crusted ono, and eggplant Parmesan to hamburger steak, beef stew, and spaghetti with meatballs. Dinner shines with blackened ono with mango–basil sauce;

tofu napoleon with ginger pesto; crab cakes with papaya beurre blanc; grilled chicken; barbecued baby back ribs; and, of course, the special of the day.

1237 Lower Main St., Wailuku. ℂ 808/244-8774. www.akscafe.com. Plate lunches $6.75–$7.40; dinners $11–$13. MC, V. Mon–Sat 10:30am–2pm and 4:30–8:30pm.

Ichiban (finds JAPANESE/SUSHI What a find: an informal neighborhood restaurant that serves inexpensive, home-cooked Japanese food *and* good sushi at realistic prices. Local residents consider Ichiban a staple for breakfast, lunch, or dinner and a haven of comforts: egg-white omelets; great saimin; combination plates of teriyaki chicken, teriyaki meat, *tonkatsu* (pork cutlet), rice, and pickled cabbage; chicken yakitori; and sushi—everything from unagi and scallop to California roll. The sushi items may not be cheap, but like the specials, such as steamed *opakapaka*, they're a good value. I love the tempura, miso soup, and spicy ahi hand roll.

Kahului Shopping Center, 47 Kaahumanu Ave., Kahului. ℂ 808/871-6977. Main courses $4.50–$5.25 breakfast, $5.95–$9.50 lunch (combination plates $8), $4.95–$28 dinner (combination dinner $12, dinner specials from $8.95). AE, DC, MC, V. Mon–Fri 7am–2pm; Sat 10:30am–2pm; Mon–Sat 5–9pm. Closed 2 weeks around Christmas and New Year's.

Maui Bake Shop BAKERY/DELI Sleepy Vineyard Street has seen many a mom-and-pop business come and go, but Maui Bake Shop is here to stay. Maui native Claire Fujii-Krall and her husband, baker José Krall (who was trained in the south of France), are turning out buttery brioches, healthful nine-grain and two-tone rye breads, focaccia, strudels, sumptuous fresh-fruit gâteaux, puff pastries, and dozens of other baked goods and confections. The breads are baked in one of Maui's oldest brick ovens, installed in 1935; a high-tech European diesel oven handles the rest. The front window displays more than 100 bakery and deli items, among them salads; a popular eggplant marinara focaccia; homemade quiches; and an inexpensive calzone filled with chicken, pesto, mushroom, and cheese. Homemade soups (clam chowder, minestrone, cream of asparagus) team up nicely with sandwiches on freshly baked bread. Save room for the Ultimate Dessert: white-chocolate macadamia-nut cheesecake.

2092 Vineyard St. (at N. Church St.), Wailuku. ℂ 808/242-0064. Most items under $5. AE, MC, V. Mon–Fri 6am–3pm; Sat 7am–1pm.

Restaurant Matsu JAPANESE/LOCAL Customers have come from Hana (more than 50 miles away) just for Matsu's California rolls, while regulars line up for the cold saimin (julienned cucumber, egg, Chinese-style sweet pork, and red ginger on noodles) and for the bento plates—various assemblages of chicken, teriyaki beef, fish, and rice. The nigiri sushi items are popular, especially among the don't-dally lunch crowd. The katsu pork and chicken, breaded and deep-fried, are other specialties of this casual Formica-style diner. I love the tempura udon and the saimin—steaming mounds of wide and fine noodles swimming in homemade broths and topped with condiments. The daily specials are a changing lineup of home-cooked classics: oxtail soup, roast pork with gravy, teriyaki ahi, miso butterfish, and breaded mahimahi.

Maui Mall, 161 Alamaha St., Kahului. ℂ 808/871-0822. Most items less than $6. No credit cards. Mon–Tues and Sat 10am–3pm; Wed–Fri 10am–8pm.

2 West Maui

LAHAINA
There's a **Maui Tacos** (p. 91) in Lahaina Square (ℂ **808/661-8883**).

VERY EXPENSIVE
David Paul's Lahaina Grill ✿ *Kids* NEW AMERICAN   Even after David Paul Johnson's departure, this Lahaina hot spot has maintained its popularity. It's still filled with chic, tanned diners in stylish aloha shirts, and there's still attitude aplenty at the entrance. The signature items remain: tequila shrimp and firecracker rice, Kona coffee–roasted rack of lamb, Maui onion–crusted seared ahi, and Kalua duck quesadilla. A special custom-designed chef's table can be arranged with 72-hour notice for larger parties. The ambience—black-and-white tile floors, pressed tin ceilings, eclectic 1890s decor—is striking, and the bar, even without an ocean view, is the busiest spot in Lahaina. The kids' menu includes spaghetti, chicken fingers, mahimahi, and more for $12.

127 Lahainaluna Rd. ℂ **808/667-5117**. Reservations required. Main courses $29–$43. AE, DC, DISC, MC, V. Daily 5:30–10pm. Bar daily 5:30pm–midnight.

The Feast at Lele ✿✿ POLYNESIAN   The owners of Old Lahaina Luau (see "A Night to Remember: Luau, Maui Style" in chapter 8) have teamed up with chef James McDonald's culinary prowess (I'o and Pacific'o), placed it in a perfect outdoor oceanfront setting, and added the exquisite dancers of the Old Lahaina Luau. The result: a culinary and cultural experience that sizzles. As if the sunset weren't heady enough, dances from Hawaii, Tonga, Tahiti, and Samoa are presented, up close and personal, in full costumed

splendor. Chanting, singing, drumming, dancing, the swish of ti-
leaf skirts, the scent of plumeria—it's a full adventure, even for the
most jaded luau aficionado. Guests sit at white-clothed, candlelit
tables set on the sand (unlike the luau, where seating is en masse)
and dine on entrees from each island: Kalua pig, tasty steamed moi,
and savory pohole ferns and hearts of palm from Hawaii; lobster-
ogo (seaweed) salad and grilled steak from Tonga; steamed chicken
and taro leaf in coconut milk from Tahiti; and grilled fish in banana
leaf from Samoa. Particularly mesmerizing is the evening's opening:
A softly lit canoe carries three people ashore to the sound of conch
shells.

505 Front St. © **886/244-5353** or 808/667-5353. www.feastatlele.com. Reservations a must. Set 5-course menu $99 for adults, $69 for children 2–12; gratuity not
included. AE, MC, V. Apr 1–Sept 30 daily 6–9pm; Oct 1–Mar 31 daily 5:30–8:30pm.

EXPENSIVE

Gerard's ✺✺✺ *Finds* FRENCH   The charm of Gerard's—soft
lighting, Edith Piaf on the sound system, excellent service—is
matched by a menu of uncompromising standards. After more than
2 decades in Lahaina, Gerard Reversade never runs out of creative
offerings, yet stays true to his French roots. A frequent winner of the
Wine Spectator Award of Excellence, Gerard's offers roasted *opakapaka* with star anise, fennel fondue, and hints of orange and ginger—
a stellar entree on a menu of winners. The Kona lobster ragout with
pasta and morels promises ecstasy, and the spinach salad with scallops is among the finest I've tasted. Gerard's has an excellent appetizer menu, with shiitake and oyster mushrooms in puff pastry; fresh
ahi and smoked salmon carpaccio; and a very rich, highly touted
escargot ragout with burgundy butter and garlic cream.

In the Plantation Inn, 174 Lahainaluna Rd. © **808/661-8939.** www.gerards
maui.com. Reservations recommended. Main courses $30–$39. AE, DC, DISC, MC,
V. Daily 6–9pm.

I'o ✺ PACIFIC RIM   I'o is a fantasy of sleek curves and etched
glass, co-owned by chef James McDonald. He offers an impressive
selection of appetizers (his strong suit) and some lavish Asian-Poly-
nesian interpretations of seafood, such as stir-fried lobster with
mango-Thai curry sauce. Unless you're sold on a particular entree,
my advice is to go heavy on the superb appetizers, especially the
silken purse, a brilliant concoction of tricolored pot stickers stuffed
with roasted peppers, mushrooms, spinach, macadamia nuts, and
silken tofu. Foie gras lovers, take heed: The foie gras fish is topped
with foie gras truffle butter over a vegetable salad. Chef McDonald

Where to Dine in Lahaina & Kaanapali

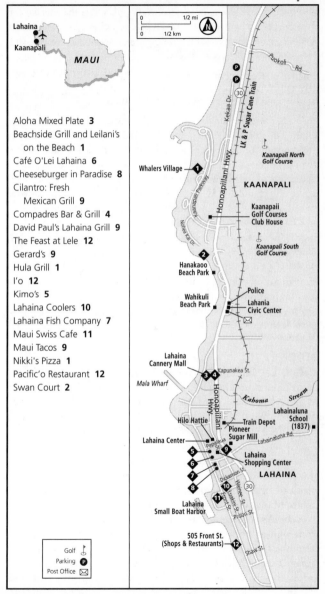

Aloha Mixed Plate **3**

Beachside Grill and Leilani's on the Beach **1**

Café O'Lei Lahaina **6**

Cheeseburger in Paradise **8**

Cilantro: Fresh Mexican Grill **9**

Compadres Bar & Grill **4**

David Paul's Lahaina Grill **9**

The Feast at Lele **12**

Gerard's **9**

Hula Grill **1**

I'o **12**

Kimo's **5**

Lahaina Coolers **10**

Lahaina Fish Company **7**

Maui Swiss Cafe **11**

Maui Tacos **9**

Nikki's Pizza **1**

Pacific'o Restaurant **12**

Swan Court **2**

Lahaina

Kaanapali

MAUI

Whalers Village ❶

Kaanapali North Golf Course

KAANAPALI

Kaanapaii Golf Courses Club House

Kaanapali South Golf Course

❷

Hanakaoo Beach Park

Police

Wahikuli Beach Park

Lahania Civic Center

Lahaina Cannery Mall

❸❹ Kapunakea St.

Mala Wharf

Kaboma Stream

Lahainaluna School (1837)

Hilo Hattie

Train Depot

Pioneer Sugar Mill

Lahaina Center

❺

❻

❼

❽

❾

Lahaina Shopping Center

LAHAINA

❿

⓫

Lahaina Small Boat Harbor

505 Front St. (Shops & Restaurants) ⓬

Golf

Parking

Post Office

83

also owns Pacific'o, the restaurant next door, and is the chef for the Feast at Lele, which is on the ocean side of I'o.

505 Front St. ⓒ **808/661-8422.** www.iomaui.com. Reservations recommended. Main courses $23–$59. AE, DC, MC, V. Daily 5:30–10pm.

Pacific'o Restaurant ⓖ PACIFIC RIM/CONTEMPORARY PACIFIC You can't get any closer to the ocean than the tables here, which are literally on the beach. With good food complementing this sensational setting, foodies and aesthetes have much to enjoy. The split-level dining starts near the entrance, with a long bar (where you can also order lunch or dinner) and a few tables along the railing. Steps lead down to the outdoor tables, where the award-winning seafood dishes come to you with the backdrop of Lanai across the channel. The prawn-and-basil won tons, fresh fish over wilted arugula and bean sprouts, and ahi and ono tempura with miso and lime-basil sauce are among Pacific'o's memorable offerings. The vegetarian special—a marinated, roasted tofu steak crowned with quinoa, Maui onions, red lentils, and a heavenly dose of shiitake mushrooms—is a longtime favorite. If you like seafood, sunsets, and touches of India and Indonesia in your fresh-from-the-sea dining choices, you should be happy here.

505 Front St. ⓒ **808/667-4341.** www.pacificomaui.com. Reservations recommended. Main courses $11–$14 lunch, $26–$32 dinner. AE, DC, MC, V. Daily 11am–4pm and 5:30–10pm.

MODERATE

Café O'Lei Lahaina ⓖⓖ *Value* AMERICAN Just over 10 years ago, restaurateurs Dana and Michael Pastula opened their first Café O'Lei in Makawao (Dana has managed such premier restaurants as Hulo'poe Court and Ihilani in Manele Bay Resort on Lanai and Pacific Grill at Four Seasons Maui, and Michael has been a chef for more than 25 years, including stints at the Swan Court in the Hyatt Regency Maui and Wailea Maui Marriott). The tiny, hidden eatery was packed from day one. The duo have brought their unique blend of island-fresh ingredients and zippy preparations to Lahaina (and also to Maalaea, Iao Valley, and Outrigger Napili Shores). The location could not be better: alfresco dining on upper and lower decks, both with an unobstructed 180-degree view of the ocean and the island of Lanai in the distance. Despite the fact that this is Front Street, Lahaina, the Pastulas still have great food and reasonable prices; the plate-lunch special is only $6.95. Because the view is so romantic, I recommend that you go here for dinner before the sun sets to take in that ocean panorama as you dine on seared ahi, sautéed mahi, macadamia-nut roast duckling, Thai coconut lobster, jumbo shrimp, or calamari.

839 Front St. ⓒ **808/661-9491**. Reservations recommended. Main courses lunch $6.50–$11, dinner $14–$23. AE, DISC, MC, V. Daily 10:30am–9:30pm.

Compadres Bar & Grill MEXICAN   Despite its concrete floor and high industrial ceilings, Compadres exudes good cheer. And that cheer has burgeoned lately with a new open-air seating area and a takeout taqueria window for diners on the run. The food is classic Tex-Mex, beginning with huevos rancheros, egg burritos, hot cakes, and omelets (the Acapulco is heroic) for breakfast and progressing to enchiladas and appetizers for the margarita-happy crowd. Stay spare (vegetable enchilada in fresh spinach tortilla), or get hefty (Texas T-bone and enchiladas). This is a carefree place with a large capacity for merrymaking. Don't miss Taco Tuesdays, from 4 to 8pm, where margaritas are just $3.

Lahaina Cannery Mall, 1221 Honoapiilani Hwy. ⓒ **808/661-7189**. Main courses $10–$23. AE, DC, DISC, MC, V. Daily 8am–10pm.

Kimo's STEAK/SEAFOOD   Kimo's has a loyal following that keeps it from falling into the faceless morass of waterfront restaurants serving surf-and-turf with great sunset views. It's a formula restaurant (sibling to Leilani's and Hula Grill) that works not only because of its oceanfront patio and upstairs dining room, but also because, for the price, there are some satisfying choices. It's always crowded, buzzing with people on a deck offering views of Molokai, Lanai, and Kahoolawe. Burgers and sandwiches are affordable and consistent, and the fresh catch in garlic-lemon and a sweet-basil glaze is a top seller. The waistline-defying hula pie—macadamia-nut ice cream in a chocolate-wafer crust with fudge and whipped cream—originated here.

845 Front St. ⓒ **808/661-4811**. www.kimosmaui.com. Reservations recommended for dinner. Main courses $8–$12 lunch, $17–$26 dinner. AE, DC, DISC, MC, V. Daily 11am–3:30pm and 5–10:30pm. Bar open 11am–1:30am.

Lahaina Fish Company SEAFOOD   This restaurant's open-air dining room is literally over the water, with flickering torches after sunset and an affordable menu that covers the seafood-pasta basics. Head to an oceanside table, and order a cheeseburger, chicken burger, fish burger, generous basket of peel-and-eat shrimp, or sashimi; lingering is highly recommended. The light lunch/grill menu offers appetizers (sashimi, seared ahi, spring rolls, and pot stickers), salads, and soups. The restaurant has spiffed up its dinner selections to include hand-carved steaks; several pasta choices; and local fare such as stir-fry dishes, teriyaki chicken, and luau-style ribs. The specialty, though, remains the fresh seafood: Four types of fresh fish are offered nightly, in three preparations. Pacific Rim specials include fresh ahi, seared spicy or cooked in a sweet ginger-soy sauce.

831 Front St. ℰ 808/661-3472. Main courses $10–$36. AE, MC, V. Daily 11am–11pm.

INEXPENSIVE

Aloha Mixed Plate ℛ ⟨Value⟩ PLATE LUNCHES/BEACHSIDE GRILL   Look for the festive turquoise-and-yellow, plantation-style front with the red corrugated-iron roof and adorable bar, tiny and busy, directly across from the Lahaina Cannery Mall. Grab a picnic table at ocean's edge, in the shade of large kiawe and milo trees, where you can watch the bobbing sailboats and two islands on the near horizon. (On the upper level, there are umbrellas and plumeria trees—just as charming.) Then tuck into inexpensive mahimahi, Kalua pig and cabbage, shoyu chicken, teriyaki beef, and other local plate-lunch specials, all at budget-friendly prices, served with macaroni salad and rice. The shoyu chicken is the best I've had, fork tender and tasty, and the spicy chicken drumettes come from a fabled family recipe. (The bestsellers are the coconut prawns and Aloha Mixed Plate of shoyu chicken, teriyaki beef, and mahimahi.) I don't know of anywhere else you can order a mai tai with a plate lunch and enjoy table service with an ocean view.

1285 Front St. ℰ 808/661-3322. www.alohamixedplate.com. Main courses $4.95–$9.95. MC, V. Daily 10:30am–10pm.

Cheeseburger in Paradise AMERICAN   Wildly successful, always crowded, highly visible, and very noisy, with live music in the evenings, Cheeseburger is a shrine to the American classic. This is burger country, tropical-style, with everything from tofu and garden burgers to the biggest, juiciest beef and chicken burgers, served on whole-wheat and sesame buns baked fresh daily. There are good reasons why the two-story green-and-white building next to the seawall is always packed: good value, good grinds, and a great ocean view. The Cheeseburger in Paradise—a hefty hunk with Jack and cheddar cheeses, sautéed onions, lettuce, fresh tomatoes, and Thousand Island dressing—is a paean to the basics. You can build your own burger by adding sautéed mushrooms, bacon, grilled Ortega chilies, and other condiments for an extra charge. Onion rings, chili-cheese fries, and cold beer complete the carefree fantasy.

811 Front St. ℰ 808/661-4855. www.cheeseburgerland.com. Burgers $7–$10. AE, DISC, MC, V. Daily 8am–10pm.

Cilantro: Fresh Mexican Grill ✦ (Kids) (Finds) MEXICAN   This is Maui's best bet for fabulous Mexican food at frugal prices. And believe it or not, this fast-food restaurant serves fresh, healthy food. The chef and owner is Pris Nabavi, creator of Maui's Pizza Paradiso Italian Kitchen. He wanted the "challenge of something different," so he took off to Mexico to find out how the Mexicans used to cook in "the old days." He's back on Maui with this unbelievably delicious eatery where everything is made from scratch. Even the corn tortillas are handmade daily. Signature dishes include the citrus-and-herb-marinated chipotle rotisserie chicken, the veggie Mariposa salad, and the popular Mother Clucker Flautas, plus lip-smacking "al pastor"-style adobo pork—all this at budget-pleasing prices. It's a great place to take the kids; the Los Ninos menu items are under $3.75.

170 Papalaua Ave. ✆ **808/667-5444.** www.cilantrogrill.com. Entrees $3.25–$8.95. MC, V. Mon–Thurs 11am–9:30pm; Fri–Sat 11am–10pm; Sun 11am–8pm.

Lahaina Coolers ✦ AMERICAN/INTERNATIONAL   A huge marlin hangs above the bar, epic wave shots and wall sconces made of surfboard fins line the walls, and open windows on three sides of this ultracasual indoor/outdoor restaurant take advantage of the shade trees to create a cheerful ambience. This is a great breakfast joint, with feta-cheese Mediterranean omelets, huevos rancheros, and fried jasmine rice with Kula vegetables and Portuguese sausage. There are three types of eggs Benedict: the classic; a vegetarian version (with Kula vegetables—excellent); and the Local, with Portuguese sausage and sweet bread. At lunch burgers rule, and the sandwiches, from grilled portobellos to the classic tuna melt, are ideal for casual Lahaina. Made fresh daily, the pasta is prepared Asian-style (chicken breast in a spicy Thai peanut sauce), with pesto, or vegetarian (in a spicy Creole sauce). Pizzas, pastas, fresh catch, steak, and enchiladas round out the entrees, and everything can be prepared vegetarian.

180 Dickensen St. ✆ **808/661-7082.** Main courses $7.50–$11 lunch, $14–$25 dinner. AE, DC, DISC, MC, V. Daily 8am–2am (full menu until midnight).

Maui Swiss Cafe SANDWICHES/PIZZA   Newly renovated and double its original size (which was tiny), Swiss Cafe now has five Internet stations and continues to serve excellent sandwiches and continental breakfast. Having gone from a sandwich-and-pizza shop to a European-style sidewalk Internet cafe, it still serves $5 lunch specials and two scoops of ice cream for $2.50 (and sometimes the ice cream is free with the lunch special). Top-quality breads are baked fresh daily, Dijon mustard, good Swiss cheese, and keen attention to sandwich fillings and pizza toppings make this a very special sandwich shop. The Swiss owner, Dominique Martin, has imbued this corner of Lahaina with a European flavor, down to the menus printed in English and German and the Swiss breakfast of sliced ham, Emmenthal cheese, hard-boiled egg, and freshly baked croissant. Watch for the "signature melt" sandwiches, with imported Emmenthal cheese baked on an Italian Parmesan crust.

640 Front St. ✆ **808/661-6776.** www.swisscafe.net. Sandwiches and 8-in. pizzas $6.50–$8.95. No credit cards. Daily 9am–8pm.

KAANAPALI
EXPENSIVE
Swan Court ✿✿ CONTINENTAL   What could be better than a fantasy restaurant in a fantasy resort? It's not exactly a hideaway (this is, after all, a Hyatt), but Swan Court is wonderful in a resorty sort of way, with a dance floor, waterfalls, flamingos, and an ocean view adding to the package. Come here as a splurge or on a bottomless expense account, and enjoy Pacific lobster coconut soup, rock shrimp crab cake, Maui sugar-cane-skewered ahi, and sautéed *opakapaka* in striking surroundings. The menu sticks to the tried and true, making Swan Court a safe choice for those who like a respectable and well-executed selection in a romantic setting with candlelight, a Japanese garden, and swans serenely gliding by—a year-round Valentine dinner.

In the Hyatt Regency Maui, 200 Nohea Kai Dr. ✆ **808/661-1234.** Reservations recommended for dinner. Main courses $30–$38. AE, DC, DISC, MC, V. Daily 6:30–11:30am (noon on Sun); Tues, Thurs, and Sat 6–10pm.

MODERATE
Beachside Grill and Leilani's on the Beach STEAK/ SEAFOOD   The Beachside Grill is the informal, less-expensive room downstairs on the beach, where folks wander in off the sand for a frothy beer and a beachside burger. Leilani's is the dinner-only room, with more expensive but still not outrageously priced steak and seafood offerings. At Leilani's you can order everything from affordable spinach, cheese, and mushroom ravioli to lobster and steak. Children can get a quarter-pound hamburger for under $5 or a broiled chicken breast for a couple of dollars more—a value, for sure. Pasta, rack of lamb, filet mignon, and Alaskan king crab at market price are among the choices in the upstairs room. Although the steak-and-lobster combinations can be pricey, the good thing about Leilani's is the strong middle range of entree prices, especially

the fresh fish for around $20 to $25. All of this, of course, comes with an ocean view. There's live Hawaiian music every afternoon except Friday, when the Rock 'n' Roll Aloha Friday set gets those decibels climbing. Free concerts are usually offered on a stage outside the restaurant on the last Sunday of the month.

In Whalers Village, 2435 Kaanapali Pkwy. © **808/661-4495.** www.leilanis.com. Reservations suggested for dinner at both restaurants. Lunch and dinner (Beachside Grill) $6.95–$13; dinner (Leilani's) $18–$25. AE, DC, DISC, MC, V. Beachside Grill daily 11am–11pm (bar daily until 12:30am). Leilani's daily 5–10pm.

Hula Grill ⚐ *Kids* HAWAII REGIONAL/SEAFOOD Who wouldn't want to tuck into crab-and-corn cakes, banana-glazed opah, mac-nut-roasted *opakapaka,* or crab won tons under a thatched umbrella, with palm trees at arm's length and a view of Lanai? Peter Merriman, one of the originators of Hawaii Regional Cuisine, segued seamlessly from his smallish, Big Island upcountry enclave to this large, high-volume, open-air dining room on the beach. Hula Grill offers a wide range of prices and choices; it can be expensive but doesn't have to be. The menu includes Merriman's signature firecracker mahimahi; seafood pot stickers; and several different fresh-fish preparations, including his famous ahi poke rolls—lightly sautéed rare ahi wrapped in rice paper with Maui onions. At lunch the menu is more limited, with a choice of sandwiches, entrees, pizza, appetizers, and salads. The kids' menu includes free pasta for kids under 4, cheese pizza, chicken, burgers, and more. There are happy-hour entertainment and Hawaiian music daily. For those wanting a more casual atmosphere, the Barefoot Bar, located on the beach, offers burgers, fish, pizza, and salads.

In Whalers Village, 2435 Kaanapali Pkwy. © **808/667-6636.** www.hulagrill.com. Reservations recommended for dinner. Lunch and Barefoot Bar menus $8–$16; dinner main courses $16–$32. AE, DC, DISC, MC, V. Daily 11am–10:30pm.

INEXPENSIVE

Whalers Village has a food court where you can buy pizza, very good Japanese food (including tempura, soba, and other noodle dishes), Korean plates, and fast-food burgers at serve-yourself counters and courtyard tables. It's an inexpensive alternative and a quick, handy stop for shoppers and Kaanapali beachgoers.

Nikki's Pizza PIZZA Formerly Pizza Paradiso, Nikki's has a full menu of pastas, pizzas, and desserts, including smoothies, coffee, and ice cream. This is a welcome addition to the Kaanapali scene, where casual is king and good food doesn't have to be fancy. The pizza reflects a simple and effective formula that has won acclaim through the years: good crust, true-blue sauces, and toppings loyal to tradition but with just enough edge for those who want it. Create your own pizza with roasted eggplant, mushrooms, anchovies, artichoke hearts, spicy sausages, cheeses, and a slew of other toppings. Nikki's offers some heroic choices, from the Veg Wedge to the Maui Wowie (ham and Maui pineapple) and the Godfather (roasted chicken, artichoke hearts, and sun-dried tomatoes).

In Whalers Village, 2435 Kaanapali Pkwy. © 808/667-0333. Gourmet pizza $3.85–$4.65 (by the slice); whole pizzas $12–$27. MC, V. Daily 11am–10pm.

HONOKOWAI, KAHANA & NAPILI
EXPENSIVE

Roy's Kahana Bar & Grill 🍴🍴 EURO-ASIAN   Despite the lack of dramatic view and an upstairs location in a shopping mall, Roy's remains crowded and extremely popular for one reason: fabulous food. It bustles with young, hip, impeccably trained servers delivering blackened ahi or perfectly seared lemon grass *shutome* (broadbill swordfish) to tables of satisfied customers. Roy's is known for its rack of lamb and fresh seafood (usually eight or nine choices) and for the chain's large, open kitchens that turn out everything from pizza to sake-grilled New York steak. If polenta is on the menu, don't resist: On my last visit, the polenta was rich and fabulous, with garlic, cream, spinach, and wild mushrooms. Large picture windows open up Roy's Kahana but don't quell the noise—another tireless trait long ago established by Roy's Restaurant in Honolulu, the flagship of Yamaguchi's burgeoning empire.

In the Kahana Gateway Shopping Center, 4405 Honoapiilani Hwy. © 808/669-6999. www.roysrestaurant.com. Reservations strongly recommended. Main courses $14–$31. AE, DC, DISC, MC, V. Daily 5:30–10pm.

Sea House Restaurant ASIAN/PACIFIC   The Sea House is not glamorous, famous, or hip, but it's worth mentioning for its spectacular view of Napili Bay. The Napili Kai Beach Club, where Sea House is located, is a charming throwback to the days when hotels blended in with their surroundings and had lush tropical foliage. Dinner entrees come complete with soup or salad, vegetables, and rice or potato. The lighter appetizer menu is a delight—more than a dozen choices ranging from sautéed or blackened crab cake to crisp Pacific Rim sushi of ahi capped in nori and cooked tempura-style.

In Napili Kai Beach Resort, 5900 Honoapiilani Hwy. © 808/669-1500. Reservations required for dinner. Main courses $18–$49; appetizer menu $5–$14. AE, DISC, MC, V. Sun–Fri 8–10:30am, noon–2pm, and 5:30–9pm. Pupu menu Sat–Thurs 2–9pm; Fri 2–9pm; Sat 5:30–9pm.

MODERATE

Fish & Game Brewing Co. & Rotisserie SEAFOOD/STEAK
This restaurant consists of an oyster bar, deli counter and retail section, and tables. The small retail section sells fresh seafood, and the sit-down menu covers basic tastes: salads (Caesar, Oriental chicken with won tons), fish and chips, fresh-fish sandwiches, cheeseburgers, and beer—lots of it. At dinner count on heavier meats and the fresh catch of the day (ahi, mahimahi, ono), with rotisserie items such as grilled chicken, steaks, and duck. The late-night menu offers shrimp, cheese fries, quesadillas, and lighter fare.

In the Kahana Gateway Shopping Center, 4405 Honoapiilani Hwy. ✆ **808/669-3474.** Reservations recommended for dinner. Main courses $7–$13 lunch, $16–$32 dinner. AE, DC, DISC, MC, V. Daily 11am–2am; late-night menu 10:30pm–1am. During football season (Sept–Jan) brunch Sat–Sun 7am–3pm.

INEXPENSIVE

Maui Tacos *Kids* MEXICAN   Mark Ellman's Maui Tacos chain has grown faster than you can say "Haleakala." Ellman put gourmet Mexican on paper plates and on the island's culinary map long before the island became known as Hawaii's center of salsa and chimichangas. Barely more than a takeout counter with a few tables, this and the six other Maui Tacos in Hawaii (four on Maui alone) are the rage of hungry surfers; discerning diners; burrito buffs; and Hollywood glitterati like Sharon Stone, whose picture adorns a wall or two. Choices include excellent fresh-fish tacos (garlicky and flavorful), chimichangas, and mouth-breaking compositions such as the Hookipa (a personal favorite): a "surf burrito" of fresh fish, black beans, and salsa. The green-spinach burrito contains four kinds of beans, rice, and potatoes—it's a knockout, requiring a siesta afterwards. Kids' menu items start at $2.75.

In Napili Plaza, 5095 Napili Hau St. ✆ **808/665-0222.** www.mauitacos.com. Items range $4–$7.50. AE, DC, DISC, MC, V. Daily 9am–9pm.

Pizza Paradiso Italian Caffe PIZZA/ITALIAN   Order at the counter (pastas, gourmet pizza whole or by the slice, salads, and desserts), and find a seat at one of the few tables. The pasta sauces—marinara, pescatore, Alfredo, Florentine, and pesto, with options and add-ons—are as popular as the pizzas and panini sandwiches. The Massimo, a pesto sauce with artichoke hearts, sun-dried tomatoes, and capers, comes with a choice of chicken, shrimp, or clams, and is so good it was a Taste of Lahaina winner in 1999. Whether you take out or dine in, this is a hot spot in the neighborhood, with free delivery.

In the Honokowai Marketplace, 3350 Lower Honoapiilani Rd. ℂ 808/667-2929. www.pizzaparadiso.com. Pastas $7.95–$9.25; pizzas $13–$27. MC, V. Daily 11am–10pm.

KAPALUA

The Banyan Tree Restaurant ☆☆☆ CONTEMPORARY AUSTRALIAN   Fasten your seat belts, food fans; this is one of the hottest, most creative chefs to come to Hawaii in decades. Australian Chef Antony Scholtmeyer said his philosophy is "dining shouldn't be safe, but a sexy blend of flavors and textures to create an exciting and sensual experience." His combinations may sound like a walk on the wild side, but once you taste his "sexy" cuisine, you'll be hooked. It takes a creative mind to come up with a signature amuse bouche of foie gras ice cream (don't laugh until you've tried it) with the taste of duck a l'orange (thanks to the confit orange zest and fresh orange segments) and the creamy taste of foie gras. Another zinger is the crispy-skin moi (the Hawaiian fish of royalty), served with lentil dhal, raita, and micro cilantro. Honey-roasted duck breast served with celery root risotto and pineapple jus is another winner. Save room for his warm bitter chocolate "meltaway" with sour cream sorbet, lilikoi sauce, and local berries. *Food and Wine* magazine has named him a "Chef to Watch." Word is out, so book a reservation at the Ritz-Carlton's signature restaurant before you leave home, or you'll never get in.

Ritz-Carlton Kapalua Resort. ℂ 808/669-6200. Reservations recommended for dinner. Main courses $32–$48. 4-course meal $80. AE, DISC, MC, V. Daily 11am–2pm and 5:30–9pm.

Plantation House Restaurant ☆☆ SEAFOOD/HAWAIIAN-MEDITERRANEAN   With its teak tables, fireplace, and open sides, Plantation House gets stellar marks for atmosphere. The 360-degree view from high among the resort's pine-studded hills takes in Molokai and Lanai, the ocean, the rolling fairways and greens, the northwestern flanks of the West Maui Mountains, and the daily sunset spectacular. Readers of the *Maui News* have deemed this the island's "Best Ambience"—a big honor on an island of wonderful views. It's the best place for breakfast in West Maui, hands down, and one of my top choices for dinner. The menu changes constantly but may include fresh fish prepared several ways—among them, Mediterranean (seared); Upcountry (sautéed with Maui onions and vegetable sauté); Island (pan-seared in sweet sake and macadamia nuts); and Rich Forest (with roasted wild mushrooms), the top seller. At breakfast, the Eggs Mediterranean is superb, and at lunch, sandwiches (open-faced smoked turkey, roasted vegetable, and goat-cheese wrap) and salads rule. When the sun sets, the menu expands to marvelous starters such as polenta and scampi-style shrimp, crab cakes, Kula and Mediterranean salads, and a hearty entree selection of fish, pork tenderloin, roast duck, and filet mignon with apple-smoked Maui onion.

2000 Plantation Club Dr. (at Kapalua Plantation Golf Course). ℂ **808/669-6299.** www.theplantationhouse.com. Reservations recommended. Main courses $24–$35. AE, DC, MC, V. Daily 8am–3pm and 5:30–10pm.

Sansei Seafood Restaurant and Sushi Bar ★★ PACIFIC RIM

Perpetual award-winner Sansei offers an extensive menu of Japanese and East-West delicacies. Part fusion, part Hawaii Regional Cuisine, Sansei is tirelessly creative, with a menu that scores higher with adventurous palates than with purists (although there are endless traditional choices as well). Maki is the mantra here. If you don't like cilantro, watch out for those complex spicy crab rolls. Other choices include panko-crusted ahi sashimi, sashimi trio, ahi carpaccio, noo-dle dishes, lobster, Asian rock-shrimp cakes, traditional Japanese tempura, and sauces that surprise, in creative combinations such as ginger-lime chile butter and cilantro pesto. But there's simpler fare as well, such as shrimp tempura, noodles, and wok-tossed upcoun-try vegetables. Desserts are not to be missed. If it's autumn, don't pass up persimmon crème brûlée made with Kula persimmons. In other seasons, opt for tempura-fried ice cream with chocolate sauce. There's karaoke every night from 10pm to 1am. *Money-saving tip:* Eat early; all food is 25% off between 5:30 and 6pm.

At the Kapalua Shops, 115 Bay Dr. ℂ **808/669-6286.** Also in Kihei at the Kihei Town Center ℂ **808/879-0004.** www.sanseihawaii.com. Reservations recom-mended. Main courses $19–$29. AE, DISC, MC, V. Daily 5:30–10pm. Thurs–Fri pupu and bar menu with karaoke until 1am.

Vino Italian Tapas & Wine Bar ★★★ (Finds) ITALIAN   Two

Japanese guys, D. K. Kodama (chef and owner of Sansei Seafood Restaurant and Sushi Bar, reviewed above) and Chuck Furuya (Hawaii's only master sommelier), teamed up to create this culinary adventure for foodies. Vino opened in August 2003 to big, big acco-lades. Probably the best Italian food on Maui is served at this exqui-site restaurant overlooking the rolling hills of the Kapalua Golf Course. Always wanting to be on the cutting edge, the duo rebranded the restaurant in December 2004 to Vino Italian Tapas & Wine Bar. The new menu features more than two dozen tapas (small plates), ranging from the signature asparagus Milanese (just $5.95) to slow butter-poached Kona lobster ($18). Plus they have retained the most popular large plate dishes, like fresh mahimahi with artichokes and grape tomatoes on capellini, Mudicca-crusted pan-fried veal stuffed with prosciutto, and *osso buco* with spinach risotto. Go to Vino early during your stay on Maui; you most likely will want to return.

Kapalua Village Course Golf Club House, Kapalua Resort. ② **808/661-VINO.** Reservations recommended. Tapas $5.95–$18; large plates $19–$25. AE, DISC, MC, V. Daily 11am–2pm and 6–9:30pm.

3 South Maui

KIHEI/MAALAEA

There's a **Maui Tacos** at Kamaole Beach Center in Kihei (② **808/ 879-5005**).

EXPENSIVE

Buzz's Wharf AMERICAN   Buzz's is another formula restaurant that offers a superb view, substantial sandwiches, meaty french fries, and surf-and-turf fare—in a word, satisfying but not sensational. Still, this bright, airy dining room is a fine way station for whale-watching over a cold beer and a fresh mahimahi sandwich with fries. Some diners opt for several appetizers (stuffed mushrooms, steamer clams, clam chowder, onion soup) and a salad, and then splurge on dessert. Buzz's prize-winning Tahitian Baked Papaya is a warm, fragrant melding of fresh papaya with vanilla and coconut—the pride of the house.

Maalaea Harbor, 50 Hauoli St. ② **808/244-5426.** Reservations recommended. Main courses $20–$33. AE, DC, DISC, MC, V. Mon–Sat 11am–9pm; Sun 10am–9pm.

Five Palms ⚑ PACIFIC RIM   This is the best lunch spot in Kihei—open-air, with tables a few feet from the beach and up-close-and-personal views of Kahoolawe and Molokini. You'll have to walk through a nondescript parking area and the modest entrance of the Mana Kai Resort to reach this unpretentious place. They feature a menu of breakfast and lunch items served from 8am to 2:30pm, so if you're jet-lagged and your stomach isn't on Hawaiian time, you can get a snow-crab omelet at 2 in the afternoon or a juicy Angus beef hamburger at 8 in the morning. At dinner, with the torches lit on the beach and the main dining room open, the ambience shifts to evening romantic but still casual. Just-caught fish is the star of the dinner menu.

In the Mana Kai Resort, 2960 S. Kihei Rd. ② **808/879-2607.** Reservations recommended for dinner. Dinner $23–$40. AE, DC, MC, V. Daily 8am–2:30pm and 5–9pm, with pupu menu daily 2:30–6pm.

The Waterfront at Maalaea 🎯🎯 SEAFOOD The family-owned Waterfront has won many prestigious awards for wine excellence, service, and seafood, but its biggest boost is word of mouth. Loyal diners rave about the friendly staff and seafood, fresh off the boat in nearby Maalaea Harbor and prepared with care. The bay and harbor view is one you'll never forget, especially at sunset. You have nine choices of preparations for the several varieties of fresh Hawaiian fish, ranging from *en papillote* (baked in buttered parchment) to Southwestern (smoked chile and cilantro butter) to Cajun spiced and island-style (sautéed, broiled, poached, or baked and paired with tiger prawns). Other choices: Kula onion soup; an excellent Caesar salad; the signature lobster chowder; and grilled eggplant layered with Maui onions, tomatoes, and spinach, served with red-pepper coulis and Big Island goat cheese. Like the seafood, it's superb.

Maalaea Harbor, 50 Hauoli St. ℭ **808/244-9028.** Reservations recommended. Main courses $19–$35. AE, DC, DISC, MC, V. Opens daily at 5pm; last seating at 8:30pm.

MODERATE

Stella Blues Cafe 🎯 *(Kids* AMERICAN Stella Blues gets going at breakfast and continues through to dinner with something for everyone—vegetarians, kids, pasta and sandwich lovers, and hefty steak eaters. Grateful Dead posters line the walls, and a covey of gleaming motorcycles is invariably parked outside. It's loud, lively, irreverent, and unpretentious. Sandwiches are the highlight, ranging from Tofu Extraordinaire to Mom's Egg Salad on a croissant to garden burgers and grilled chicken. Tofu wraps and mountain-size Cobb salads are popular, and for the reckless, there are large coffee shakes with mounds of whipped cream. Daily specials include fresh seafood, and everything's made from scratch, down to the pesto mayonnaise and herb bread. At dinner, selections range from affordable full dinners to pastas and burgers.

Azeka II Shopping Center, 1279 S. Kihei Rd. ℭ **808/874-3779.** Main courses $7–$23. AE, DC, DISC, MC, V. Daily 7:30am–10pm.

INEXPENSIVE

The Coffee Store COFFEEHOUSE This simple, classic coffeehouse for caffeine connoisseurs serves two dozen different types of coffee and coffee drinks, from mochas and lattes to cappuccinos, espressos, and toddies. Breakfast items include smoothies, lox and bagels, quiches, granola, and assorted pastries. Pizza, salads, vegetarian lasagna, veggie-and-shrimp quesadillas, and sandwiches (garden burger, tuna, turkey, ham, grilled veggie panini) also move briskly from the takeout counter. The turkey-and-veggie wraps are a local legend. There are only a few small tables, and they fill up fast, often with musicians and artists who've spent the previous evening entertaining at the Wailea and Kihei resorts.

In Azeka Place II, 1279 Kihei Rd. ✆ **808/875-4244.** www.mauicoffee.com. All items less than $8.50. AE, MC, V. Mon–Sat 6:30am–8pm; Sun 6:30am–7pm.

Peggy Sue's *(Kids* AMERICAN   Just for a moment, forget that diet, and take a leap. It's Peggy Sue's to the rescue! This 1950s-style diner has oodles of charm and is a swell place to spring for the best chocolate malt on the island. You'll also find sodas, shakes, floats, egg creams, milkshakes, and scoops of made-on-Maui Roselani-brand gourmet ice cream—14 flavors. Old-fashioned soda-shop stools, an Elvis Presley Boulevard sign, and jukeboxes on every Formica table serve as a backdrop for the famous burgers (and garden burgers), brushed with teriyaki sauce and served with all the goodies. The fries are great, too. Kids' meals go for just $3.95.

In Azeka Place II, 1279 S. Kihei Rd. ✆ **808/875-8944.** Burgers $7–$11; plate lunches $6–$12. AE, DISC, MC, V. Sun–Thurs 11am–9pm; Fri–Sat 11am–10pm.

Shaka Sandwich & Pizza PIZZA   How many "best pizzas" are there on Maui? It depends on which shore you're on, the west or the south. At this south-shore old-timer, which recently moved to a new (and much larger) location, they still are serving those award-winning pizzas, New York–style heroes and Philly cheese steaks, calzones, salads, homemade garlic bread, and homemade meatball sandwiches. Shaka uses fresh Maui produce, long-simmering sauces, and homemade Italian bread. Choose thin or Sicilian thick crust with gourmet toppings: Maui onions, spinach, anchovies, jalapeños, and a spate of other vegetables. Try the white pizza; with the perfectly balanced flavors of olive oil, garlic, and cheese, you won't even miss the tomato sauce. Clam-and-garlic pizza, spinach pizza (with olive oil, spinach, garlic, and mozzarella), and the Shaka Supreme (with at least 10 toppings) should satisfy even the biggest appetites.

1770 S. Kihei Rd. ✆ **808/874-0331.** Sandwiches $4.35–$11; pizzas $13–$26. No credit cards. Daily 10:30am–9pm.

WAILEA

The Shops at Wailea, a sprawling location between the Grand Wailea Hotel and Outrigger Wailea Resort, has added a spate of new shops and restaurants to this stretch of south Maui. **Ruth's Chris Steak House** is here, as are **Tommy Bahama's Tropical Cafe & Emporium; Honolulu Coffee Company; Cheeseburger, Mai**

Tai's and Rock-n-Roll; and **Longhi's.** Next door at the Outrigger Wailea, **Hula Moons,** the retro-Hawaiian-themed restaurant, has reopened after a $3 million renovation and moved to the upper level of the lobby building, giving it an ocean view.

VERY EXPENSIVE

Spago ☆☆☆ HAWAIIAN/CALIFORNIA/PACIFIC REGIONAL This contemporary restaurant features fresh, local Hawaiian ingredients prepared under the culinary watch of master chef Wolfgang Puck. The room has an open-air setting overlooking the Pacific Ocean. The menu features traditional Hawaiian dishes with Puck's own brand of cutting-edge innovations, including an unbelievable coconut soup with local lobster, keffir, chili, and galangal. For entrees, try the whole steamed fish served with chili, ginger, and baby choy sum; the incredible Kona lobster with sweet-and-sour banana curry, coconut rice, and dry-fried green beans; or the grilled *côte de boeuf* with braised celery, armagnac, peppercorns, and *pommes aligot.* An extensive wine list rounds out the menu. Save room for the warm guanaja chocolate tart. Make reservations early; this place is popular. And bring plenty of cash or your platinum card.

Four Seasons Resort Maui, 3900 Wailea Alanui Dr., Wailea, 96753. ⓒ **808/879-2999.** www.wolfgangpuck.com. Reservations required. Entrees $27–$48. AE, DC, DISC, MC, V. Daily 5:30–9pm.

EXPENSIVE

Joe's Bar & Grill ☆☆ AMERICAN GRILL The 270-degree view spans the golf course, tennis courts, ocean, and Haleakala—a worthy setting for Beverly Gannon's style of American home cooking with a regional twist. The hearty staples include fresh fish and filet mignon, but the meatloaf upstages them all. The Tuscan white-bean soup is superb, and the tenderloin, with roasted portobellos, garlic mashed potatoes, and a pinot noir demiglace, is American home cooking at its best. Daily specials could be grilled ahi with white truffle–Yukon gold mashed potatoes or sautéed mahimahi with shrimp bisque and sautéed spinach. If apple-pumpkin cheesecake is on the menu, you should definitely spring for it.

In the Wailea Tennis Club, 131 Wailea Ike Place. ⓒ **808/875-7767.** Reservations recommended. Main courses $23–$33. AE, DC, DISC, MC, V. Daily 5:30–9:30pm.

Longhi's ☆☆ ITALIAN This is a great alternative to the high-priced restaurants in the surrounding resorts. Breakfasts here are something you want to wake up to: perfect baguettes, fresh-baked cinnamon rolls (one is enough for two people), and eggs Benedict or Florentine with hollandaise. Lunch is either an Italian banquet (ahi torino, prawns amaretto, and a wide variety of pastas) or fresh salads and sandwiches. Dinner (overlooking the water) is where Longhi's shines, with a long list of fresh-made pasta dishes, seafood platters, and beef and chicken dishes (like filet mignon with béarnaise or veal sauté). Leave room for the daily dessert specials. There's live music Saturday nights until 1:30am.

The Shops at Wailea, 3750 Wailea Alanui Dr., Wailea. ℂ 808/891-8883. www.longhi-maui.com. Reservations for dinner recommended. Main courses $18–$35. AE, DC, MC, V. Mon–Fri 8am–10pm; Sat 7:30am–1:30am; Sun 7:30am–10pm.

Nick's Fishmarket Maui *ᏌᏌᏌ* SEAFOOD   I do love Nick's. This is a classic seafood restaurant that sticks to the tried and true (in other words, *not* an overwrought menu) but stays fresh with excellent ingredients and a high degree of professionalism in service and preparation. I love the onion vichyssoise with taro swirl and a hint of *tobiko* (flying-fish roe) and the bow-tied servers with almond-scented cold towels. The Greek Maui Wowie salad gets my vote as one of the top salads in Hawaii. The wonderful blackened mahimahi has been a Nick's signature for eons. Fresh opah (moonfish), salmon, scallops, Hawaiian lobster tails, and chicken, beef, and lamb choices offer ample choices for diners enjoying the fantasy setting on the south Maui shoreline. The round bar, where you can sit facing the ocean, has a warm, friendly feel.

In the Fairmont Kea Lani Hotel, 4100 Wailea Alanui. ℂ 808/879-7224. www.tristar-restaurants.com. Reservations recommended. Main courses $25–$50; prix-fixe dinners $55 to market price. AE, DC, DISC, MC, V. Mon–Thurs 5:30–10pm; Fri–Sat 5:30–10:30pm; bar until 11pm.

MODERATE

Caffé Ciao *Ꮜ* ITALIAN   There are two parts to this charming trattoria: the deli, with a takeout section, and the cafe, with tables under the trees, next to the bar. Rare and wonderful wines, such as Vine Cliff, are sold in the deli, along with ultraluxe rose soaps and other bath products, assorted pastas, pizzas, roasted potatoes, vegetable panini, vegetable lasagna, abundant salads, and an appealing selection of microwavable and takeout goodies. On the terrace under the trees, the tables are cheerfully accented with Italian herbs growing in cachepots. *A fave:* the linguine pomodoro, with fresh tomatoes, spinach-tomato sauce, and a dollop of mascarpone. Unfortunately, lunch is seasonal (summer and mid-Dec to mid-Mar, when most of the tourists are around).

In the Kea Lani Hotel, 4100 Wailea Alanui. ℂ 808/875-4100. Reservations recommended. Main courses $13–$20 lunch, $17–$36 dinner; pizzas $17–$19. AE,

DC, DISC, MC, V. Lunch (seasonally) daily noon–3pm; dinner daily 5:30–10pm. Bar daily 11am–10pm.

SeaWatch ✹ ISLAND CUISINE   Under the same ownership as Kapalua's Plantation House (reviewed earlier in this chapter), Sea-Watch is one of the more affordable stops in tony Wailea. You'll dine on the terrace or in a high-ceilinged room, on a menu that carries the tee-off-to-19th-hole crowd with ease. For breakfast, try bagels and lox with Maui onions, scrambled eggs with Kalua pork and Maui onions, or crab cake Benedict with roasted-pepper hollandaise. Lunchtime sandwiches, pastas, salads, wraps, and soups are moderately priced, and you get 360-degree views to go with them. The cashew chicken wrap with mango chutney is a winner, as are the tropical-fish quesadilla and the grilled fresh-catch sandwich with Kula lime aioli. Save room for the bananas Foster.

100 Wailea Golf Club Dr. ✆ **808/875-8080.** www.seawatchrestaurant.com. Reservations required for dinner. Main courses $4–$12 breakfast, $6.50–$15 lunch, $23–$30 dinner. AE, DC, MC, V. Daily 8am–10pm.

MAKENA

Prince Court ✹✹ CONTEMPORARY ISLAND   Half of the Sunday brunch experience here is the head-turning view of Makena Beach, Molokini islet, and Kahoolawe island. The bountiful Sunday buffet includes pasta, omelets, cheeses, pastries, sashimi, crab legs, smoked salmon, fresh Maui produce, and a smashing array of ethnic and Continental foods. The dinner menu changes regularly; the current winners are the steamed Manila clams scampi with roasted garlic, diced tomatoes, and fried basil; Dungeness crab and goat-cheese won ton with Maui-onion guacamole; and the Prince Court Sampler with Kona lobster cakes, Kalua duck lumpia, and sugar-cane-speared grilled prawns. Game entrees (venison, rack of lamb, breast of duck) come in highly acclaimed preparations, such as poha compote and black cherry cabernet sauce.

In the Maui Prince Hotel, 5400 Makena Alanui. ✆ **808/874-1111.** Reservations recommended. Main courses $19–$38; kids 6 and under eat free. Fri prime rib and seafood buffet $42 ($25 children); Sun brunch $42. AE, MC, V. Sun 9am–2pm (with last seating at noon); daily 6–9:30pm (Fri buffet 2 seatings: 6–6:30pm and 8–8:30pm).

4 Upcountry Maui

HALIIMAILE (ON THE WAY TO UPCOUNTRY MAUI)
EXPENSIVE

Haliimaile General Store ✹✹✹ AMERICAN   Bev Gannon, one of the 12 original Hawaii Regional Cuisine chefs, is still going strong at her foodie haven in the pineapple fields. You'll dine at tables set on old wood floors under high ceilings, with works by local artists hanging on the walls. Sip the lilikoi lemonade and nibble the sashimi napoleon or the house salad (island greens with mandarin oranges, onions, toasted walnuts, and blue-cheese crumble)—all are notable items on a menu that bridges Hawaii with Gannon's Texas roots. Kids can enjoy "kid cocktails" like kiwi soda and a special menu featuring pizza, ribs, chicken, and spaghetti.

Haliimaile Rd., Haliimaile. ⓒ 808/572-2666. www.haliimailegeneralstore.com. Reservations recommended for dinner. Lunch $10–$20; dinner $20–$30. AE, DC, DISC, MC, V. Mon–Fri 11am–2:30pm; daily 5:30–9:30pm.

MAKAWAO & PUKALANI

Casanova Italian Restaurant ⓐ ITALIAN Makawao's nightlife center contains a stage, dance floor, restaurant, and bar—and food to love and remember. This is pasta heaven: Try the spaghetti fra diavolo or the spinach gnocchi in a fresh tomato-Gorgonzola sauce. Other choices include a huge pizza selection, grilled lamb chops in an Italian mushroom marinade, lots more pasta dishes, and luscious desserts. My personal picks on a stellar menu: garlic spinach topped with Parmesan and pine nuts; polenta with radicchio (the mushroom-and-cream sauce is fabulous!); and tiramisu, the best on the island.

1188 Makawao Ave. ⓒ 808/572-0220. Reservations recommended for dinner. Main courses $10–$24; 12-in. pizzas from $10. AE, DC, DISC, MC, V. Mon–Sat 11:30am–2pm; daily 5:30–9pm; dancing Wed–Sat 9:45pm–1am. Lounge daily 5:30pm–12:30am. Deli Mon–Sat 7:30am–6pm, Sun 8:30am–6pm.

'Aha'aina Upcountry Cafe AMERICAN/LOCAL Pukalani's inexpensive, casual, and very popular cafe features simple, home-cooked comfort food, such as humongous hamburgers, chicken katsu, fresh-fish tacos, sesame-crusted ahi-and-chicken tortilla soup, plus home-baked bread, oven-fresh muffins, and local faves such as saimin, loco moco, and shoyu chicken. The dreamy breakfast menu features fluffy pancakes and big egg dishes.

In the Andrade Building, 7 Aewa Place (just off Haleakala Hwy.), Pukalani. ⓒ 808/572-2395. Breakfast $5–$10; lunch $6–$15. MC, V. Tues–Sat 7am–2pm; Sun 7am–1pm.

KULA (AT THE BASE OF HALEAKALA NATIONAL PARK)

Cafe 808 AMERICAN/LOCAL Despite its out-of-the-way location, Cafe 808 has become a universal favorite among upcountry residents of all ages. Here, you'll enjoy tasty home-style cooking with no pretensions: chicken lasagna, smoked-salmon omelets, famous burgers (teriyaki, hamburger, garden burger, mahimahi, taro), roast pork, smoked turkey, and a huge selection of local-style specials. Regulars rave about the chicken katsu, saimin, and beef stew. The few tables are sprinkled around a room with linoleum-tile floors, hardwood benches, plastic patio chairs, and old-fashioned booths—rough around the edges in a pleasing way, and very camp.

Lower Kula Rd., past Holy Ghost Church, across from Morihara Store. © **808/878-6874.** Burgers from $4; main courses $5.50–$9.95. No credit cards. Daily 6am–8pm.

Grandma's Coffee House ® COFFEEHOUSE/AMERICAN

Alfred Franco's grandmother started what is now a five-generation coffee business back in 1918, when she was 16 years old. Today this tiny wooden coffeehouse, still serving homegrown Haleakala coffee, is the quintessential roadside oasis. Grandma's offers espresso, hot and cold coffees, home-baked pastries, inexpensive pasta, sandwiches (including sensational avocado and garden burgers), homemade soups, fresh juices, and local plate-lunch specials that change daily. Rotating specials include Hawaiian beef stew, ginger chicken, saimin, chicken curry, lentil soup, and sandwiches piled high with Kula vegetables. The lemon squares and the pumpkin bread are standouts.

At the end of Hwy. 37, Keokea (about 6 miles before the Tedeschi Vineyards in Ulu-palakua). © **808/878-2140.** Most items less than $8.95. MC, V. Daily 7am–5pm.

Kula Lodge ® HAWAII REGIONAL/AMERICAN   Don't let

the dinner prices scare you: The Kula Lodge is equally enjoyable at breakfast and lunch, when the prices are lower and the views through the picture windows have an eye-popping intensity. The million-dollar vista spans the flanks of Haleakala, central Maui, the ocean, and the West Maui Mountains. The Kula Lodge has always been known for its breakfasts: fabulous eggs Benedict; legendary banana–mac-nut pancakes; and a highly recommended tofu scramble with green onions, Kula vegetables, and garlic chives. If possible, go for sunset cocktails. When darkness descends, a roaring fire and lodge atmosphere add to the coziness of the room. The dinner menu features "small plates" of Thai summer rolls, seared ahi, and other starters. Top seafood dishes include sesame-seared ono, Cuban-style spicy swordfish with rum-soaked bananas, and miso salmon with wild mushrooms. There are also pasta, rack of lamb, filet mignon, and free-range chicken breast.

Haleakala Hwy. (Hwy. 377). © **808/878-2517.** Reservations recommended for dinner. Breakfast $7.50–$16; lunch $11–$18; dinner main courses $14–$28. AE, DC, DISC, MC, V. Daily 6:30am–9pm.

Kula Sandalwoods Restaurant ☆ AMERICAN   This is Kula cuisine, with produce from the backyard and everything made from scratch, including French toast with home-baked Portuguese sweet bread, hotcakes or Belgian waffles with fresh fruit, baguettes, open-faced country omelets, hamburgers drenched in a sharp cheddar cheese sauce, and an outstanding veggie burger. The grilled-chicken-breast sandwich is marvelous, served with the soup of the day and Kula mixed greens. Dine in the gazebo or on the terrace, with dazzling views in all directions, including, in the spring, a yard dusted with lavender jacaranda flowers and a hillside ablaze with fields of orange akulikuli blossoms.

15427 Haleakala Hwy. (Hwy. 377). ⓒ **808/878-3523.** Breakfast $6.95–$9.75; lunch $7.25–$13; Sun brunch $6.95–$9.75. MC, V. Mon–Sat 6:30am–2pm; Sun 6:30am–noon.

5 East Maui: On the Road to Hana

PAIA
MODERATE

Jacques North Shore ☆☆ (Value) SEAFOOD/SUSHI   Jacques is difficult to pin down: Some have called it a hipper, cheaper version of the upscale Mama's Fish House. The clientele tends to be trendy, hard-body windsurfers; blonde, tan surfers; and chic North Shore residents. The decor is patio dining under a big circus tent. Some might be distracted by the hostess and servers (20-something beauty queens dressed in "barely there" clothes), but the main attraction is the food. Do not miss the North Shore pumpkin fish (fish, bananas, and oranges served with a ginger-pumpkin sauce and miso butter), Greek pasta (roasted bell peppers, roasted garlic, and feta cheese over orrechiette pasta), or one of the fabulous vegetarian entrees like the vegetable curry (with tofu, bananas, and oranges). The sushi bar (closed Sun–Mon) whips out a mean spicy ahi roll and a died-and-gone-to-heaven California roll.

120 Hana Hwy., Paia. ⓒ **808/579-8844.** No reservations. Main courses $11–$20. AE, DC, DISC, MC, V. Daily 11:30am–3pm and 5–10pm. Sushi bar Tues–Sat 5:30–10pm.

Milagros Food Company ☆ SOUTHWESTERN/SEAFOOD Milagros has gained a following with its great home-style cooking, upbeat atmosphere, and highly touted margaritas. Sit outdoors for some great people-watching as you tuck into dishes created with a combination of Southwestern and Pacific Rim styles and flavors accompanied by fresh veggies and Kula greens. Blackened ahi taquitos; pepper-crusted ono pasta; blue shrimp tostadas; and sandwiches, salads, and combination plates are some of the offerings here. For breakfast, I recommend the Olive Oyl spinach omelet or the huevos rancheros, served with home fries. I love Paia's tie-dyes, beads, and hippie flavor, and this is the front-row seat for it all. Watch for happy hour, with cheap and fabulous margaritas.

Hana Hwy. and Baldwin Ave., Paia. ℂ 808/579-8755. Breakfast around $7; lunch $6–$10; dinner $15–$20. AE, MC, V. Daily 8am–10pm.

Moana Bakery & Cafe *☆☆* LOCAL/EUROPEAN   Moana gets high marks for its stylish concrete floors, high ceilings, booths and cafe tables, and fabulous food. Don Ritchey, formerly a chef at Haliimaile General Store, has created the perfect Paia eatery, a casual bakery–cafe that highlights his stellar skills. All the bases are covered: saimin, omelets, wraps, pancakes, and fresh-baked goods in the morning; soups, sandwiches, pasta, and satisfying salads for lunch; and for dinner, varied selections with Asian and European influences and fresh island ingredients. The lemon-grass-grilled prawns with green-papaya salad are an explosion of flavors and textures, and the roasted vegetable napoleon is gourmet fare. Ritchey has a special gift with fish, especially the nori-sesame-crusted *opakapaka* with wasabi beurre blanc. There's entertainment 3 nights a week, ranging from jazz to vintage Hawaiian to Latin.

71 Baldwin Ave. ℂ 808/579-9999. Reservations recommended for dinner. Breakfast $4.60–$9.95; lunch $5.95–$9.95; dinner main courses $7.95–$24. MC, V. Tues–Sun 8am–9pm; Mon 8am–2:30pm.

INEXPENSIVE

Cafe des Amis *☆* CREPES/SALADS   This Paia newcomer has quickly become known as the place for healthy and tasty lunches that are easy on the wallet. Crepes are the star here, and they are popular: spinach with feta cheese; scallops with garlic and chipotle chile; shrimp curry with coconut milk; and dozens more choices, including breakfast crepes and dessert crepes (like banana and chocolate or caramelized apples with rum). Equally popular are the salads (including Niçoise, Greek, and Caesar) and smoothies. The crepes come with a house salad—a great deal.

42 Baldwin Ave. ℂ 808/579-6323. Crepes $6.50–$8.50. MC, V. Open daily 8:30am–8:30pm.

Paia Fish Market *☆* SEAFOOD   This really is a fish market, with fresh fish to take home and cooked seafood, salads, pastas, fajitas, and quesadillas to take out or enjoy at the few picnic tables inside the restaurant. It's an appealing and budget-friendly selection: Cajun-style fresh catch, fresh-fish specials (usually ahi or salmon), fresh-fish tacos and quesadillas, and seafood and chicken pastas. You can also order hamburgers, cheeseburgers, fish and chips (or shrimp and chips), and wonderful lunch and dinner plates, cheap and tasty. Peppering the walls are photos of the number-one sport here, windsurfing.

110 Hana Hwy. ⓒ **808/579-8030.** Lunch and dinner plates $6.95–$20. DISC, MC, V. Daily 11am–9:30pm.

ELSEWHERE ON THE ROAD TO HANA

Mama's Fish House 🐟🐟🐟 SEAFOOD   If you love fish, this is the place for you. The interior features curved lauhala-lined ceilings, walls of split bamboo, lavish arrangements of tropical blooms, and picture windows to let in the view. With servers wearing Polynesian prints and flowers behind their ears, and the sun setting in Kuau Cove, Mama's mood is hard to beat. The fish is fresh (the fishermen are even credited by name on the menu) and prepared Hawaiian-style with tropical fruit; baked in a macadamia-nut-and-vanilla-bean crust; or in a number of preparations involving ferns, seaweed, Maui onions, and roasted kukui nut. My favorite menu item is mahimahi laulau with luau leaves (taro greens) and Maui onions, baked in ti leaves and served with Kalua pig and Hanalei poi. You can get deep-water ahi seared with coconut and lime, or ono "caught by Keith Nakamura along the 40-fathom ledge near Hana" in Hana ginger teriyaki with mac-nuts and crisp Maui onion. Other special touches include the use of Molokai sweet potato, Hana breadfruit, organic lettuces, Haiku bananas, and fresh coconut.

799 Poho Place, just off the Hana Hwy., Kuau. ⓒ **808/579-8488.** Reservations recommended for lunch, required for dinner. Main courses $29–$36 lunch, $32–$49 dinner. AE, DC, DISC, MC, V. Opens daily at 11am, last seating at 9pm (light menu 2:30–4:45pm).

Nahiku Coffee Shop, Smoked Fish Stand, and Ti Gallery 🐟 *Finds* SMOKED KABOBS   What a delight to stumble across this trio of comforts on the long drive to Hana! The small coffee shop sells locally made baked goods, Maui-grown coffee, banana bread, organic tropical-fruit smoothies, and locally made coconut candy. Next door the Ti Gallery sells locally made Hawaiian arts and crafts, such as pottery and koa-wood vessels.

The barbecue smoker is my favorite part of the operation. It puts out superb smoked and grilled fish, fresh and locally caught. The teriyaki-based marinade, made by the owner, adds a special touch to the fish (ono, ahi, marlin). One of the biggest sellers is the Kalua pig sandwich. Also hits are the fish, beef, and chicken tacos, served with cheese, jalapeños, and salsa. When available, fresh corn on the cob from Kipahulu is also served. You can sit at one of the roadside picnic tables, or you can take your lunch to go.

Hana Hwy., ½ mile past mile marker 28. No phone. Kabobs $3 each. No credit cards. Coffee shop daily 9am–5:30pm. Fish stand Fri–Wed 10am–5pm. Gallery daily 10am–5pm.

Pauwela Cafe ⭐ *Finds* INTERNATIONAL   It's easy to get lost on the way to this wonderful cafe, but it's worth the search. I never dreamed you could dine so well with such pleasing informality. Nearly everything in this tiny cafe is made from scratch. Breakfasts feature such scrumptious items as pain perdu (French bread in orange-vanilla custard), veggie frittata, and Belgian waffles. Lunch is a great collection of salads and sandwiches, where the scene-stealing Kalua turkey sandwich consists of moist, smoky shredded turkey with cheese on home-baked French bread and covered with a green-chili-and-cilantro sauce. Also available are burgers (including a vegetarian taro burger), chicken quesadillas, and veggie burritos. Dinner entrees include a range of items, from chicken quesadillas to veggie lasagna to Cajun-grilled mahi. The cafe is a little less than 1½ miles past the Haiku turn-off and ½ mile up on the left.

375 W. Kuiaha Rd., off Hana Hwy., past Haiku Rd., Haiku. ℂ **808/575-9242.** Breakfast $4.25–$7; lunch $5.25–$7.50; dinner $6.50–$9. MC, V. Mon–Fri 7am–2:30pm; Tues–Fri 5–8pm; Sun 8am–2pm.

HANA

Hotel Hana Maui ⭐⭐⭐ ECLECTIC   The ingredients-driven menu here features fresh fish caught by local fishermen, produce brought in by nearby farmers, and fruits that are in season. The result is true "Hawaiian" food, grown right on the island. Breakfast features an omelet with local Maui onions and a Hana fern salad, almond-crusted French toast, or local papaya with yogurt and homemade granola. Lunch ranges from Maui Cattle Company burgers to just-caught fish sandwiches. Dinner, which changes daily, can include just-picked lettuce for salads (Kula-grown baby romaine with Gruyere crostini and sherry-thyme vinaigrette, or baby lettuces with Kula citrus, local radishes, and Kalamata olives), a range of soups (like a chilled Kula cucumber soup), and a range of entrees (seared rare Hana-caught ahi with smoked bacon, forest mushrooms, and wilted greens, or oven-roasted chicken breast with crispy polenta, Nihiku bush beans, and mole sauce). Try the three- or four-course tasting menu or, even better, the Chef's Choice custom tasting.

Hana Hwy. ⓒ **808/248-8211.** Reservations recommended for Fri–Sat dinner. Entrees $10–$14 breakfast, $12–$16 lunch, $31–$35 dinner; tasting menu $55 for 3-courses, $65 for 4-courses, $105 for Chef's Choice. AE, DISC, MC, V. Daily 7:30–10:30am, 11:30am–2:30pm, and 6–8:30pm. Friday buffet and Hawaiian show 6-8:30pm.

5

Fun on & off the Beach

This is why you've come to Maui—the sun, the sand, and the surf. In this chapter, I'll tell you about the best beaches, from where to soak up the rays to where to plunge beneath the waves. I've covered a range of ocean activities on Maui, as well as my favorite places and outfitters for these marine adventures. Also in this chapter are things to do on dry land, including the best spots for hiking and camping and the greatest golf courses.

1 Beaches

Hawaii's beaches belong to the people. All beaches (even those in front of exclusive resorts) are public property, and you are welcome to visit. Hawaii state law requires all resorts and hotels to offer public right-of-way access to the beach, along with public parking. For beach toys and equipment, contact the **Activity Warehouse** (© 800/343-2087; www.travelhawaii.com), which has branches in Lahaina at 578 Front St., near Prison Street (© 808/667-4000), and in Kihei at Azeka Place II, on the mountain side of Kihei Road near Lipoa Street (© 808/875-4000). Beach chairs rent for $2 a day, coolers (with ice) for $2 a day, and a host of toys (Frisbees, volleyballs, and more) for $1 a day.

WEST MAUI
KAANAPALI BEACH 👭👭

Four-mile-long Kaanapali is one of Maui's best beaches, with grainy gold sand as far as the eye can see. The beach parallels the sea channel through most of its length, and a paved beach walk links hotels and condos, open-air restaurants, and Whalers Village shopping center. Because Kaanapali is so long, the beach is crowded only in pockets; there's plenty of room to find seclusion. Summertime swimming is excellent.

There's fabulous snorkeling around **Black Rock,** in front of the Sheraton; the water is clear, calm, and populated with clouds of tropical fish. You might even spot a turtle or two.

Facilities include outdoor showers; you can use the restrooms at the hotel pools. Beach-activity vendors line up in front of the hotels, offering various water activities and equipment.

Parking is a problem, though. There are two public entrances: At the south end, turn off Honoapiilani Highway into the Kaanapali Resort, and pay for parking there, or continue on Honoapiilani Highway, turn off at the last Kaanapali exit at the stoplight near the Maui Kaanapali Villas, and park next to the beach signs indicating public access (this is limited to only a few cars, so to save time you might want to just head to the Sheraton or Whalers Village and plunk down your money).

KAPALUA BEACH 𝔊𝔊𝔊

The beach cove that fronts the Kapalua Bay Hotel is the stuff of dreams: a golden crescent bordered by two palm-studded points, with crystal-clear water and a gently sloping sandy bottom. Protected from strong winds and currents by the lava-rock promontories, Kapalua's calm waters are great for snorkelers and swimmers of all ages and abilities, and the bay is big enough to paddle a kayak around without getting into the more challenging channel that separates Maui from Molokai. Waves come in just right for riding.

The beach is accessible from the hotel on one end, which provides sun chairs with shades and a beach-activities center for its guests, and a public access way on the other. The inland side is edged by a shady path and cool lawns. Outdoor showers are stationed at both ends. You'll also find restrooms, lifeguards, a rental shack, and plenty of shade.

Parking is limited to about 30 spaces in a small lot off Lower Honoapiilani Road, by Napili Kai Beach Club, so arrive early.

SOUTH MAUI
KAMAOLE III BEACH PARK 𝔊

Three beach parks—Kamaole I, II, and III—stand like golden jewels in the front yard of the funky seaside town of Kihei. All three are popular with local residents and visitors because they're easily accessible. On weekends they're jam-packed with fishermen, picnickers, swimmers, and snorkelers.

The most popular is Kamaole III, or "Kam-3," as locals say. Swimming is safe here, but scattered lava rocks are toe-stubbers at the water line, and parents should watch to make sure that kids don't venture too far out, because the bottom slopes off quickly. Both the north and south shores are rocky fingers with a surge big enough to attract fish and snorkelers, and the winter waves attract bodysurfers. Kam-3 is also a wonderful place to watch the sunset. Facilities include restrooms, showers, picnic tables, barbecue grills, and lifeguards. There's also plenty of parking on South Kihei Road, across from the Maui Parkshore condos.

WAILEA BEACH 🏝🏝

Wailea is the best golden-sand crescent on Maui's sunbaked southwestern coast. One of five beaches within Wailea Resort, Wailea is big, wide, and protected on both sides by black-lava points. It's the front yard of the Four Seasons Wailea and the Grand Wailea Resort Hotel and Spa. From the beach, the view out to sea is magnificent, framed by neighboring Kahoolawe and Lanai and the tiny crescent of Molokini. The clear waters tumble to shore in waves just the right size for gentle riding, with or without a board. From shore, you can see Pacific humpback whales in season (Dec–Apr) and unreal sunsets nightly. Facilities include restrooms; outdoor showers; and limited free parking at the blue SHORELINE ACCESS sign, on Wailea Alanui Drive, the main drag of this resort.

ULUA BEACH 🏝

One of the most popular beaches in Wailea, Ulua is a long, wide, crescent-shaped gold-sand beach between two rocky points. When the ocean is calm, Ulua offers Wailea's best snorkeling; when it's rough, the waves are excellent for bodysurfers. The ocean bottom is shallow and gently slopes down to deeper waters, making swimming generally safe. In high season (Christmas–Mar and June–Aug), the beach is carpeted with towels. Facilities include showers and restrooms. A variety of equipment is available for rent at the nearby Wailea Ocean Activity Center. To find Ulua, look for the blue SHORELINE ACCESS sign on South Kihei Road, near Stouffer Wailea Beach Resort. A tiny parking lot is nearby.

MALUAKA BEACH (MAKENA BEACH) 🏝🏝

On the southern end of Maui's resort coast, development falls off dramatically, leaving a wild, dry countryside of green kiawe trees. Maluaka Beach, often called Makena, is notable for its beauty and its views of Molokini Crater; the offshore islet; and Kahoolawe, the so-called "target" island. It's a short, wide, palm-fringed crescent of golden, grainy sand set between two black-lava points and bounded by big sand dunes topped by a grassy knoll. Swimming in this mostly calm bay is considered the best on Makena Bay, which is bordered on the south by Puu Olai cinder cone and historic Keawala'i Congregational Church. Facilities include restrooms, showers, a landscaped park, lifeguards, and roadside parking. Along Makena Alanui, look for the SHORELINE ACCESS sign near the Maui Prince hotel, turn right, and head down to the shore.

ONELOA BEACH (BIG BEACH) 🦀🦀

Oneloa, which means "long sand" in Hawaiian, is one of the most popular beaches on Maui. Locals call it Big Beach; it's 3,300 feet long and more than 100 feet wide. Mauians come here to swim, fish, sunbathe, surf, and enjoy the view of Kahoolawe and Lanai. Snorkeling is good around the north end at the foot of Puu Olai, a 360-foot cinder cone. During storms, however, big waves and a strong rip current make swimming dangerous. There are no facilities except portable toilets, but there's plenty of parking. To get here, drive past the Maui Prince Hotel to the second dirt road, which leads through a kiawe thicket to the beach.

On the other side of Puu Olai is **Little Beach,** a small pocket beach where nudists work on their all-over tans, to the chagrin of uptight authorities who take a dim view of public nudity.

EAST MAUI
HOOKIPA BEACH PARK 🦀

Two miles past Paia on the Hana Highway, you'll find one of the most famous windsurfing sites in the world. Due to its constant winds and endless waves, Hookipa attracts top windsurfers and wave jumpers from around the globe. Surfers and fishermen also enjoy this small, gold-sand beach at the foot of a grassy cliff, which provides a natural amphitheater for spectators. Except when international competitions are being held, weekdays are the best time to watch the daredevils fly over the waves. When the water is flat, snorkelers and divers explore the reef. Facilities include restrooms, showers, pavilions, picnic tables, barbecue grills, and a parking lot.

WAIANAPANAPA STATE PARK 🦀

Four miles before Hana, off the Hana Highway, is this beach park. The park's 120 acres have 12 cabins (see p. 75), a caretaker's residence, a beach park, picnic tables, barbecue grills, restrooms, showers, a parking lot, a shoreline hiking trail, and a black-sand beach (it's actually small black pebbles). This is a wonderful area for both shoreline hikes (mosquitoes are plentiful, so bring insect repellent) and picnicking. Swimming is generally unsafe due to powerful rip currents and strong waves breaking offshore, which roll into the beach unchecked. Waianapanapa is crowded on weekends with local residents and their families, as well as tourists; weekdays are generally a better bet.

HAMOA BEACH 🏖🏖

This half-moon-shaped, gray-sand beach (a mix of coral and lava) in a truly tropical setting is a favorite among sunbathers seeking rest and refuge. The Hotel Hana-Maui maintains the beach and acts as though it's private, which it isn't—so just march down the lava-rock steps and grab a spot on the sand. The 100-foot-wide beach is three football fields long and sits below 30-foot black-lava sea cliffs. Hamoa is often swept by powerful rip currents. Surf breaks offshore and rolls ashore, making this a popular surfing and bodysurfing area. The calm left side is best for snorkeling in summer. The hotel has numerous facilities for guests; there are an outdoor shower and restrooms for nonguests. Parking is limited. Look for the Hamoa Beach turn-off from Hana Highway.

2 Watersports

Activity Warehouse (℃ 800/343-2087; www.travelhawaii.com), which has branches in Lahaina at 578 Front St., near Prison Street (℃ 808/667-4000), and in Kihei at Azeka Place II, on the mountain side of Kihei Road near Lipoa Street (℃ 808/875-4000), rents everything from beach chairs and coolers to kayaks, boogie boards, and surfboards.

Snorkel Bob's (www.snorkelbob.com) has snorkel gear, boogie boards, and other ocean toys at four locations: 1217 Front St., Lahaina (℃ 808/661-4421); Napili Village, 5425-C Lower Honoapiilani Hwy., Napili (℃ 808/669-9603); in North Kihei at Azeka Place II, 1279 S. Kihei Rd. #310 (℃ 808/875-6188); and in South Kihei/ Wailea at the Kamaole Beach Center, 2411 S. Kihei Rd., Kihei (℃ 808/879-7449). All locations are open daily from 8am to 5pm.

BOATING & SAILING

Later in this section, you can find information on snorkel cruises to Molokini under "Snorkeling"; fishing charters under "Sport Fishing"; and trips that combine snorkeling with whale-watching under "Whale-Watching Cruises."

America II 🏆 This U.S. contender in the 1987 America's Cup race is a true racing boat, a 65-foot sailing yacht offering 2-hour **morning sails, afternoon sails,** and **sunset sails** year-round, plus **whale-watching** in winter. These are sailing trips, so there's no snorkeling—just the thrill of racing with the wind. Complimentary bottled water, soda, and chips are available.

Lahaina Harbor, slip 5. ℂ **888/667-2133** or 808/667-2195. www.galaxymall.com/ stores/americaii. Trips $33 adults, $17 children 12 and under. Whale-watching $25 adults, $13 children.

Scotch Mist Sailing Charters   This 50-foot Santa Cruz sailboat offers 2-hour sailing adventures. Prices include snorkel gear, juice, fresh pineapple spears, Maui chips, beer, wine, and soda.

Lahaina Harbor, slip 2. ℂ **808/661-0386**. www.scotchmistsailingcharters.com. Sail trips $35 adults, $18 children ages 5–12, free for children under 5; sunset sail $45.

OCEAN KAYAKING

Gliding silently over the water, propelled by a paddle, seeing Maui from the sea the way the early Hawaiians did—that's what ocean kayaking is all about. One of Maui's best kayak routes is along the **Kihei Coast,** where there's easy access to calm water. Early mornings are always best, because the wind comes up around 11am, making seas choppy and paddling difficult.

The island's cheapest kayak rentals are at the **Activity Warehouse** (ℂ **800/343-2087;** www.travelhawaii.com), which has branches in Lahaina at 578 Front St., near Prison Street (ℂ **808/667-4000**), and in Kihei at Azeka Place II, on the mountain side of Kihei Road near Lipoa Street (ℂ **808/875-4000**), where one-person kayaks are $10 a day and two-person kayaks are $15 a day.

For the uninitiated, my favorite kayak-tour operator is **Makena Kayak Tours** (ℂ **877/879-8426** or 808/879-8426; makenakyak@ aol.com). Professional guide Dino Ventura leads a 2½-hour trip from Makena Landing and loves taking first-timers over the secluded coral reefs and into remote coves. His wonderful tour will be a highlight of your vacation. It costs $55, including refreshments and snorkel and kayak equipment.

South Pacific Kayaks, 2439 S. Kihei Rd., Kihei (ℂ **800/776-2326** or 808/875-4848; www.mauikayak.com), is Maui's oldest kayak-tour company. Its expert guides lead ocean-kayak trips that include lessons, a guided tour, and snorkeling. Tours run from 2½ to 5 hours and range in price from $65 to $139. South Pacific also offers kayak rentals starting at $30 a day.

In Hana, **Hana-Maui Sea Sports** (ℂ **808/248-7711;** www. hana-maui-seasports.com) runs 2-hour tours of Hana's coastline on wide, stable "no roll" kayaks, with snorkeling, for $89 per person. They also feature kayak surfing lessons for $89.

SCUBA DIVING

Some people come to Maui for the sole purpose of plunging into the tropical Pacific and exploring the underwater world. You can see the great variety of tropical marine life, explore sea caves, and swim with sea turtles and monk seals in the clear tropical waters off the island. Trade winds often rough up the seas in the afternoon, so most dive operators schedule early-morning dives that end at noon.

Most operators offer no-experience-necessary dives, ranging from $95 to $125. You can learn from this glimpse into the sea world whether diving is for you.

Everyone dives **Molokini.** This crescent-shaped crater has three tiers of diving: a 35-foot plateau inside the crater basin (used by beginning divers and snorkelers), a wall sloping to 70 feet just beyond the inside plateau, and a sheer wall on the outside and backside of the crater that plunges 350 feet. This underwater park is very popular thanks to calm, clear, protected waters and an abundance of marine life.

Ed Robinson's Diving Adventures ⊛ (© **800/635-1273** or 808/879-3584; www.mauiscuba.com) is the only Maui company rated one of *Scuba Diver* magazine's top five best dive operators for 7 years straight. Ed, a widely published underwater photographer, offers specialized charters for small groups. Two-tank dives are $120 ($135 with equipment); his dive boats depart from Kihei Boat Ramp.

If Ed is booked, call **Mike Severns Diving** (© **808/879-6596;** www.mikesevernsdiving.com), for small (maximum 12 people, divided into two groups of six), personal diving tours on a 38-foot Munson/Hammerhead boat with freshwater shower. Mike and his wife, Pauline Fiene-Severns, are both biologists who make diving in Hawaii not only fun, but also educational (they have a spectacular underwater photography book called *Molokini Island*). Two-tank dives are $110 (with equipment).

Stop by any location of **Maui Dive Shop** ⊛ (www.maui diveshop.com), Maui's largest diving retailer, with everything from rentals to scuba-diving instruction to dive-boat charters, for a free copy of the 24-page *Maui Dive Guide,* which has maps and details about the 20 best shoreline and offshore dives and snorkeling sites, all ranked for beginner, intermediate, or advanced snorkelers/divers. Maui Dive Shop has branches in Kihei at Azeka Place II Shopping Center, 1455 S. Kihei Rd. (© **808/879-3388**), Kamaole Shopping Center (© **808/879-1533**), and Shops at Wailea (© **808/875-9904**); in Lahaina at Lahaina Cannery Mall (© **808/661-5388**); and in the Honokowai Market Place (© **808/661-6166**). Other locations include Whalers Village, Kaanapali (© **808/661-5117**); Kaanapali Fairway Shops (© **808/551-9663**); Maalaea Village (© **808/244-5514**); and Kahana Gateway, Kahana (© **808/669-3800**).

SNORKELING

Snorkeling is the main attraction in Maui—and almost anyone can do it. All you need are a mask, a snorkel, fins, and some basic swimming skills. In many places all you have to do is wade into the water and look down. Most resorts and excursion boats offer instruction for first-time snorkelers, but it's plenty easy to figure it out for yourself.

Some snorkel tips: Always go with a buddy. Look up every once in a while to see where you are, how far offshore you are, and whether there's any boat traffic. Don't touch anything; not only can you damage coral, but camouflaged fish and shells with poisonous spines might also surprise you. Always check with a dive shop, lifeguards, and others on the beach about the area in which you plan to snorkel: Are there any dangerous conditions you should know about? What are the current surf, tide, and weather conditions? If you're not a good swimmer, wear a life jacket or other flotation device.

Snorkel Bob's *(R)* (www.snorkelbob.com) and the **Activity Warehouse** will rent you everything you need; see the introduction to this section for locations. Also see "Scuba Diving" (above) for Maui Dive Shop's free booklet on great snorkeling sites.

When the whales aren't around, **Capt. Steve's Rafting Excursions** (*(C)* **808/667-5565;** www.captainsteves.com) offers 7-hour snorkel trips from Mala Wharf in Lahaina to the waters around **Lanai** (you don't actually land on the island). Rates of $150 for adults and $115 for children 12 and under include breakfast, lunch, snorkel gear, and wet suits.

Maui's best snorkeling beaches include **Kapalua Beach; Black Rock,** at Kaanapali Beach, in front of the Sheraton; along the Kihei coastline, especially at **Kamaole III Beach Park;** and along the Wailea coastline, particularly at **Ulua Beach.** Mornings are best, because local winds don't kick in until around noon. **Olowalu** has great snorkeling around the **14-mile marker,** where there is a turtle-cleaning station about 150 to 225 feet out from shore. Turtles line up here to have cleaner wrasses pick off small parasites.

Ahihi-Kinau Natural Preserve is another terrific place; it requires more effort to reach it, but it's worth it, because it's home to Maui's tropical marine life at its best. You can't miss in Ahihi Bay, a 2,000-acre state natural area reserve in the lee of Cape Kinau, on Maui's rugged south coast, where Haleakala spilled red-hot lava that ran to the sea in 1790. Fish are everywhere in this series of rocky coves and black-lava tide pools. The black, barren, lunarlike land stands in stark contrast to the green-blue water. To get here, drive south of Makena past Puu Olai to Ahihi Bay, where the road turns to gravel and sometimes seems like it'll disappear under the waves. At Cape Kinau, there are three four-wheel-drive trails that lead across the lava flow; take the shortest one, nearest La Pérouse Bay. If you have a standard car, drive as far as you can, park, and walk the remainder of the way.

SNORKEL CRUISES TO MOLOKINI

The crater of **Molokini** 𝒢 sits almost midway between Maui and the uninhabited island of Kahoolawe. Tilted so that only the thin rim of its southern side shows above water in a perfect semicircle, Molokini serves, on its concave side, as a natural sanctuary for tropical fish and snorkelers, who commute daily to this marine-life preserve. Note that in high season, Molokini can be crowded with dozens of boats, each carrying scores of snorkelers.

Maui Classic Charters 𝒢𝒢   Maui Classic Charters offers morning and afternoon **snorkel-sail cruises to Molokini** on *Four Winds II,* a 55-foot glass-bottom catamaran, for $79 adults ($49 children 3–12) for the morning sail and $40 adults ($30 children) in the afternoon. *Four Winds* trips include a continental breakfast; a barbecue lunch; complimentary beer, wine, and soda; complimentary snorkeling gear and instruction; and sport fishing along the way.

In the fast, state-of-the-art catamaran *Maui Magic,* you can take a 5-hour snorkel journey to both Molokini and La Pérouse for $99 for adults and $79 for children ages 5 to 12, including a continental breakfast, barbecue lunch, drinks (beer, wine, and soda), snorkel gear, and instruction. During **whale season** (Dec–Apr) the Maui Magic Whale Watch, a 1½-hour trip with beverages, is $40 for adults and $30 for children ages 3 to 12.

Maalaea Harbor, slip 55 and slip 80. ⓒ **800/736-5740** or 808/879-8188. www. mauicharters.com. Prices vary depending on cruise.

Pacific Whale Foundation   This not-for-profit foundation supports its whale research by offering **whale-watch cruises** and **snorkel tours,** some to Molokini and Lanai. It operates a 65-foot power catamaran called *Ocean Spirit,* a 50-foot sailing catamaran called *Manute'a,* and a fleet of other boats. There are 15 daily trips to choose among, offered from December through May, out of both Lahaina and Maalaea harbors.

101 N. Kihei Rd., Kihei. ⓒ **800/942-5311** or 808/879-8811. www.pacificwhale. org. Trips from $20 adults, $15 children ages 7–12, free for ages 6 and under; snorkeling cruises from $30.

Pride of Maui   For a high-speed, action-packed snorkel-sail experience, consider the *Pride of Maui*. These 5½-hour **snorkel cruises** take in not only **Molokini,** but also Turtle Bay and Makena for more snorkeling, and cost $86 for adults and $53 for children ages 3 to 12. Continental breakfast, barbecue lunch, gear, and instruction are included. They also have an afternoon Molokini cruise ($35 adults, $27 children, plus an optional lunch for an additional $5); an evening cocktail cruise ($47 adults, $20 children); and, during whale season, a whale-watching cruise ($26 adults, $17 children).

Maalaea Harbor. (✆ **877/TO-PRIDE** or 808/875-0955. www.prideofmaui.com. Prices vary; see above.

SPORT FISHING

Marlin (as big as 1,200 lb.), tuna, ono, and mahimahi await the baited hook in Maui's coastal and channel waters. No license is required; just book a sport-fishing vessel out of Lahaina or Maalaea harbors. Most charter boats that troll for big-game fish carry a maximum of six passengers. You can walk the docks, inspecting boats and talking to captains and crews, or book through an activities desk or one of the outfitters recommended below.

Shop around: Prices vary widely. A shared boat for a half day of fishing starts at $100; a shared full day of fishing starts at around $140. A half-day exclusive (you get the entire boat) is around $400 to $700; a full-day exclusive can range from $500 to $1,000. Also, many boat captains tag and release marlin or keep the fish for themselves. If you want to eat your mahimahi for dinner or have your marlin mounted, tell the captain before you go.

The best way to book a sport-fishing charter is through the experts: The best booking desk in the state is **Sportfish Hawaii** ⋒ (✆ **877/388-1376** or 808/396-2607; www.sportfishhawaii.com), which books boats not only on Maui, but also on all the islands. These fishing vessels have been inspected and must meet rigorous criteria. Prices range from $850 to $950 for a full-day exclusive charter for up to six people; it's $599 to $750 for a half-day exclusive.

SURFING

The ancient Hawaiian sport of *hee nalu* (wave sliding) is probably the sport most people picture when they think of the islands. If you'd like to give it a shot, just sign up at any one of the recommended surfing schools listed below.

Tide and Kiva Rivers, two local boys (actually twins) who have been surfing since they could walk, operate **Rivers to the Sea** (✆ **808/280-8795** or 808/280-6236; www.riverstothesea.com), one of the best surfing schools on Maui. Rates are $75 each for a group of three or more, $200 for a couple, and $150 for a private lesson. All lessons are 2 hours long and include equipment and instruction.

I also recommend the **Nancy Emerson School of Surfing,** 358 Papa Place, Suite F, Kahului (© **808/244-SURF** or 808/662-4445; fax 808/662-4443; www.surfclinics.com). Nancy has been surfing since 1961 and has even been a stunt performer for various movies, including *Waterworld.* It's $75 per person for a 2-hour group lesson; private 2-hour classes are $160.

In Hana, **Hana-Maui Sea Sports** (© **808/248-7711;** www. hana-maui-seasports.com) has 2-hour long-board lessons taught by a certified ocean lifeguard for $89.

WHALE-WATCHING

Every winter, pods of Pacific humpback whales make the 3,000-mile swim from the chilly waters of Alaska to bask in Maui's summery shallows. The humpback is the star of the annual whale-watching season, which usually begins in December or January and lasts until April or sometimes May. About 1,500 to 3,000 humpback whales appear in Hawaiian waters each year.

WHALE-WATCHING FROM SHORE

Between mid-December and April, you can just look out to sea. There's no best time of day for whale-watching, but the whales seem to appear when the sea is glassy and the wind calm. Once you see one, keep watching in the same vicinity; a whale might stay down for 20 minutes. Bring a book and binoculars, which you can rent for $2 a day at the **Activity Warehouse** (© **800/343-2087;** www.travel hawaii.com), which has branches in Lahaina at 578 Front St., near Prison Street (© **808/667-4000**), and in Kihei at Azeka Place II, on the mountain side of Kihei Road near Lipoa Street (© **808/875-4000**). Some good whale-watching points on Maui are:

McGregor Point   On the way to Lahaina, there's a scenic lookout at mile marker 9 (just before you get to the Lahaina Tunnel). It's a good viewpoint to scan for whales.

Outrigger Wailea Resort   On the Wailea coastal walk, stop at this resort to look for whales through the telescope installed as a public service by the Hawaiian Islands Humpback Whale National Marine Sanctuary.

Olowalu Reef   Along the straight part of Honoapiilani Highway, between McGregor Point and Olowalu, you'll often spot whales leaping out of the water. Sometimes their appearance brings traffic to a screeching halt: People abandon their cars and run down to the sea to watch, causing a major traffic jam. If you stop, pull off the road so that others can pass.

Puu Olai It's a tough climb up this coastal landmark near the Maui Prince Hotel, but you're likely to be well rewarded: This is the island's best spot for offshore whale-watching. On the 360-foot cinder cone overlooking Makena Beach, you'll be at the right elevation to see Pacific humpbacks as they dodge Molokini and cruise up Alalakeiki Channel between Maui and Kahoolawe. If you don't see one, you'll at least have a whale of a view.

WHALE-WATCHING CRUISES

For a closer look, take a whale-watching cruise. The **Pacific Whale Foundation,** 101 N. Kihei Rd., Kihei (© **800/942-5311** or 808/ 879-8811; www.pacificwhale.org), is a not-for-profit foundation in Kihei that supports its whale research by offering cruises and snorkel tours, some to Molokini and Lanai. They operate a 65-foot power catamaran called the *Ocean Spirit,* a 50-foot sailing catamaran called the *Manute'a,* and a sea kayak. They have 15 daily trips to choose among, and their rates for a 2-hour whale-watching cruise would make Captain Ahab smile (starting at $20 for adults, $15 for children). Cruises are offered from December through May, out of both Lahaina and Maalaea harbors.

If you want to combine ocean activities, a snorkel or dive cruise to Molokini, the sunken crater off Maui's south coast, might be just the ticket. You can see whales on the way there, at no extra charge. See "Scuba Diving" and "Boating & Sailing" earlier in this section.

WINDSURFING

Maui has Hawaii's best windsurfing beaches. In winter windsurfers from around the world flock to the town of **Paia** to ride the waves. **Hookipa Beach,** known all over the globe for its brisk winds and excellent waves, is the site of several world-championship contests. **Kanaha,** west of Kahului Airport, also has dependable winds. When the winds turn northerly, **Kihei** is the spot to be. The northern end of Kihei is best: **Ohukai Park,** the first beach as you enter South Kiehi Road from the northern end, has not only good winds, but also parking, a long strip of grass to assemble your gear, and good access to the water. Experienced windsurfers here are found in front of the **Maui Sunset** condo, 1032 S. Kihei Rd., near Waipuilani Street (a block north of McDonald's), which has great windsurfing conditions but a very shallow reef (not good for beginners).

Hawaiian Island Surf and Sport, 415 Dairy Rd., Kahului (© **800/231-6958** or 808/871-4981; www.hawaiianisland.com), offers lessons (from $79), rentals, and repairs. Other shops that offer rentals and lessons are **Hawaiian Sailboarding Techniques,** 425 Koloa St., Kahului (© **800/968-5423** or 808/871-5423; www.hst windsurfing.com), with 2½-hour lessons from $79; and **Maui Windsurf Co.,** 22 Hana Hwy., Kahului (© **800/872-0999** or 808/ 877-4816; www.maui-windsurf.com), which has complete equipment rental (board, sail, rig harness, and roof rack) from $45 and lessons starting at $75.

For daily reports on wind and surf conditions, call the **Wind and Surf Report** at © **808/877-3611.**

3 Hiking

In the past 3 decades, Maui has grown from a rural island to a fast-paced resort destination, but its natural beauty largely remains; there are still many places that can be explored only on foot. Those interested in seeing the backcountry—complete with virgin waterfalls, remote wilderness trails, and quiet meditative settings—should head for Haleakala's upcountry or the tropical Hana coast.

For more information on Maui hiking trails and to obtain free maps, contact **Haleakala National Park,** P.O. Box 369, Makawao, HI 96768 (© **808/572-4400;** www.nps.gov/hale), and the **State Division of Forestry and Wildlife,** 54 S. High St., Wailuku, HI 96793 (© **808/984-8100;** www.hawaii.gov). For information on trails, hikes, and camping, and permits for state parks, contact the **Hawaii State Department of Land and Natural Resources,** State Parks Division, P.O. Box 621, Honolulu, HI 96809 (© **808/587-0300;** www.state.hi.us/dlnr); note that you can get information from the website but cannot obtain permits there. For information on Maui County Parks, contact **Maui County Parks and Recreation,** 1580-C Kaahumanu Ave., Wailuku, HI 96793 (© **808/243-7380;** www.mauimapp.com).

TIPS ON SAFE HIKING   Water might be everywhere in Hawaii, but it more than likely isn't safe to drink. Most stream water must be treated, because cattle, pigs, and goats have probably contaminated the water upstream. Bacterium leptospirosis, which is found in freshwater streams throughout the state, enters the body through breaks in the skin or through the mucous membranes. It produces flulike symptoms and can be fatal. Carry enough drinking water with you on your hikes, or use tablets with hydroperiodide to purify water. Also, don't forget there is very little twilight in Maui when the sun sets; it gets dark quickly.

GUIDED HIKES   If you'd like a knowledgeable guide to accompany you on a hike, call **Maui Hiking Safaris** ℛ (© **888/445-3963** or 808/573-0168; www.mauihikingsafaris.com), **Hike Maui** ℛ (© **808/879-5270;** fax 808/893-2515; www.hikemaui.com), or **Maui Eco-Adventures** (© **877/661-7720** or 808/661-7720; www.ecomaui.com).

Ekahi Tours (© **888/292-2422** or 808/877-9775; www.ekahi.com) offers hikes through the verdant Kahakuloa Valley by a Kahakuloa resident and Hawaiiana expert. For information on hikes given by the **Hawaii Sierra Club** on Maui, call © **808/573-4147** (www.hi.sierraclub.org).

HALEAKALA NATIONAL PARK ℛℛℛ

For complete coverage of the national park, see "House of the Sun: Haleakala National Park" in chapter 6.

DAY HIKES FROM THE MAIN ENTRANCE

In addition to the difficult hike into the crater, the park has a few shorter and easier options. Anyone can take a ½-mile walk down the **Hosmer Grove Nature Trail** ℛ, or you can start down **Sliding Sands Trail** for a mile or two to get a hint of what lies ahead. Even this short hike can be exhausting at the high altitude. A good day hike is **Halemauu Trail** to Holua Cabin and back, an 8-mile, half-day trip. A 20-minute orientation presentation is given daily in the Summit Building at 9:30, 10:30, and 11:30am. The park rangers offer two **guided hikes.** The 2-hour, 2-mile **Cinder Desert Hike** takes place Tuesday and Friday at 10am and starts from the Sliding Sands Trailhead at the end of the Haleakala Visitor Center parking lot. The 3-hour, 3-mile **Waikamoi Cloud Forest Hike** leaves every Monday and Thursday at 9am; it starts at the Hosmer Grove, just inside the park entrance, and traverses the Nature Conservancy's Waikamoi Preserve. *Always call in advance:* The hikes and briefing sessions may be canceled, so check first. For details, call the park at © **808/572-4400** or visit www.nps.gov/hale.

THE EAST MAUI SECTION OF THE PARK AT KIPAHULU (NEAR HANA)

APPROACHING KIPAHULU FROM HANA   If you drive to Kipahulu, you'll have to approach it from the Hana Highway; it's not accessible from the summit. Always check in at the ranger station before you begin your hike; the staff can inform you of current conditions and share their wonderful stories about the history, culture, flora, and fauna of the area.

There are two hikes you can take here. The first is a short, easy half-mile loop along the **Kaloa Point Trail** (Kaloa Point is a windy bluff overlooking **Oheo Gulch**), which leads toward the ocean along pools and waterfalls and back to the ranger station. The clearly marked path leaves the parking area and rambles along the flat, grassy peninsula. Crashing surf and views of the Big Island of Hawaii are a 5-minute walk from the ranger station.

The second hike is for the more hardy. Although just a 4-mile round-trip, the trail is steep, and you'll want to stop and swim in the pools, so allow 3 hours. You'll be climbing over rocks and up steep trails, so wear hiking boots. Take water, snacks, swim gear, and insect repellent. Always be on the lookout for flash-flood conditions. This walk will pass two magnificent waterfalls: the 181-foot **Makahiku Falls** and the even bigger 400-foot **Waimoku Falls** ⭐. There's a pool on the top of the Makahiku Falls that's safe to swim in as long as the waters aren't rising. The trail starts at the ranger station.

GUIDED HIKES The rangers at Kipahulu conduct a 1-mile hike to the **Bamboo Forest** ⭐ at 9am daily; half-mile hikes or orientation talks are given at noon, 1:30, 2:30, and 3:30pm daily; and a 4-mile round-trip hike to **Waimoku Falls** takes place on Saturday at 9:30am. All programs and hikes begin at the ranger station. Call in advance to make sure the hike will take place that day by contacting the **Kipahulu Ranger Station** (✆ **808/248-7375**).

SKYLINE TRAIL, POLIPOLI SPRINGS STATE RECREATION AREA ⭐

This is some hike—strenuous but worth every step. It's 8 miles, all downhill, with a dazzling 100-mile view of the islands dotting the blue Pacific, plus the West Maui Mountains.

The trail is located just outside Haleakala National Park at Polipoli Springs National Recreation Area; however, you access it by going through the national park to the summit. The Skyline Trail starts just beyond the Puu Ulaula summit building on the south side of Science City and follows the southwest rift zone of Haleakala from its lunarlike cinder cones to a cool redwood grove. The trail drops 3,800 feet on a 4-hour hike to the recreation area in the 12,000-acre Kahikinui Forest Reserve. If you'd rather drive, you'll need a four-wheel-drive vehicle to access the trail.

THE POLIPOLI LOOP, POLIPOLI STATE PARK ⚑

The **Polipoli Loop** ⚑ is an easy, 5-mile hike that takes about 3 hours. Dress warmly; the loop is up at 5,300 to 6,200 feet, so it's cold even in summer. To get here, take the Haleakala Highway (Hwy. 37) to Keokea and turn right onto Highway 337; after less than a half mile, turn on Waipoli Road, which climbs swiftly. After 10 miles, Waipoli Road ends at the Polipoli State Park campground. The well-marked trailhead is next to the parking lot, near a stand of Monterey cypress; the tree-lined trail offers the best view of the island.

The Polipoli Loop is really a network of three trails: Haleakala Ridge, Plum Trail, and Redwood Trail. After a half mile of meandering through groves of eucalyptus, blackwood, swamp mahogany, and hybrid cypress, you'll join the Haleakala Ridge Trail, which, about a mile into the trail, joins with the Plum Trail (named for the plums that ripen in June and July). It passes through massive redwoods and by an old Conservation Corps bunkhouse and a run-down cabin before joining up with the Redwood Trail, which climbs through Mexican pine, tropical ash, Port Orford cedar, and redwood.

HANA-WAIANAPANAPA COAST TRAIL ⚑

This is an easy, 6-mile hike that takes you back in time. Allow 4 hours to walk along this relatively flat trail, which parallels the sea, along lava cliffs and a forest of lauhala trees. The best time of day is either the early morning or the late evening, when the light on the lava and surf makes for great photos. Join the route at any point along the Waianapanapa Campground, and go in either direction. Along the trail, you'll see remains of an ancient *heiau* (temple), stands of lauhala trees, caves, and a blowhole.

WAIHEE RIDGE ⚑

This strenuous 3- to 4-mile hike, with a 1,500-foot climb, offers spectacular views of the valleys of the West Maui Mountains. Allow 3 to 4 hours for the round-trip hike. Pack a lunch, carry water, and pick a dry day, as this area is very wet. There's a picnic table at the summit, with great views.

To get here from Wailuku, turn north on Market Street, which becomes the Kahekilii Highway (Hwy. 340) and passes through Waihee. Go just over 2½ miles from the Waihee Elementary School, and look for the turnoff to the Boy Scouts' Camp Maluhia on the left. Turn into the camp, and drive nearly a mile to the trailhead on the jeep road. About ⅓ mile in, there will be another gate, marking the entrance to the West Maui Forest Reserve. A foot trail, kept in good shape by the State Department of Land and Natural Resources, begins here. The trail climbs to the top of the ridge, offering great views of the various valleys. The trail is marked by a number of switchbacks and can be extremely muddy and wet. In some areas it's so steep that you have to grab onto the trees and bushes for support.

4 Great Golf

Golfers new to Maui should know that it's windy here, especially between 10am and 2pm, when winds of 10 to 15 mph are the norm. Play two to three clubs up or down to compensate for the wind factor. I also recommend bringing extra balls; the rough is thicker here, and the wind will pick your ball up and drop it in very unappealing places (like water hazards).

If your heart is set on playing on a resort course, book at least a week in advance. For the ardent golfer on a tight budget: Play in the afternoon, when discounted twilight rates are in effect. There's no guarantee you'll get 18 holes in, especially in winter, when it's dark by 6pm, but you'll have an opportunity to experience these world-famous courses at half the usual fee.

For last-minute and discount tee times, call **Stand-by Golf** (© **888/645-BOOK** or 808/874-0600; www.stand-bygolf.com) between 7am and 9pm. Stand-by offers discounted (up to 50% off greens fees), guaranteed tee times for same-day or next-day golfing.

Golf Club Rentals (© **808/665-0800;** www.mauiclubrentals.com) has custom-built clubs for men, women, and juniors (both right- and left-handed), which can be delivered island-wide; the rates are just $20 to $25 a day. The company also offers lessons with pros starting at $150 for 9 holes plus greens fees.

WEST MAUI

Kaanapali Courses ⊛ Both courses at Kaanapali offer a challenge to all golfers. The par-72, 6,305-yard **North Course** is a true Robert Trent Jones design: an abundance of wide bunkers; several long, stretched-out tees; and the largest, most contoured greens on Maui. The par-72, 6,250-yard **South Course** is an Arthur Jack Snyder design; although shorter than the North Course, it requires more accuracy on the narrow, hilly fairways.

Off Hwy. 30, Kaanapali. © **808/661-3691.** www.kaanapali-golf.com. Greens fees: $160 (North Course), $130 (South Course); Kaanapali guests pay $130 (North), $117 (South); twilight rates $77 (North), $74 (South) for everyone. At the 1st stoplight in Kaanapali, turn onto Kaanapali Pkwy.; the 1st building on your right is the clubhouse.

Kapalua Resort Courses ⭐⭐⭐ The views from these three championship courses are worth the greens fees alone. The par-72, 6,761-yard **Bay Course** (© 808/669-8820) was designed by Arnold Palmer and Ed Seay. This course is a bit forgiving, with its wide fairways; the greens, however, are difficult to read. The par-71, 6,632-yard **Village Course** (© 808/669-8830), another Palmer/Seay design, is the most scenic of the three courses. The **Plantation Course** (© 808/669-8877), site of the Mercedes Championships, is a Ben Crenshaw/Bill Coore design. This 6,547-yard, par-73 course, set on a rolling hillside, is excellent for developing your low shots and precise chipping.

Off Hwy. 30, Kapalua. © 877/KAPALUA. www.kapaluamaui.com. Greens fees: Village Course $185 ($130 for hotel guests), $85 twilight rate; Bay Course $200 ($140 for hotel guests), $90 twilight rate; Plantation Course $250 ($160 for hotel guests), $100 twilight rate.

SOUTH MAUI

Elleair Maui Golf Club (formerly Silversword Golf Club) Sitting in the foothills of Haleakala, just high enough to afford spectacular ocean vistas from every hole, this is a course for golfers who love the views as much as the fairways and greens. It's very forgiving. *Just one caveat:* Go in the morning. Not only is it cooler, but—more important—it's also less windy.

1345 Piilani Hwy. (near Lipoa St. turnoff), Kihei. © 808/874-0777. Greens fees: $100; twilight rates $80; 9-hole rates $60.

Makena Courses ⭐⭐ Here, you'll find 36 holes of "Mr. Hawaii Golf"—Robert Trent Jones, Jr.—at its best. Add to that spectacular views: Molokini islet looms in the background, humpback whales gambol offshore in winter, and the tropical sunsets are spectacular. The par-72, 6,876-yard **South Course** has a couple of holes you'll never forget. The view from the par-four 15th hole, which shoots from an elevated tee 183 yards downhill to the Pacific, is magnificent. The par-72, 6,823-yard **North Course** is more difficult and more spectacular. The 13th hole, located partway up the mountain, has a view that makes most golfers stop and stare. The next hole is even more memorable: a 200-foot drop between tee and green.

On Makena Alanui Dr., just past the Maui Prince Hotel. © 808/879-3344. www.maui.net/~makena. Greens fees: North Course $170 ($95–$140 for Makena Resort guests), twilight rates $95 ($80 for guests); South Course $180 ($105–$150 for resort guests), twilight rates $105 ($90 for guests); guest rates vary seasonally, with higher rates in the winter.

Wailea Courses ★★ There are three courses to choose among at Wailea. The **Blue Course,** a par-72, 6,758-yard course designed by Arthur Jack Snyder and dotted with bunkers and water hazards, is for duffers and pros alike. The wide fairways appeal to beginners, while the undulating terrain makes it a course everyone can enjoy. A little more difficult is the par-72, 7,078-yard championship **Gold Course,** with narrow fairways, several tricky dogleg holes, and the classic Robert Trent Jones, Jr., challenges: natural hazards, like lava-rock walls. The **Emerald Course,** also designed by Robert Trent Jones, Jr., is Wailea's newest, with tropical landscaping and a player-friendly design.

Wailea Alanui Dr. (off Wailea Iki Dr.), Wailea. ℭ **888/328-MAUI** or 808/875-7450. www.waileagolf.com. Greens fees: Blue Course $175 ($135 resort guests), twilight $100 ($90 resort guests); Gold Course $185 ($145 resort guests); Emerald Course $185 ($145 resort guests).

UPCOUNTRY MAUI

Pukalani Country Club This cool, par-72, 6,962-yard course at 1,100 feet offers a break from the resorts' high greens fees, and it's really fun to play. The 3rd hole offers golfers two different options: a tough (especially into the wind) iron shot from the tee, across a gully (yuck!) to the green; or a shot down the side of the gully across a second green into sand traps below. (Most people choose to shoot down the side of the gully; it's actually easier than shooting across a ravine.) High handicappers will love this course, and more experienced players can make it more challenging by playing from the back tees.

360 Pukalani St., Pukalani. ℭ **808/572-1314.** www.pukalanigolf.com. Greens fees, including cart $60 for 18 holes before 11am; $55 11am–2pm; $45 after 2pm. 9 holes $35. Take the Hana Hwy. (Hwy. 36) to Haleakala Hwy. (Hwy. 37) to the Pukalani exit; turn right onto Pukalani St. and go 2 blocks.

5 Biking, Horseback Riding & Tennis

BIKING

Cruising down Haleakala, from the lunarlike landscape at the top, past flower farms, pineapple fields, and eucalyptus groves, is quite an experience—and you don't have to be an expert cyclist to do it. This is a safe, comfortable bicycle trip, although it requires some stamina in the colder, wetter months between November and March. Wear layers of warm clothing, because there may be a 30°F (16°C) change in temperature from the top of the mountain to the ocean. Generally, tour groups will not take riders under 12, but younger children can ride along in the van that accompanies the groups, as can pregnant women. The trip usually costs between $100 and $140, which includes hotel pickup, transport to the top, bicycle and safety equipment, and meals.

Maui's oldest downhill company is **Maui Downhill** ⚲ (© 800/ 535-BIKE or 808/871-2155; www.mauidownhill.com), which offers a sunrise safari bike tour, including continental breakfast and brunch, starting at $150 (book online and save $48). If it's all booked up, try **Maui Mountain Cruisers** (© 800/232-6284 or 808/871-6014; www.mauimountaincruisers.com), which has sunrise trips at $130 (book online and save $35), or **Mountain Riders Bike Tours** (© 800/706-7700 or 808/242-9739; www.mountain riders.com), with sunrise rides for $115 (book online and save $17). All rates include hotel pickup, transport to the top, bicycle, safety equipment, and meals.

If you want to avoid the crowd and go down the mountain at your own pace, call **Haleakala Bike Company** (© 888/922-2453; www.bikemaui.com), which will outfit you with the latest gear, take you up to the top, make sure you are secure on the bike, and then let you ride down by yourself at your own pace. Trips range from $65 to $85; they also have bicycle rentals to tour other parts of Maui on your own (from $47 a day).

If you want to venture out on your own, rentals—$10 a day for cruisers and $20 a day for mountain bikes—are available from the **Activity Warehouse** (© 800/343-2087; www.travelhawaii.com), which has branches in Lahaina at 602 Front St., near Prison Street (© 808/667-4000), and in Kihei at Azeka Place II, on the mountain side of Kihei Road near Lipoa Street (© 808/875-4000).

For information on bikeways and maps, get a copy of the *Maui County Bicycle Map,* which has information on road suitability, climate, trade winds, mileage, elevation changes, bike shops, safety tips, and various bicycling routes. The map is available for $7.50 ($6.25 for the map and $1.25 postage), bank checks or money orders only, from Tri Isle R, C, and D Council, Attn: Bike Map Project, 200 Imi Kala St., Suite 208, Wailuku, HI 96793.

HORSEBACK RIDING

Maui offers spectacular adventure rides through rugged ranch lands, into tropical forests, and to remote swimming holes. One of my favorites is **Piiholo Ranch,** in Makawao (© 866/572-5544 or 808/357-5544; www.piiholo.com). If you're out in Hana, don't pass up the **Maui Stables** ⚲⚲ in Kipahulu (a mile past Oheo Gulch;

© **808/248-7799;** www.mauistables.com). For those horse lovers who are looking for the ultimate equine experience, check out Frank Levinson's **"Maui Horse Whisperer Experience"** (*©* **808/572-6211;** www.mauihorses.com), which includes a seminar on the language of the horse.

If you'd like to ride down into Haleakala's crater, contact **Pony Express Tours** *⚐* (*©* **808/667-2200** or 808/878-6698; www.pony expresstours.com), which offers a variety of rides down to the crater floor and back up. I also recommend riding with **Mendes Ranch & Trail Rides** *⚐*, 3530 Kahekili Hwy., 4 miles past Wailuku (*©* **808/ 244-7320;** www.mendesranch.com), on the 300-acre Mendes Ranch.

TENNIS

Maui has excellent public tennis courts; all are free and available from daylight to sunset (a few are even lit for night play until 10pm). The courts are available on a first-come, first-served basis; when someone's waiting, limit your play to 45 minutes. For a complete list of public courts, call **Maui County Parks and Recreation** (*©* **808/243-7230**). Because most public courts require a wait and are not conveniently located near the major resort areas, most visitors pay a fee to play at their own hotels. The exceptions to that rule are in Kihei (which has courts in Kalama Park on S. Kihei Rd. and in Waipualani Park on W. Waipualani Rd., behind the Maui Sunset Condo), in Lahaina (courts are in Malu'uou o lele Park, at Front and Shaw sts.), and in Hana (courts are in Hana Park, on the Hana Hwy.).

Private tennis courts are available at most resorts and hotels on the island. The **Kapalua Tennis Garden and Village Tennis Center,** Kapalua Resort (*©* **808/669-5677;** www.kapaluamaui.com), is home to the Kapalua Open, which features the largest purse in the state, on Labor Day weekend. Court rentals are $10 per person for resort guests and $12 per person for nonguests. The staff will match you up with a partner if you need one. In Wailea try the **Wailea Tennis Club,** 131 Wailea Iki Place (*©* **808/879-1958;** www.wailea resort.com), with 11 Plexipave courts. Court fees are $12 per player.

6

Seeing the Sights

There is far more to the Valley Isle than just sun, sand, and surf. Get out and see for yourself the otherworldly interior of a 10,000-foot volcanic crater; watch endangered sea turtles make their way to nesting sites in a wildlife sanctuary; wander back in time to the days when whalers and missionaries fought for the soul of Lahaina; and feel the energy of a thundering waterfall cascade into a serene mountain pool.

1 Central Maui

Central Maui isn't exactly tourist central; this is where real people live. You'll most likely land here and head directly to the beach. However, there are a few sights worth checking out if you need a respite from the sun and surf.

KAHULUI

Under the airport flight path, next to Maui's busiest intersection and across from Costco in Kahului's new business park, is the most unlikely place: **Kanaha Wildlife Sanctuary,** Haleakala Highway Extension and Hana Highway (© 808/984-8100). In the parking area off Haleakala Highway Extension (behind the mall, across the Hana Hwy. from Cutter Automotive), you'll find a 150-foot trail that meanders along the shore to a shade shelter and lookout. Watch for the sign proclaiming this the permanent home of the endangered black-neck Hawaiian stilt, whose population is now down to about 1,000 to 1,500. Naturalists say this is a good place to see endangered Hawaiian Koloa ducks, stilts, coots, and other migrating shorebirds. For a quieter, more natural-looking wildlife preserve, try the **Kealia Pond National Wildlife Preserve** in Kihei (see "South Maui," later in this chapter).

WAILUKU & WAIKAPU

Wailuku is worth a visit for some terrific shopping (see chapter 7) and a brief stop at the **Bailey House Museum** ℛ, 2375-A Main St. (© 808/244-3326; www.mauimuseum.org). Missionary and sugar

Flying High: Helicopter Rides

Only a helicopter can bring you face to face with remote sites like Maui's little-known Wall of Tears, near the summit of Puu Kukui in the West Maui Mountains. You'll glide through canyons etched with 1,000-foot waterfalls and over dense rainforests; you'll climb to 10,000 feet, high enough to glimpse the summit of Haleakala.

Helicopter pilots are an interesting hybrid: part Hawaiian historian, part DJ, part tour guide, and part amusement-ride operator. As you soar through the clouds, you'll learn about the island's flora, fauna, history, and culture.

Among the many helicopter-tour operators on Maui, the best is **Blue Hawaiian** 🐟🐟, at Kahului Airport (© **800/ 745-BLUE** or 808/871-8844; www.bluehawaiian.com), with prices ranging from $125 to $280. If Blue Hawaiian is booked, try **Sunshine Helicopters** (© **800/544-2520** or 808/871-0722; www.sunshinehelicopters.com), with prices ranging from $125 to $320.

planter Edward Bailey's 1833 home is a treasure trove of Hawaiiana. Inside you'll find an eclectic collection, from precontact artifacts like scary temple images, dog-tooth necklaces, and a rare lei made of tree-snail shells to latter-day relics like Duke Kahanamoku's 1919 redwood surfboard. It's open Monday through Saturday from 10am to 4pm. Admission is $5 adults, $4 seniors, and $1 children 7 to 12.

About 3 miles south of Wailuku on the Honoapiilani Highway, lies the tiny, one-street village of Waikapu, which has two attractions that are worth a peek. Relive Maui's past by taking a 40-minute narrated tram ride around fields of pineapple, sugar cane, and papaya trees at **Maui Tropical Plantation,** 1670 Honoapiilani Hwy., Waikapu (© **800/451-6805** or 808/244-7643), a real working plantation (open daily 9am–5pm). A shop sells fresh and dried fruit, and a restaurant serves lunch. Admission is free; the tram tours, which start at 10am and leave about every 45 minutes, are $9.50 for adults and $3.50 for kids 3 to 12.

Marilyn Monroe and Frank Lloyd Wright meet for dinner every night (well, sort of) at the **Waikapu Golf and Country Club,** 2500 Honoapiilani Hwy. (© **808/244-2011**), one of Maui's most unusual buildings. Neither actually set foot on Maui, but these icons of glamour and architecture share a Hawaiian legacy. Wright designed this place for a Pennsylvania family in 1949, but it was never constructed. In 1957 Marilyn and husband Arthur Miller wanted it built for them in Connecticut, but they separated the following year. When Tokyo billionaire Takeshi Sekiguchi went shopping at Taliesen West for a signature building to adorn his 18-hole golf course, he found the blueprints and had Marilyn's Wright house cleverly redesigned as a clubhouse. It doesn't quite fit the setting, but it's still the best-looking building on Maui today. You can walk in and look around at Wright's architecture and the portraits of Marilyn in Monroe's, the restaurant.

IAO VALLEY

A couple of miles north of Wailuku, past the Bailey House Museum, where the little plantation houses stop and the road climbs ever higher, Maui's true nature begins to reveal itself. The transition between suburban sprawl and raw nature is so abrupt that most people who drive up into the valley don't realize they're suddenly in a rainforest. The walls of the canyon begin to close around them, and a 2,250-foot needle pricks gray clouds scudding across the blue sky. The air is moist and cool, and the shade is a welcome comfort. This is Iao Valley, a 6-acre state park whose great nature, history, and beauty have been enjoyed by millions of people from around the world for more than a century.

Iao ("Supreme Light") Valley, 10 miles long and encompassing 4,000 acres, is the eroded volcanic caldera of the West Maui Mountains. The head of the Iao Valley is a broad circular amphitheater where four major streams converge into Iao Stream. At the back of the amphitheater is rain-drenched Puu Kukui, the West Maui Mountains' highest point. No other Hawaiian valley lets you go from seacoast to rainforest so easily. This peaceful valley, full of tropical plants, rainbows, waterfalls, swimming holes, and hiking trails, is a place of solitude, reflection, and escape for residents and visitors alike. From Wailuku, take Main Street and then turn right on Iao Valley Road to the entrance to the state park. The park is open daily from 7am to 7pm.

For information, contact **Iao Valley State Park,** State Parks and Recreation, 54 S. High St., Room 101, Wailuku, HI 96793 (© **808/984-8109;** www.hawaii.gov). The **Hawaii Nature Center** , 875 Iao Valley Rd. (© **808/244-6500;** www.hawaiinaturecenter.org), home of the Iao Valley Nature Center, features hands-on, interactive exhibits and displays relating the story of Hawaiian natural history;

it's an important stop for all who want to explore Iao Valley. Hours are daily from 10am to 4pm. Admission is $6 for adults, $4 for children 4 to 12, and free for children under 4.

Two paved walkways loop into the massive green amphitheater, across the bridge of Iao Stream, and along the stream itself. The 0.33-mile loop on a paved trail is an easy walk; you can even take your grandmother on this one. A leisurely stroll will allow you to enjoy lovely views of the Iao Needle and the lush vegetation. Others often proceed beyond the state park border and take two trails deeper into the valley, but the trails enter private land, and NO TRESPASSING signs are posted.

The feature known as **Iao Needle** is an erosional remnant composed of basalt dikes. The phallic rock juts an impressive 2,250 feet above sea level. Youngsters play in **Iao Stream,** a peaceful brook that belies its bloody history. In 1790 King Kamehameha the Great and his men engaged in the bloody battle of Iao Valley to gain control of Maui. When the battle ended, so many bodies blocked Iao Stream that the battle site was named Kepaniwai, or "damming of the waters." An architectural heritage park of Hawaiian, Japanese, Chinese, Filipino, and New England–style houses stands in harmony by Iao Stream at **Kepaniwai Heritage Garden.** This is a good picnic spot, with plenty of picnic tables and benches. You can see ferns, banana trees, and other native and exotic plants in the **Iao Valley Botanic Garden** along the stream.

2 Lahaina & West Maui

HISTORIC LAHAINA

Located between the West Maui Mountains and the deep azure ocean offshore, Lahaina stands out as one of the few places in Hawaii that has managed to preserve its 19th-century heritage while still accommodating 21st-century guests. This is no quiet seaside village, but a vibrant, cutting-edge kind of place, filled with a sense of history—but definitely with its mind on the future.

Baldwin Home Museum The oldest house in Lahaina, this coral-and-rock structure was built in 1834 by Rev. Dwight Baldwin, a doctor with the fourth company of American missionaries to sail to Hawaii. Like many missionaries, he came to Hawaii to do good—and did very well for himself. After 17 years of service, Baldwin was granted 2,600 acres in Kapalua for farming and grazing. His ranch manager experimented with what Hawaiians called *hala-kahiki,* or pineapple, on a 4-acre plot. The rest is history. The house

Lahaina

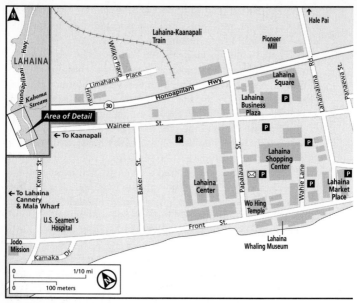

looks as if Baldwin has just stepped out for a minute to tend a sick neighbor down the street.

Next door is the **Masters' Reading Room,** Maui's oldest building. This became visiting sea captains' favorite hangout once the missionaries closed down all of Lahaina's grog shops and banned prostitution. By 1844, once hotels and bars started reopening, it lost its appeal. It's now the headquarters of the **Lahaina Restoration Foundation** (✆ **808/661-3262**), a plucky band of historians who try to keep this town alive and antique at the same time. Stop in and pick up a self-guided walking-tour map of Lahaina's most historic sites.

120 Dickenson St. (at Front St.). ✆ **808/661-3262**. www.lahainarestoration.org. Admission $3 adults, $2 seniors, $5 families. Daily 10am–4:30pm.

Banyan Tree *Kids* Of all the banyan trees in Hawaii, this is the greatest of all—so big that you can't get it in your camera's viewfinder. It was only 8 feet tall when it was planted in 1873 by Maui Sheriff William O. Smith to mark the 50th anniversary of Lahaina's first Christian mission. Now it's more than 50 feet tall, has 12 major trunks, and shades ⅔ acre in Courthouse Square.

At the Courthouse Building, 649 Wharf St.

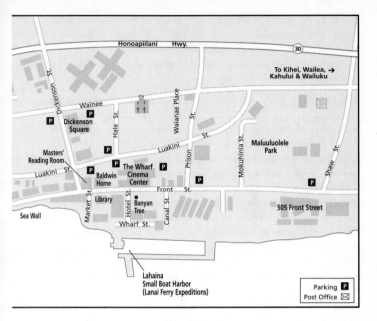

Hale Pai When the missionaries arrived in Hawaii to spread the word of God, they found the Hawaiians had no written language. They quickly rectified the situation by converting the Hawaiian sounds into a written language. They then built the first printing press in order to print educational materials that would assist them on their mission. Hale Pai was the printing house for the Lahainaluna Seminary, the oldest American school west of the Rockies. Today Lahainaluna is the public high school for the children of West Maui.

Lahainaluna High School Campus, 980 Lahainaluna Rd. (at the top of the mountain). ℂ 808/661-3262. www.lahainarestoration.org/halepai. Free admission. Mon–Fri by appointment only.

Lahaina Jodo Mission This site has long been held sacred. The Hawaiians called it Puunoa Point, which means "the hill freed from taboo." Once a small village named *Mala* (garden), this peaceful place was a haven for Japanese immigrants who came to Hawaii in 1868 as laborers for the sugar-cane plantations. They eventually built a small wooden temple to worship here. In 1968, on the 100th anniversary of Japanese presence in Hawaii, a Great Buddha statue (some 12 ft. high and weighing 3½ tons) was brought here from Japan. The immaculate grounds also contain a replica of the original wooden temple and a 90-foot-tall pagoda.

12 Ala Moana St. (off Front St., near the Mala Wharf). © **808/661-4304.** Free admission. Daily during daylight hours.

Maluuluolele Park *(Kids)* At first glance this Front Street park appears to be only a hot, dry, dusty softball field. But under home plate is the edge of Mokuula, where a royal compound once stood more than 100 years ago; it's now buried under tons of red dirt and sand. Here, Prince Kauikeaolui, who ascended the throne as King Kamehameha III when he was only 10, lived with the love of his life, his sister Princess Nahienaena. Missionaries took a dim view of incest, which was acceptable to Hawaiian nobles in order to preserve the royal bloodlines. Torn between love for her brother and the new Christian morality, Nahienaena grew despondent and died at the age of 21. King Kamehameha III, who reigned for 29 years—longer than any other Hawaiian monarch—presided over Hawaii as it went from kingdom to constitutional monarchy, and absolute power over the islands began to transfer from island nobles to missionaries, merchants, and sugar planters. Kamehameha died in 1854 at the age of 39. In 1918 his royal compound, containing a mausoleum and artifacts of the kingdom, was demolished and covered with dirt to create a public park. The baseball team from Lahainaluna School now plays games on the site of this royal place, still considered sacred to many Hawaiians.

Front and Shaw sts.

Wo Hing Temple ✿ The Chinese were among the various immigrants brought to Hawaii to work in the sugar-cane fields. In 1909 several Chinese workers formed the Wo Hing society, a chapter of the Chee Kun Tong society, which dates from the 17th century. In 1912 they built this social hall for the Chinese community. Completely restored, the Wo Hing Temple contains displays and artifacts on the history of the Chinese in Lahaina. Next door in the old cookhouse is a theater with movies of Hawaii taken by Thomas Edison in 1898 and 1903.

Front St. (between Wahie Lane and Papalaua St.). © **808/661-3262.** Admission by donation. Daily 10am–4pm.

A WHALE OF A PLACE IN KAANAPALI

Heading north from Lahaina, the next resort area you'll come to is Kaanapali, which boasts a gorgeous stretch of beach. If you haven't seen a real whale yet, go to **Whalers Village,** 2435 Kaanapali Pkwy., a shopping center that has adopted the whale as its mascot. You can't miss it: A huge, almost life-size metal sculpture of a mother whale and two nursing calves greets you. A few more steps, and you're met by the looming, bleached-white bony skeleton of a 40-foot sperm whale. It's pretty impressive.

On the second floor of the mall is the **Whale Center of the Pacific** (© 808/661-5992), a museum celebrating the "Golden Era of Whaling" (1825–60). Harpoons and scrimshaw are on display; the museum has even re-created the cramped quarters of a whaler's seagoing vessel. Open during mall hours, daily from 9:30am to 10pm; admission is free.

THE SCENIC ROUTE FROM WEST MAUI TO CENTRAL OR UPCOUNTRY MAUI: THE KAHEKILI HIGHWAY

The usual road from West Maui to Wailuku is the Honoapiilani Highway (Hwy. 30), which runs along the coast and then turns inland at Maalaea. But those in search of a back-to-nature driving experience should go the other way, along the **Kahekili Highway (Hwy. 340)** ⚘. (*Highway* is a bit of a euphemism for this paved but somewhat precarious narrow road. Check your rental-car agreement before you head out; some don't allow cars on this road. If it is raining or has been raining, skip this road due to mud and rock slides.) It was named after the great chief Kahekili, who built houses from the skulls of his enemies.

You'll start out on the Honoapiilani Highway (Hwy. 30), which becomes the Kahekili Highway (Hwy. 340) after Honokohau, at the northernmost tip of the island. Around this point are **Honolua** ⚘ and **Mokuleia** ⚘ **bays,** which have been designated as Marine Life Conservation Areas (the taking of fish, shells, or anything else is prohibited).

From this point, the quality of the road deteriorates, and you may share the way with roosters, goats, cows, and dogs. The narrow road weaves along for the next 20 miles, following an ancient Hawaiian coastal footpath and showing you the true wild nature of Maui. These are photo opportunities from heaven: steep ravines, rolling pastoral hills, tumbling waterfalls, exploding blowholes, crashing surf, jagged lava coastlines, and a tiny Hawaiian village straight off a postcard.

Just before mile marker 20, look for a small turnoff on the mauka side of the road (just before the guardrail starts). Park here and walk across the road, and on your left you'll see a spouting **blowhole.** In winter this is an excellent spot to look for whales.

About 3 miles farther along the road, you'll come to a wide turnoff providing a great photo op: a view of the jagged coastline down to the crashing surf.

Less than ½ mile farther along, just before mile marker 16, look for the POHAKU KANI sign, marking the huge, 6×6-foot, bell-shaped stone. To "ring" the bell, look on the side facing Kahakuloa for the deep indentations, and strike the stone with another rock.

Along the route, nestled in a crevice between two steep hills, is the picturesque village of **Kahakuloa** ✿ ("the tall hau tree"), with a dozen weather-worn houses, a church with a red-tile roof, and vivid green taro patches. From the northern side of the village, you can look back at the great view of Kahakuloa, the dark boulder beach, and the 636-foot Kahakuloa Head rising in the background.

At various points along the drive are artists' studios, nestled into the cliffs and hills. One noteworthy stop is the **Kaukini Gallery,** which features work by more than two dozen local artists, with lots of gifts and crafts to buy in all price ranges. (You may also want to stop here to use one of the few restrooms along the drive.)

When you're approaching Wailuku, stop at the **Halekii and Pihanakalani Heiau,** which visitors rarely see. To get here from Wailuku, turn north from Main Street onto Market Street. Turn right onto Mill Street and follow it until it ends; then make a left on Lower Main Street. Follow Lower Main until it ends at Waiehu Beach Road (Hwy. 340), and turn left. Turn left on Kuhio Street and again at the first left onto Hea Place; drive through the gates, and look for the Hawaii Visitor's Bureau marker.

These two *heiau,* built in 1240 from stones carried up from the Iao Stream below, sit on a hill with a commanding view of central Maui and Haleakala. Kahekili, the last chief of Maui, lived here. After the bloody battle at Iao Stream, Kamehameha I reportedly came to the temple here to pay homage to the war god, Ku, with a human sacrifice. *Halekii (House of Images)* is made of stone walls with a flat grassy top, whereas *Pihanakalani* (gathering place of supernatural beings) is a pyramid-shaped mount of stones. If you sit quietly nearby (never walk on any *heiau*—it's considered disrespectful), you'll see that the view alone explains why this spot was chosen.

3 South Maui

MAALAEA

At the bend in the Honopiilani Highway (Hwy. 30), Maalaea Bay runs along the south side of the isthmus between the West Maui

Mountains and Haleakala. This is the windiest area on Maui: Trade winds blowing between the two mountains are funneled across the isthmus, and by the time they reach Maalaea, gusts of 25 to 30 mph are not uncommon.

This creates ideal conditions for **windsurfers** out in Maalaea Bay. Surfers are also seen just outside the small boat harbor in Maalaea, which has one of the fastest breaks in the state.

Maui Ocean Center 𝕶𝕶 *Kids*   This 5-acre facility houses the largest aquarium in Hawaii and features one of Hawaii's largest predators: the tiger shark. Exhibits are geared toward the residents of Hawaii's ocean waters. As you walk past the three dozen or so tanks and numerous exhibits, you'll slowly descend from the "beach" to the deepest part of the ocean without ever getting wet. Start at the surge pool, where you'll see shallow-water marine life like spiny urchins and cauliflower coral; then move on to the reef tanks, turtle pool, "touch" pool (with starfish and urchins), and eagle-ray pool before reaching the star of the show: the 100-foot-long, 600,000-gallon main tank, featuring tiger, gray, and white-tip sharks, as well as tuna, surgeonfish, triggerfish, and numerous other tropicals. A walkway goes right through the tank, so you'll be surrounded on three sides by marine creatures. A very cool place and well worth the time. Some new additions are a hammerhead exhibit and the Shark Dive Maui Program; if you're a certified scuba diver, you can plunge into the aquarium with sharks, stingrays, and tropical fish while friends and family watch safely from the other side of the glass. *Helpful hint:* Buy your tickets online to avoid the long admission lines.

Maalaea Harbor Village, 192 Maalaea Rd. (the triangle between Honoapiilani Hwy. and Maalaea Rd.) ⓒ **808/270-7000.** www.mauioceancenter.com. Admission $21 adults, $18 seniors, $14 children 3–12. Daily 9am–5pm (until 6pm July–Aug).

KIHEI

Capt. George Vancouver landed at Kihei in 1778, when it was only a collection of fishermen's grass shacks on the hot, dry, dusty coast (hard to believe, eh?). A **totem pole** stands today where he's believed to have landed, across from Aston Maui Lu Resort, 575 S. Kihei Rd. Vancouver sailed on to what later became British Columbia, where a great international city and harbor now bear his name.

West of the junction of Piilani Highway (Hwy. 31) and Mokulele Highway (Hwy. 350) is **Kealia Pond National Wildlife Preserve** (ⓒ **808/875-1582**), a 700-acre U.S. Fish and Wildlife wetland preserve where endangered Hawaiian stilts, coots, and ducks hang out and splash. These ponds work two ways: as bird preserves and as sedimentation basins that keep the coral reefs from silting from runoff. You can take a self-guided tour along a boardwalk dotted with interpretive signs and shade shelters, through sand dunes, and around ponds to Maalaea Harbor. The boardwalk starts at the outlet of Kealia Pond on the ocean side of North Kihei Road (near mile marker 2 on Piilani Hwy.). Among the Hawaiian waterbirds seen here are the black-crowned high heron, Hawaiian coot, Hawaiian duck, and Hawaiian stilt. There are also shorebirds like sanderling, Pacific golden plover, ruddy turnstone, and wandering tattler. From July to December, the hawksbill turtle comes ashore here to lay her eggs. *Tip:* If you're bypassing Kihei, take the Piilani Highway (Hwy. 31), which parallels strip-mall–laden South Kihei Road, and avoid the hassle of stoplights and traffic.

WAILEA
The dividing line between arid Kihei and artificially green Wailea is distinct. Wailea once had the same kiawe-strewn, dusty landscape as Kihei until Alexander & Baldwin, Inc. (of sugar-cane fame), began developing a resort here in the 1970s (after piping water from the other side of the island to the desert terrain of Wailea). Today the manicured 1,450 acres of this affluent resort stand out like an oasis along the normally dry leeward coast.

The best way to explore this golden resort coast is to rise with the sun and head for Wailea's 1.5-mile **coastal nature trail** 𝑅, stretching between the Kea Lani Hotel and the kiawe thicket just beyond the Renaissance Wailea. It's a great morning walk, a serpentine path that meanders uphill and down past native plants, old Hawaiian habitats, and a billion dollars' worth of luxury hotels. You can pick up the trail at any of the resorts or from clearly marked SHORELINE ACCESS points along the coast. The best times to go are early morning or sunset; by midmorning, it gets crowded with joggers and later with beachgoers. As the path crosses several bold black-lava points, it affords vistas of islands and ocean. Benches allow you to pause and contemplate the view across Alalakeiki Channel, where you might see **whales** in season.

MAKENA
A few miles south of Wailea, the manicured coast changes over to the wilderness of *Makena* (abundance). In the 1800s cattle were driven down the slope from upland ranches and loaded onto boats that waited to take them to market. Now **Makena Landing** 𝑅 is a beach park with boat-launching facilities, showers, toilets, and picnic

tables. It's great for snorkeling and for launching kayaks bound for Pérouse Bay and Ahihi-Kinau preserve.

From the landing, go south on Makena Road; on the right is **Keawali Congregational Church** ✸ (✆ **808/879-5557**), built in 1855 with walls 3 feet thick. Surrounded by ti leaves, which by Hawaiian custom provides protection, and built of lava rock with coral used as mortar, this Protestant church sits on its own cove with a gold-sand beach. It always attracts a Sunday crowd for its 9:30am Hawaiian-language service. Take some time to wander through the cemetery; you'll see some tombstones with ceramic pictures of the deceased on them, which is an old custom.

A little farther south on the coast is **La Pérouse Monument** ✸, a pyramid of lava rocks that marks the spot where French explorer Admiral Comte de La Pérouse set foot on Maui in 1786. The first Westerner to "discover" the island, La Pérouse described the "burning climate" of the leeward coast, observed several fishing villages near Kihei, and sailed on into oblivion, never to be seen again; some believe he may have been eaten by cannibals in what is now Vanuatu. To get here, drive south past Puu Olai to Ahihi Bay, where the road turns to gravel. Go another 2 miles along the coast to La Pérouse Bay; the monument sits amid a clearing in black lava at the end of the dirt road.

The rocky coastline and sometimes rough seas contribute to the lack of appeal for water activities here; **hiking** opportunities, however, are excellent. Bring plenty of water and sun protection, and wear hiking boots that can withstand walking on lava. From La Pérouse Bay, you can pick up the old King's Highway trail, which at one time circled the island. Walk along the sandy beach at La Pérouse and look for the trail indentation in the lava, which leads down to the lighthouse at the tip of Cape Hanamanioa, about ¾ miles round-trip. Or you can continue on the trail as it climbs up the hill for 2 miles and then ventures back toward the ocean, where there are quite a few old Hawaiian home foundations and rocky/coral beaches.

4 House of the Sun: Haleakala National Park ✸✸✸

At once forbidding and compelling, **Haleakala National Park** is Maui's main natural attraction (*Haleakala* means "house of the sun"). More than 1.3 million people a year ascend the 10,023-foot-high mountain to peer down into the crater of the world's largest dormant volcano. (Haleakala is officially considered to be "active, but not currently erupting," even though it has not rumbled or spewed lava since 1790.) That hole would hold Manhattan: 3,000 feet deep, 7½ miles long by 2½ miles wide, and encompassing 19 square miles.

The Hawaiians recognized the mountain as a sacred site. Ancient chants tell of Pele, the volcano goddess, and one of her siblings doing battle on the crater floor where *Kawilinau* (Bottomless Pit) now stands. Commoners in ancient Hawaii didn't spend much time here, though. The only people allowed into this sacred area were the kahunas, who took their apprentices to live for periods of time in this intensely spiritual place. Today New Agers also revere Haleakala as one of the earth's powerful energy points, and even the U.S. Air Force has a not-very-well-explained presence here.

But there's more to do here than simply stare into a big black hole: Just going up the mountain is an experience in itself. Where else on the planet can you climb from sea level to 10,000 feet in just 37 miles, or a 2-hour drive? The snaky road passes through big, puffy, cumulus clouds to offer magnificent views of the isthmus of Maui, the West Maui Mountains, and the Pacific Ocean.

Many drive up to the summit in predawn darkness to watch the **sunrise** over Haleakala. Writer Mark Twain called it "the sublimest spectacle" of his life. Others take a trail ride inside the bleak lunar landscape of the wilderness inside the crater or coast down the 37-mile road from the summit on a bicycle with special brakes (see "Biking" and "Horseback Riding" in chapter 5). Hardy adventurers hike and camp inside the crater's wilderness (see "Hiking" in chapter 5). Those bound for the interior bring their survival gear because the terrain is raw, rugged, and punishing. However you choose to experience Haleakala National Park, it will prove memorable— guaranteed.

JUST THE FACTS

Haleakala National Park extends from the summit of Mount Haleakala into the crater, down the volcano's southeast flank to Maui's eastern coast, beyond Hana. There are actually two separate and distinct destinations within the park: **Haleakala Summit** 🔆 and the **Kipahulu** 🔆 coast (see "Tropical Haleakala: Oheo Gulch at Kipahulu," later in this chapter). The summit gets all the publicity, but Kipahulu draws crowds too; it's lush, green, and tropical, and home to Oheo Gulch (also known as Seven Sacred Pools). No road links the summit and the coast; you have to approach them separately, and you need at least a day to see each place.

WHEN TO GO   At the 10,023-foot summit, weather changes fast. With wind chill, temperatures can be below freezing any time of year. Summer can be dry and warm; winters, wet, windy, and cold. Before you go, get current weather conditions from the park (© **808/572-4400**) or the **National Weather Service** (© **808/871-5054**).

From sunrise to noon, the light is weak, but the view is usually free of clouds. The best time for photos is in the afternoon, when the sun lights the crater and clouds are few. Go on full-moon nights for spectacular viewing. However, even when the forecast is promising, the weather at Haleakala can change in an instant; be prepared.

ACCESS POINTS   **Haleakala Summit** is 37 miles, or about a 2-hour drive, from Kahului. To get here, take Highway 37 to Highway 377 to Highway 378. For details on the drive, see "The Drive to the Summit," later in this chapter. Pukalani is the last town for water, food, and gas.

The **Kipahulu** section of the national park is on Maui's east end near Hana, 60 miles from Kahului on Highway 36 (the Hana Hwy.). Due to traffic and rough road conditions, plan on 4 hours for the drive from Kahului (see "Driving the Road to Hana," later in this chapter). Hana is the only nearby town for services, water, gas, food, and overnight lodging; some facilities may not be open after dark.

At both entrances to the park, the admission fee is $5 per person or $10 per car, good for a week of unlimited entry.

INFORMATION, VISITOR CENTERS & RANGER PRO-GRAMS   For information before you go, contact **Haleakala National Park,** P.O. Box 369, Makawao, HI 96768 (© **808/572-4400;** www.nps.gov/hale).

One mile from the park entrance, at 7,000 feet, is **Haleakala National Park Headquarters** (© **808/572-4400**), open daily from 7am to 4pm. You can pick up information on park programs and activities, get camping permits, and occasionally see a *nene* (Hawaiian goose)—one or more are often here to greet visitors. Restrooms, a pay phone, and drinking water are available.

The **Haleakala Visitor Center,** open daily from sunrise to 3pm, is near the summit, 11 miles from the park entrance. It offers a panoramic view of the volcanic landscape, with photos identifying the various features and exhibits that explain its history, ecology, geology, and volcanology. Park staff members are often handy to answer questions. The only facilities are restrooms and water.

Rangers offer excellent, informative, and free **naturalist talks** at 9:30, 10:30, and 11:30am daily in the summit building. For information on **hiking** (including guided hikes), see "Hiking" in chapter 5

THE DRIVE TO THE SUMMIT

If you look on a Maui map, almost in the middle of the part that resembles a torso, there's a black wiggly line that looks like this: **WWWWW**. That's **Highway 378,** also known as **Haleakala Crater Road**—one of the fastest-ascending roads in the world. This grand corniche has at least 33 switchbacks; passes through numerous climate zones; goes under, in, and out of clouds; takes you past rare silversword plants and endangered Hawaiian geese sailing through the clear, thin air; and offers a view that extends for more than 100 miles.

Going to the summit takes about 2 hours from Kahului. No matter where you start out, you'll follow Highway 37 (Haleakala Hwy.) to Pukalani, where you'll pick up Highway 377 (which is also Haleakala Hwy.), which you take to Highway 378. Along the way, expect fog, rain, and wind. You might encounter stray cattle and downhill bicyclists. Fill up your gas tank before you go; the only gas available is 27 miles below the summit at Pukalani. There are no facilities beyond the ranger stations, so bring your own food and water.

Remember, you're entering a high-altitude wilderness area. Some people get dizzy due to the lack of oxygen; you might also suffer lightheadedness, shortness of breath, nausea, or worse: severe headaches, flatulence, and dehydration. People with asthma, pregnant women, heavy smokers, and those with heart conditions should be especially careful in the rarefied air. Bring water and a jacket or a blanket, especially if you go up for sunrise. Or you might want to go up to the summit for sunset, which is also spectacular.

As you go up the slopes, the temperate drops about 3°F (2°C) every 1,000 feet, so the temperature at the top can be 30°F (16°C) cooler than it was at sea level. Come prepared with sweaters, jackets, and rain gear.

At the **park entrance,** you'll pay an entrance fee of $10 per car (or $2 for a bicycle). About a mile from the entrance is **Park Headquarters,** where an endangered **nene,** or Hawaiian goose, might greet you with its unique call. With its black face, buff cheeks, and partially webbed feet, the gray-brown bird looks like a small Canada goose with zebra stripes; it brays out "nay-nay" (thus its name), doesn't migrate, and prefers lava beds to lakes. The unusual goose clings to a precarious existence on these alpine slopes. Vast populations of more than 25,000 once inhabited Hawaii, but hunters, pigs, feral cats and dogs, and mongooses preyed on the nene; coupled with habitat destruction, these predators nearly caused its extinction. By 1951 there were only 30 left. Now protected as Hawaii's state bird, the wild nene on Haleakala number fewer than 250—and the species remains endangered.

Beyond headquarters are **two scenic overlooks** on the way to the summit. **Leleiwi Overlook** ⚑ is just beyond mile marker 17. From the parking area, a short trail leads you to a panoramic view of the lunarlike crater. Two miles farther along is **Kalahaku Overlook** ⚑, the best place to see a rare **silversword.** You can turn into this overlook only when you are descending from the top. The silversword is the punk of the plant world, its silvery bayonets displaying tiny purple bouquets—like a spacey artichoke with attitude. Silverswords grow only in Hawaii; take from 4 to 50 years to bloom; and then, usually between May and October, send up a 1- to 6-foot stalk with a purple bouquet of sunflowerlike blooms. They're now very rare, so don't even think about taking one home.

Continue on, and you'll quickly reach the **Haleakala Visitor Center** ⚑, which offers spectacular views. You'll feel as if you're at the edge of the earth. But don't turn around here: The actual summit's a little farther on, at **Puu Ulaula Overlook** ⚑ (also known as Red Hill), the volcano's highest point. If you do go up for sunrise, the building at Puu Ulaula Overlook, a triangle of glass that serves as a windbreak, is the best viewing spot. After sunrise you can see all the way across Alenuihaha Channel to the often-snowcapped summit of Mauna Kea on the Big Island.

MAKING YOUR DESCENT   Put your car in low gear; that way, you won't destroy your brakes by riding them the whole way down.

5 More in Upcountry Maui

On the slopes of Haleakala, cowboys, planters, and other country people make their homes in serene, neighborly communities like **Makawao** and **Kula,** a world away from the bustling beach resorts. Even if you can't spare a day or two in the cool upcountry air, there are some sights that are worth a look on your way to or from the crater. Shoppers and gallery-hoppers especially might want to make the effort; see chapter 7 for details.

Kula Botanical Garden ⚑   You can take a self-guided, informative, leisurely stroll through more than 700 native and exotic plants—including three unique collections of orchids, proteas, and bromeliads—at this 5-acre garden. It offers a good overview of Hawaii's exotic flora in one small, cool place.

Hwy. 377, south of Haleakala Crater Rd. (Hwy. 378), ½ mile from Hwy. 37. ✆ 808/ 878-1715. Admission $5 adults, $1 children 6–12. Daily 9am–4pm.

Tedeschi Vineyards and Winery ⚔ On the southern shoulder of Haleakala is **Ulupalakua Ranch,** a 20,000-acre spread once owned by legendary sea captain James Makee, celebrated in the Hawaiian song and dance *Hula O Makee.* Wounded in a Honolulu waterfront brawl in 1843, Makee moved to Maui and bought Ulu-palakua. He renamed it Rose Ranch, planted sugar as a cash crop, and grew rich. Still in operation, the ranch is now home to Maui's only winery, established in 1974 by Napa vintner Emil Tedeschi, who began growing California and European grapes here and pro-ducing serious still and sparkling wines, plus a silly wine made of pineapple juice. The rustic grounds are the perfect place for a pic-nic. Pack a basket before you go, and enjoy it with a bottle of Tedeschi wine.

Across from the winery are the remains of the three smokestacks of the **Makee Sugar Mill,** built in 1878. This is home to Maui artist Reems Mitchell, who carved the mannequins on the front porch of the Ulupalakua Ranch Store: a Filipino with his fighting cock, a cowboy, a farmhand, and a sea captain, all representing the people of Maui's history.

Off Hwy. 37 (Kula Hwy.). ✆ 808/878-6058. www.mauiwine.com. Daily 9am–5pm. Free tastings; tours given 10:30am–1:30pm.

6 East Maui & Heavenly Hana

DRIVING THE ROAD TO HANA ⚔⚔⚔

Top down, sunscreen on, radio tuned to a little Hawaiian music on a Maui morning: It's time to head out to Hana along the Hana Highway (Hwy. 36), a wiggle of a road that runs along Maui's northeastern shore. The drive takes at least 3 hours, but plan to take all day. Going to Hana is about the journey, not the destination.

In all of Hawaii, no road is more celebrated than this one. It winds for 50 miles past taro patches, magnificent seascapes, water-fall pools, botanical gardens, and verdant rainforests, and it ends at one of Hawaii's most beautiful tropical places.

The outside world discovered the little village of Hana in 1926, when the narrow coastal road, carved by pickax-wielding convicts, opened. The mud-and-gravel road, often subject to landslides and washouts, was paved in 1962, when tourist traffic began to increase;

today more than 1,000 cars traverse the road each day, according to storekeeper Harry Hasegawa. That equals about 500,000 people a year on this road, which is way too many. Go at the wrong time ,and you'll be stuck in a bumper-to-bumper rental-car parade; peak traffic hours are midmorning and midafternoon year-round, especially on weekends.

In the rush to "do" Hana in a day, most visitors spin around town in 10 minutes flat and wonder what all the fuss is about. It takes time to take in Hana, play in the waterfalls, sniff the tropical flowers, hike to bamboo forests, and marvel at the spectacular scenery; stay overnight if you can. However, if you really must do the Hana Highway in a day, go just before sunrise and return after sunset.

THE JOURNEY BEGINS IN PAIA   Before you even start out, fill up your gas tank. Gas in Paia is very expensive (even by Maui standards), and it's the last place for gas until you get to Hana, some 42 miles, 54 bridges, and 600 hairpin turns down the road.

The former plantation village of Paia was once a thriving sugar-mill town. The mill is still here, but the population shifted to Kahului in the 1950s, when subdivisions opened there, leaving Paia to shrivel up and die. But the town refused to give up and has proved its ability to adapt to the times. Now chic eateries and trendy shops stand next door to the mom-and-pop establishments that have been serving generations of Paia customers.

Plan to be here early, around 7am, when **Charley's** *Ȓ*, 142 Hana Hwy. (© **808/579-9453**), opens. Enjoy a big, hearty breakfast for a reasonable price.

After you leave Paia, just before the bend in the road, you'll pass the Kuau Mart on your left; a small general store, it's the only reminder of the once-thriving sugar plantation community of **Kuau.** The road then bends into an S-turn; in the middle of the S is the entrance to **Mama's Fish House,** marked by a restored boat with Mama's logo on the side. Just past the truck on the ocean side

---

Tips Hana Highway Etiquette

Practice aloha: Give way at the one-lane bridges, wave at oncoming motorists, and let the big guys in four-by-fours have the right of way; it's just common sense, brah. If the guy behind you blinks his lights, let him pass. And don't honk your horn; in Hawaii it's considered rude.

The Road to Hana

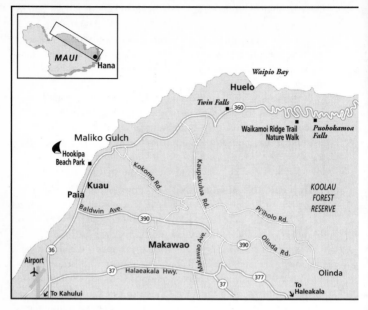

is the entrance to Mama's parking lot and adjacent small sandy cove in front of the restaurant. It's not good for swimming—ocean access is over very slippery rocks into strong surf—but the beach is a great place to sit and soak up some sun.

WINDSURFING MECCA   A mile from Mama's, just before mile marker 9, is a place known around the world as one of the greatest windsurfing spots on the planet, **Hookipa Beach Park** ⚑. *Hookipa* (hospitality) is where the top-ranked windsurfers come to test themselves against the forces of nature: thunderous surf and forceful wind. World-championship contests are held here (see "Maui Calendar of Events" in chapter 1), but on nearly every windy afternoon (the board surfers have the waves in the morning), you can watch dozens of windsurfers twirling and dancing in the wind like colorful butterflies. To watch the windsurfers, go past the park and turn left at the entrance on the far side of the beach. You can either park on the high grassy bluff or drive down to the sandy beach and park alongside the pavilion. The park also has restrooms, a shower, picnic tables, and a barbecue area.

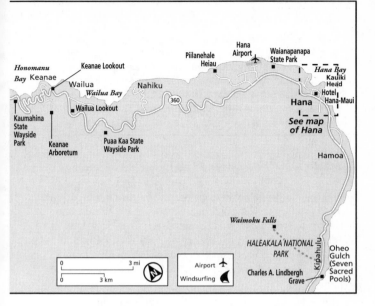

Honomanu Bay
Keanae
Keanae Lookout
Wailua
Wailua Bay
Wailua Lookout
Nahiku
360
Kaumahina State Wayside Park
Keanae Arboretum
Puaa Kaa State Wayside Park
Piilanehale Heiau
Hana Airport
Waianapanapa State Park
Hana Bay
Kauiki Head
Hana
Hotel Hana-Maui
See map of Hana
Hamoa
Waimoku Falls
HALEAKALA NATIONAL PARK
Kipahulu
Oheo Gulch (Seven Sacred Pools)
Charles A. Lindbergh Grave

0   3 mi
0   3 km

Airport ✈
Windsurfing 🏄

INTO THE COUNTRY Past Hookipa Beach the road winds down into *Maliko* **(Budding) Gulch** at mile marker 10. At the bottom of the gulch, look for the road on your right, which will take you out to **Maliko Bay.** Take the first right, which goes under the bridge and past a rodeo arena (scene of competitions by the Maliko Roping Club in summer) and on to the rocky beach. There are no facilities here except a boat-launch ramp. In the 1940s Maliko had a thriving community at the mouth of the bay, but its residents rebuilt farther inland after a strong tidal wave wiped it out. The bay may not look that special, but if the surf is up, it's a great place to watch the waves.

Back on the Hana Highway, as you leave Maliko Gulch, around mile marker 11, you'll pass through the rural area of **Haiku,** with banana patches; cane grass blowing in the wind; and forests of guava trees, avocados, kukui trees, palms, and Christmas berry. Just before mile marker 15 is the **Maui Grown Market and Deli (📞 808/ 572-1693),** a good stop for drinks or snacks for the ride.

A GREAT PLUNGE ALONG THE WAY A dip in a waterfall pool is everybody's tropical-island fantasy. A great place to stop is

---

Tips   **Travel Tip**

If you'd like to know exactly what you're seeing as you head down the road to Hana, I suggest renting a cassette tour, available from **Activity Warehouse** (www.travelhawaii.com), which has branches in Lahaina at 602 Front St., near Prison Street (© **808/667-4000**), and in Kihei at Azeka Place II, on the mountain side of Kihei Road near Lipoa Street (© **808/ 875-4000**), for $10 a day.

Twin Falls 🍴, at mile marker 2. Just before the wide concrete bridge, pull over on the mountain side and park. There is a NO TRES-PASSING sign on the gate. Although you will see several cars parked in the area and a steady line of people going up to the falls, be aware that this is private property, and trespassing is illegal in Hawaii. If you decide that you want to "risk it," you will walk about 3 to 5 minutes to the waterfall and pool, or continue on another 10 to 15 minutes to the second, larger waterfall and pool (don't go in if it has been raining).

HIDDEN HUELO   Just before mile marker 4 on a blind curve, look for a double row of mailboxes on the left side by the pay phone. Down the road lies a hidden Hawaii of an earlier time, where an indescribable sense of serenity prevails. Hemmed in by Waipo and Hoalua bays is the remote community of **Huelo** 🍴. This fertile area once supported a population of 75,000; today only a few hundred live among the scattered homes here, where a handful of B&Bs and exquisite vacation rentals cater to a trickle of travelers (see chapter 3).

The only reason Huelo is even marked is the historic 1853 **Kaulanapueo Church.** Reminiscent of New England architecture, this coral-and-cement church, topped with a plantation-green steeple and a gray tin roof, is still in use, although services are held just once or twice a month. It still has the same austere, stark inte-rior of 1853: straight-backed benches, a no-nonsense platform for the minister, and no distractions on the walls to tempt you away from paying attention to the sermon. Next to the church is a small graveyard, a personal history of this village in concrete and stone.

KOOLAU FOREST RESERVE   After Huelo, the vegetation seems lusher, as though Mother Nature had poured Miracle-Gro on everything. This is the edge of the **Koolau Forest Reserve.** *Koolau* means "windward," and this certainly is one of the greatest examples of a lush windward area: The coastline here gets about 60 to 80 inches of rain a year, as well as runoff from the 200 to 300 inches that fall farther up the mountain. Here you'll see trees laden with guavas, as well as mangoes, java plums, and avocados the size of soft-balls. The spiny, long-leafed plants are *hala* trees, which the Hawaiians used for weaving baskets, mats, and even canoe sails.

From here on out, there's a waterfall (and one-lane bridge) around nearly every turn in the road, so drive slowly, and be prepared to stop and yield to oncoming cars.

DANGEROUS CURVES   About ½ mile after mile marker 6, there's a sharp U-curve in the road, going uphill. The road is practically one-lane here, with a brick wall on one side and virtually no maneuvering room. Sound your horn at the start of the U-curve to let approaching cars know you're coming. Take this curve, as well as the few more coming up in the next several miles, very slowly.

Just before mile marker 7 is a forest of waving **bamboo.** The sight is so spectacular that drivers are often tempted to take their eyes off the road. Be very cautious. Wait until just after mile marker 7, at the **Kaaiea Bridge** and stream below, to pull over and take a closer look at the hand-hewn stone walls. Then turn around to see the vista of bamboo.

A GREAT FAMILY HIKE   At mile marker 9 there's a small state wayside area with restrooms, picnic tables, and a barbecue area. The sign says KOOLAU FOREST RESERVE, but the real attraction here is the **Waikamoi Ridge Trail** ⚑, an easy 0.75-mile loop. The start of the trail is just behind the QUIET TREES AT WORK sign. The well-marked trail meanders through eucalyptus, ferns, and *hala* trees.

SAFETY WARNING   I used to recommend another waterfall, **Puohokamoa Falls,** at mile marker 11, but not anymore. Unfortunately, what once was a great thing has been overrun by hordes of not-so-polite tourists. You will see cars parking on the already dangerous, barely two-lane Hana Highway a half a mile before the waterfall. Slow down after the 10-mile marker. As you get close to the 11-mile marker, the road becomes a congested one-lane road due to visitors parking on this narrow highway. Don't add to the congestion by trying to park: There are plenty of other great waterfalls; just drive slowly and safely through this area.

CAN'T-MISS PHOTO OPS   Just past mile marker 12 is the **Kaumahina State Wayside Park** ⚑. This is not only a good pit stop (restrooms are available) and a wonderful place for a picnic (with tables and a barbecue area), but also a great vista point. The view of the rugged coastline makes an excellent shot; you can see all the way down to the jutting Keanae Peninsula.

Another mile and a couple of bends in the road, and you'll enter the Honomanu Valley, with its beautiful bay. To get to the **Honomanu Bay County Beach Park** 𝒜, look for the turnoff on your left, just after mile marker 14, as you begin your ascent on the other side of the valley. The rutted dirt-and-cinder road takes you down to the rocky black-sand beach. There are no facilities here. Because of the strong rip currents offshore, swimming is best in the stream inland from the ocean. You'll consider the drive down worthwhile as you stand on the beach, well away from the ocean, and turn to look back on the steep cliffs covered with vegetation.

MAUI'S BOTANICAL WORLD Farther along the winding road, between mile markers 16 and 17, is a cluster of bunkhouses composing the YMCA Camp Keanae. A quarter-mile down is the **Keanae Arboretum** 𝒜𝒜, where the region's botany is divided into three parts: native forest, introduced forest, and traditional Hawaiian plants, food, and medicine. You can swim in the pools of Piinaau Stream or press on along a mile-long trail into Keanae Valley, where a lovely tropical rainforest waits at the end (see "Hiking" in chapter 5).

KEANAE PENINSULA The old Hawaiian village of **Keanae** 𝒜𝒜 stands out against the Pacific like a place time forgot. Here, on an old lava flow graced by an 1860 stone church and swaying palms, is one of the last coastal enclaves of native Hawaiians. They still grow taro in patches and pound it into poi, the staple of the old Hawaiian diet. And they still pluck *opihi* (limpet) from tide pools along the jagged coast and cast throw-nets at schools of fish. The turnoff to the Keanae Peninsula is on the left, just after the arboretum.

WAIANAPANAPA STATE PARK 𝒜𝒜 At mile marker 32, just on the outskirts of Hana, shiny black-sand Waianapanapa Beach appears like a vivid dream, with bright-green jungle foliage on three sides and cobalt-blue water lapping at its feet. The 120-acre park on an ancient *aa* lava flow includes sea cliffs, lava tubes, arches, and the beach, plus 12 cabins, tent camping, picnic pavilions, restrooms, showers, drinking water, and hiking trails. If you're interested in staying here, see chapter 3; also see "Beaches" and "Hiking" in chapter 5.

HANA 𝒜𝒜

Green, tropical Hana is a destination all its own, a small coastal village that's probably what you came to Maui in search of. Here you'll

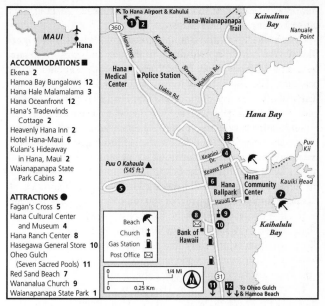

find a rainforest dotted with cascading waterfalls and sparkling blue pools, skirted by red- and black-sand beaches.

Beautiful Hana enjoys more than 90 inches of rain a year—more than enough to keep the scenery lush. Banyans, bamboo, breadfruit trees—everything seems larger than life in this small town, especially the flowers, such as wild ginger and plumeria.

The last unspoiled Hawaiian town on Maui is, oddly enough, the home of Maui's first resort, which opened in 1946. Paul Fagan, owner of the San Francisco Seals baseball team, bought an old inn and turned it into the **Hotel Hana-Maui,** which gave Hana its first taste of tourism.

As you enter Hana, the road splits about ½ mile past mile marker 33, at the police station. Both roads will take you to Hana, but the lower road, Uakea Road, is more scenic. Just before you get to Hana Bay, you'll see the old wood-frame **Hana District Police Station and Courthouse.** Next door is the **Hana Cultural Center and Museum** ⌖, on Uakea Road (© **808/248-8622;** http://hookele. com/hccm), usually open daily from 10am to 4pm. This small building has an excellent collection of Hawaiian quilts, artifacts, books, and photos. Also on the grounds are Kauhala O Hana, composed of four *hale* (houses) for living, meeting, cooking, and canoe building or canoe storage.

Cater-corner from the cultural center is the entrance to **Hana Bay** 𝒜. You can drive right down to the pier and park. There are restrooms, showers, picnic tables, barbecue areas, and even a snack bar here. The 386-foot, red-faced cinder cone beside the bay is **Kauiki Hill,** the scene of numerous fierce battles in ancient Hawaii and the birthplace of Queen Kaahumanu in 1768. A short, 5-minute walk will take you to the spot. Look for the trail along the hill on the wharf side, and follow the path through the ironwood trees; the lighthouse on the point will come into view, and you'll see pocket beaches of red cinder below. Grab onto the ironwood trees for support because the trail has eroded in some areas. This is a perfect place for a secluded picnic, or you can continue on the path out to the lighthouse. To get to the lighthouse, which sits on a small island, watch the water for about 10 minutes to get a sense of how often and from which direction the waves are coming. Between wave sets, either swim or wade in the shallow, sandy bottom channel or hop across the rocks to the island.

To get to the center of town, leave Hana Bay, cross Uakea Road, and drive up Keawa Place; turn left on Hana Highway, and on the corner will be the **Hotel Hana-Maui,** the once-luxurious hotel established by Paul Fagan in 1946. It has been neglected of late, but new management has taken over, and I'm hoping this historic hotel gets the care and maintenance it deserves. On the green hills above Hotel Hana-Maui stands a 30-foot-high white cross made of lava rock. Citizens erected the cross in memory of Paul Fagan, who founded the Hana Ranch as well as the hotel and helped keep the town alive. The hike up to **Fagan's Cross** provides a gorgeous view of the Hana coast, especially at sunset, when Fagan himself liked to climb this hill. Ask at the hotel for details on the hike.

Back on the Hana Highway, just past Hauoli Road, is the majestic **Wananalua Congregation Church.** It's on the National Historic Register not only because of its age (it was built in 1838–42 from coral stones), but also because of its location atop an old Hawaiian *heiau.*

Just past the church, on the right side of the Hana Highway, is the turnoff to the **Hana Ranch Center,** the commercial center for Hana, with a post office, bank, general store, the Hana Ranch Stables, and a restaurant and snack bar. But the real shopping experience is across the Hana Highway at the **Hasegawa General Store** 𝒜, a Maui institution (p. 171), which carries oodles of merchandise from soda and fine French wines to fishing line to name-brand clothing, plus everything you need for a picnic or a gourmet meal. This is also the place to find out what's going on in Hana: The bulletin board at the entrance has fliers and handwritten notes advertising everything from fundraising activities to classes to communitywide events. Don't miss this unique store.

If you need gas before heading back, fill up at the **Chevron Service Station** on the right side of the Hana Highway as you leave town. *Warning:* The price of gas here will take your breath away.

OUTDOOR ACTIVITIES

Hana is one of the best areas on Maui for ocean activities and also boasts a wealth of nature hikes, remote places to explore on horseback, and waterfalls to discover.

Beaches & Ocean Activities

Call **Hana-Maui Sea Sports** (© **808/248-7711;** www.hana-maui seasports.com) if you'd like to snorkel or kayak, or venture out on your own at one of my favorite beaches:

HANA   The waters in the Hana Bay are calm most of the time and great for swimming. There's excellent snorkeling and diving by the lighthouse. Strong currents can run through here, so don't venture farther than the lighthouse. See the description of Hana Bay in the introduction to this section, above, for more details.

RED SAND BEACH   The Hawaiian name for this beach is *Kaihalulu* (roaring sea) Beach. It's truly a sight to see. The beach is on the ocean side of Kauiki Hill, just south of Hana Bay, in a wild, natural setting on a pocket cove, where the volcanic cinder cone lost its seaward wall to erosion and spilled red cinders everywhere to create the red sands. Before you put on your bathing suit, there are three things to know about this beach: You have to trespass to get here (which is against the law); due to recent heavy rains, there have been several serious injuries on the muddy, slippery terrain (enter at your own risk, it can be extremely dangerous); and nudity (also illegal in Hawaii—arrests have been made) is common here.

If you are determined to go, ask for permission at the Hotel Hana-Maui. And ask about conditions on the trail (which drops several stories down to the ocean rocks). To reach the beach, put on solid walking shoes (no flip-flops), and walk south on Uakea Road, past Haoli Street and the Hotel Hana-Maui, to the parking lot for the hotel's Sea Ranch Cottages. Turn left, and cross the open field next to the Hana Community Center. Look for the dirt trail, and follow it to the huge ironwood tree, where you turn right (do not go ahead to the old Japanese cemetery). Use the ironwood trees to maintain your balance as you follow the ever-eroding cinder foot-path a short distance along the shoreline, down the narrow cliff trail (do not attempt this if it's wet). The trail suddenly turns the corner, and into view comes the burnt-red beach, set off by the turquoise waters, black lava, and vivid green ironwood trees.

The lava outcropping protects the bay and makes it safe for swimming. Snorkeling is excellent, and there's a natural whirlpool area on the Hana Bay side of the cove. Stay away from the surge area where the ocean enters the cove.

HAMOA BEACH 🚴🚴   For one of Hana's best beaches—great for swimming, boogie boarding, and sunbathing—continue another ½ mile down the Haneoo Road loop to Hamoa Beach. There is easy access from the road down to the sandy beach, and facilities include a small restroom and an outdoor shower. The large pavilion and beach accessories are for Hotel Hana-Maui guests.

Hiking

Hana is woven with hiking trails along the shoreline, through the rainforest, and up in the mountains. See "Hiking" in chapter 5 for a discussion of hiking in Waianapanapa.

Another excellent hike that takes you back in time is through Kahanu Gardens and to **Piilanihale Heiau** 🚴🚴, one of the largest ancient Hawaiian temples in the state. Turn toward the ocean on Ulaino Road, by mile marker 31. Drive down the paved road (which turns into a dirt road but is still drivable) to the first stream (about 1½ miles). If the stream is flooded, turn around and go back. If you can forge the stream, cross it and park on the right side of the road by the huge breadfruit trees. The trees are part of the 122-acre **Kahanu Garden** 🚴🚴 (📞 **808/248-8912**), owned and operated by the National Tropical Botanical Garden (www.ntbg.org), which also has two gardens on Kauai. Open Monday through Friday from 10am to 2pm, admission is $10 for self-guided tours. Allow at least an hour and a half to explore the gardens and *heiau*.

The 122 acres encompass plant collections from the Pacific Islands, concentrating on plants of value to the people of Polynesia, Micronesia, and Melanesia. Kahanu Garden contains the largest known collection of breadfruit cultivars from more than 17 Pacific Island groups and Indonesia, the Philippines, and the Seychelles.

The real draw here is the *Piilanihale Heiau* (**House of Piilani**), one of Maui's greatest chiefs. Believed to be the largest heiau in the state, it measures 340 feet by 415 feet, and it was built in a unique terrace design not seen anywhere else in Hawaii. The walls are some 50 feet tall and 8 to 10 feet thick. Historians believe that Piilani's two sons and his grandson built the mammoth temple, which was dedicated to war, sometime in the 1500s.

TROPICAL HALEAKALA: OHEO GULCH AT KIPAHULU ☆☆

If you're thinking about heading out to the so-called Seven Sacred Pools, out past Hana at the Kipahulu end of Haleakala National Park, let's clear this up right now: There are more than seven pools—about 24, actually—and *all* water in Hawaii is considered sacred. It's all a PR scam that has spun out of control into contemporary myth. Folks here call the attraction by its rightful name, **Oheo Gulch,** and visitors sometimes refer to it as Kipahulu, which is actually the name of the area where Oheo Gulch is located. No matter what you call it, it's a beautiful sight. The dazzling series of waterfall pools and cataracts cascading into the sea is so popular that it now has its own roadside parking lot.

Even though Oheo is part of Haleakala National Park, you cannot drive here from the summit. Even hiking from Haleakala to Oheo is tricky: The access trail out of Haleakala is down Kaupo Gap, which ends at the ocean, a good 6 miles down the coast from Oheo. To drive to Oheo, head for Hana, some 60 miles from Kahului on the Hana Highway (Hwy. 36). Oheo is about 30 to 50 minutes beyond Hana, along Highway 31. The Highway 31 bridge passes over pools near the ocean; the other pools, plus magnificent 400-foot Waimoku falls, are reachable via an often-muddy, but rewarding, hour-long uphill hike (see "Hiking" in chapter 5). Expect showers on the Kipahulu coast. The admission fee is $5 per person or $10 per car.

The **Kipahulu Ranger Station** (© **808/248-7375**) is staffed from 9am to 5pm daily. Restrooms are available, but there's no drinking water. Kipahulu rangers offer safety information, exhibits, books, and a variety of walks and hikes year-round; check at the station for current activities. There are a number of hiking trails in the park; see "Hiking " in chapter 5 for details.

Check with the Haleakala Park rangers before hiking up to or swimming in the pools, and always keep one eye on the water in the streams; the sky can be sunny near the coast, but floodwaters from Kipahulu Valley can cause the pools to rise 4 feet in less than 10 minutes.

7

Shops & Galleries

Maui is a shopaholic's dream as well as an arts center, with a large number of resident artists who show their works in dozens of galleries and countless gift shops. Maui is also the queen of specialty products, an agricultural cornucopia that includes Kula onions, upcountry protea, Kaanapali coffee, world-renowned potato chips, and many other tasty treats that are shipped worldwide.

As with any popular visitor destination, you'll have to wade through bad art and mountains of trinkets, particularly in Lahaina and Kihei, where touristy boutiques line the streets between rare pockets of treasures. If you shop in South or West Maui, expect to pay resort prices, clear down to a bottle of Evian or sunscreen.

Central Maui is home to some first-rate boutiques. Watch Wailuku, which is poised for a resurgence. The town has its own antiques alleys; the new Sig Zane Designs has brought a delightful infusion of creative energy; and a major promenade/emporium on Main Street is in the works. The Kaahumanu Center, in neighboring Kahului, is becoming more fashionable by the month.

Upcountry, Makawao's boutiques are worth seeking out, despite some attitude and high prices. The charm of shopping on Maui has always rested in the small, independent shops and galleries that crop up in surprising places.

1 Central Maui

KAHULUI

Kahului's best shopping is concentrated in two places. Almost all of the shops listed below are at one of the following centers:

The once-rough-around-the-edges **Maui Mall,** 70 E. Kaahumanu Ave. (© **808/877-7559**), is the talk of Kahului. Newly renovated, it's now bigger and better, and has retained some of my favorite stores while adding a 12-screen movie megaplex that features current releases as well as art-house films. The mall is still a place of everyday good things, from **Long's Drugs** to **Star Market** to **Tasaka Guri Guri,** the decades-old purveyor of inimitable icy treats, neither ice cream nor shave ice but something in between.

Queen Kaahumanu Center, 275 Kaahumanu Ave. (© 808/877-3369), 5 minutes from the Kahului Airport on Highway 32, offers more than 100 shops, restaurants, and theaters. Its second-floor Plantation District offers home furnishings and accessories, and gift and accessories shops. Kaahumanu covers all the bases, from arts and crafts to a **Foodland Supermarket** and everything in between: a thriving food court; the island's best beauty supply, **Lisa's Beauty Supply & Salon** (© 808/877-6463), and its sister store for cosmetics, **Madison Avenue Day Spa and Boutique** (© 808/873-0880); mall standards like **Sunglass Hut, Radio Shack,** and **Local Motion** (surf and beach wear); standard department stores like **Macy's** and **Sears;** and great specialty shops like **Sharper Image.**

Cost Less Imports Natural fibers are ubiquitous in this newly expanded corner of the Maui Mall, which is three times larger than before. Household accessories include lauhala; bamboo blinds; grassy floor and window coverings; shoji-style lamps; burlap yardage; baskets; Balinese cushions; Asian imports; *noreng* (Japanese folk curtains); and top-of-the-line, made-on-Maui soaps and handicrafts. A good source of tropical and Asian home decor. In the Maui Mall. © 808/877-0300.

Maui County Store Attention, T-shirt collectors: Here's your chance to get official Maui County Police and Fire logo T-shirts and other Maui County logo shirts, plus logo wear from the University of Hawaii and other made-in-Maui items. This fundraising store (it helps the police and fire departments) is staffed by students from Maui Community College learning retail sales. Prices are great; money goes to a good cause; the students get to learn a trade; and you get to take home excellent souvenirs from your Maui vacation. Maui Mall, 70 Kaahumanu Ave., Kahului. © 808/877-6669. www.mauicountystore.com.

Maui Swap Meet The Maui Swap Meet is a large and popular event. After Thanksgiving and throughout December, the activity reaches fever pitch. The colorful Maui specialties include vegetables from Kula and Keanae; fresh taro; plants; proteas; crafts; household items; homemade ethnic foods; and baked goods, including some fabulous fruit breads. Every Saturday from 7am to noon, vendors spread out their wares in booths and under tarps, in a festival-like atmosphere. Between the cheap Balinese imports and New Age crystals and incense, you may find some vintage John Kelly prints and 1930s collectibles. Admission is 50¢, and if you go early while the vendors are setting up, no one will turn you away. As we went to press, the Maui Swap Meet owners were in negotiations to stay in their longtime location on Puunene Avenue, but they may be forced to move. Please contact them first to make sure they are still there. S. Puunene Ave. (next to the Kahului Post Office). ✆ **808/877-3100.**

Summerhouse   Sleek and chic, tiny Summerhouse is big on style: casual and party dresses; separates by Russ Berens, FLAX, and Kiko; and Tencel jeans by Signatur—the best. During the holiday season the selection gets dressy and sassy, but it's a fun browse year-round. I adore the hats, accessories, easy-care clothing, and up-to-the-minute evening dresses that Summerhouse carries in abundance. The high-quality T-shirts are always a cut above. The casual selection is well suited to the island lifestyle. In the Dairy Center, 395 Dairy Rd. ✆ 808/871-1320. Also on the west side at 4405 Honoapiilani Hwy. ✆ 808/669-6616.

EDIBLES

Down to Earth Natural Foods, 305 Dairy Rd. (✆ **808/877-2661**), a health-food staple for many years, has fresh organic produce, a bountiful salad bar, sandwiches and smoothies, vitamins and supplements, fresh-baked goods, snacks, whole grains, and several packed aisles of vegetarian and health foods.

Maui's produce has long been a source of pride for islanders, and **Ohana Farmers Market,** in the Kahului Shopping Center (✆ **808/871-8347**), is the place to find a fresh, inexpensive selection of Maui-grown fruit, vegetables, flowers, and plants. Crafts and gourmet foods add to the event, and the large monkeypod trees provide welcome shade.

WAILUKU

Located at the gateway to Iao Valley, Wailuku is the county seat, the part of Maui where people live and work. Wailuku's attractive vintage architecture, smattering of antiques shops, and mom-and-pop eateries imbue the town with a down-home charm noticeably absent in Maui's resort areas. The community spirit fuels festivals throughout the year and is slowly attracting new businesses, but Wailuku is still a work in progress. It's a mixed bag—of course, there's junk, but a stroll along Main and Market streets usually turns up a treasure or two.

Bailey House Gift Shop   For made-in-Hawaii items, Bailey House is a must-stop. Gracious gardens, rare paintings of early Maui, wonderful programs in Hawaiian arts and culture, and a restored hand-hewn koa canoe await visitors. The small shop packs a wallop with its selection of remarkable gift items, from Hawaiian music to exquisite woods, traditional Hawaiian games to pareus and books. Prints by the legendary Hawaii artist Madge Tennent, lauhala hats hanging in midair, hand-sewn pheasant hatbands, jams and jellies, Maui cookbooks, and an occasional Hawaiian quilt are some of the treasures to be found here. Bailey House Museum Shop, 2375-A Main St. ℂ 808/244-3326.

Bird of Paradise Unique Antiques   Owner Joe Myhand loves furniture, old Matson liner menus, blue willow china, kimonos for children, and anything nostalgic that happens to be Hawaiian. The furniture ranges from 1940s rattan to wicker and old koa—those items tailor-made for informal island living. Myhand also collects bottles and license plates. The collection ebbs and flows with his finds, keeping buyers waiting in the wings for his Depression glass, California pottery from the 1930s and 1940s, old dinnerware, perfume bottles, vintage aloha shirts, and vintage Hawaiian music on cassettes. 56 N. Market St. ℂ 808/242-7699.

Brown-Kobayashi   Graceful living is the theme here. Antique stone garden pieces mingle quietly with Asian antiques and old and new French, European, and Hawaiian objects. Although the collection is eclectic, there's a cohesive aesthetic that sets Brown-Kobayashi apart from other Maui antiques stores. Japanese kimonos and obi, Bakelite and Peking glass beads, breathtaking Japanese lacquerware, cricket carriers, precious Chinese woods, and cloisonné are among the delights here. 160-A N. Market St. ℂ 808/242-0804.

Gottling Ltd.   Karl Gottling's shop specializes in Asian antique furniture, but you can also find smaller carvings, precious stones, jewelry, netsuke, opium weights, and finds in all sizes. I saw a cabinet with 350-year-old doors and a 17th-century Buddha lending an air of serenity next to a 150-year-old Chinese cabinet. Ming dynasty ceramics, carved wooden apples for $15, and a Persian rug for $65,000 give you an idea of the range of possibilities here. 34 N. Market St. ℂ 808/244-7779.

Old Daze   Nineteenth-century Americana and Hawaiian collectibles are nicely wedded in this charming shop. The collection features a modest furniture selection, Hawaiian pictures, 1960s ashtrays, Depression glass, old washboards, and souvenir plates from county fairs. Choices range from hokey to rustic to pleasantly nostalgic, with many items for the kitchen. Some recent finds: an 1850s German sideboard, a Don Blanding teapot, Royal Worcester china, an antique kimono, and framed vintage music sheets. Owner Geni

Dowling's love of nostalgia fills every corner of this tiny shop. 7 North Market St. (close to Main St.). © 808/249-0014.

Sig Zane Designs As we went to press, designer Sig Zane was considering moving his Wailuku store to Kahului, so be sure to call first if you plan to stop by. Whether it's a T-shirt, golf shirt, pareu, duffel bag, aloha shirt, or muumuu, a Sig Zane design has depth and sizzle. Zane and co-owner Punawai Rice have redefined Hawaiian wear by creating an inimitable style in clothing, textiles, furnishings, bedding, and lifestyle accessories. Zane's strong, graphic fabrics are made into aloha shirts and women's wear, and used in interiors and furnishings that evoke the gracious Hawaii of an earlier time. The staff is knowledgeable and helpful. 53 Market St. © 808/ 249-8997.

EDIBLES

Located in the northern section of Wailuku, **Takamiya Market,** 359 N. Market St. (© 808/244-3404), is much loved by local folks and visitors with adventurous palates. Unpretentious home-cooked foods from East and West are prepared daily. From the chilled-fish counter come fresh sashimi and poke, and in the renowned assortment of prepared foods are mounds of shoyu chicken, tender fried squid, roast pork, Kalua pork, laulau, Chinese noodles, fiddlehead ferns, and comfort foods such as cornbread and potato salad. Fresh produce and paper products are also available.

2 West Maui

LAHAINA

Lahaina's merchants and art galleries go all out from 7 to 9pm on Friday, when **Art Night** brings an extra measure of hospitality and community spirit. The Art Night openings are usually marked with live entertainment, refreshments, and a lively street scene.

   If you're in Lahaina on the second or last Thursday of the month, stroll by the front lawn of the **Baldwin Home,** 120 Dickenson St. (at Front St.), for demonstrations of lei-making (you can even buy the results).

   What was formerly a big, belching pineapple cannery is now a maze of shops and restaurants at the northern end of Lahaina town, known as the **Lahaina Cannery Mall,** 1221 Honoapiilani Hwy. (© 808/661-5304). Find your way through the T-shirt and sportswear shops to coffee at **Sir Wilfred's Coffee House,** where you can unwind with espresso and croissants, or head for **Compadres Bar &**

Grill (p. 85), where the margaritas flow freely. For film, water, aspirin, groceries, sunscreen, and other necessities, nothing beats **Long's Drugs** and **Safeway,** two old standbys. **Roland's** may surprise you with its selection of footwear—everything from Cole Haan to inexpensive sandals. At the recently expanded food court, the new **Compadres Taquería** sells Mexican food to go, while **L & L Drive-Inn** sells plate lunches.

The **Lahaina Center,** 900 Front St. (📞 **808/667-9216**), is still a work in progress. It's located north of Lahaina's most congested strip, where Front Street begins. Across the street from the center, the seawall is a much-sought-after front-row seat to the sunset. There are plenty of free validated parking and easy access to more than 30 shops, a salon, restaurants, a nightclub, and a four-plex movie-theater complex. You can get a meal at **Ruth's Chris Steak House** or **Maui Brews.** Among the shopping stops: **Banana Republic,** the **Hilo Hattie Fashion Center** (a dizzying emporium of aloha wear), and **ABC Discount Store.**

The conversion of 10,000 square feet of parking space into the re-creation of a traditional Hawaiian village is a welcome touch of Hawaiiana at Lahaina Center. The village, called **Hale Kahiko** (www.lahainacenter.com/hale_kahiko.html), features three main houses, called *hale:* a sleeping house, the men's dining house, and the crafts house, where women pounded *hala* (pandanus) strips to weave into mats and baskets. Artifacts, weapons, a canoe, and indigenous trees are among the authentic touches in this village, which can be toured privately or with a guide.

David Lee Galleries   This gallery is devoted to the works of David Lee, who uses natural powder colors to paint on silk. The pigments and technique create a luminous, ethereal quality. 712 Front St. 📞 808/667-7740.

Lahaina Arts Society Galleries   With its membership of more than 185 Maui artists, the nonprofit Lahaina Arts Society is an excellent community resource. Changing monthly exhibits in the Banyan Tree and Old Jail galleries offer a good look at the island's artistic well: two-dimensional art, fiber art, ceramics, sculpture, prints, jewelry, and more. In the shade of the humongous banyan tree in the square across from Pioneer Inn, "Art in the Park" fairs are offered every second and fourth weekend of the month. 648 Wharf St. 📞 808/661-3228.

Lei Spa Maui   Expanded to include two massage rooms and shower facilities, this day spa offers facials and other therapies.

About 95% of the beauty and bath products sold here are made on Maui. Aromatherapy body oils and perfumes are popular, as are the handmade soaps and fragrances of torch ginger, plumeria, coconut, tuberose, and sandalwood. Scented candles in coconut shells make great, inexpensive gifts. 505 Front St. ℂ 808/661-1178.

Maggie Coulombe *(Finds)* Maggie's latest couture, jersey, linen, pareo, and shoes, plus accessories, jewelry, purses, and a few surprises, are available here. 505 Front St. ℂ 808/662-0696. www.maggie coulombe.com.

Martin Lawrence Galleries The front is garish, with pop art; kinetic sculptures; and bright, carnivalesque glass objects. Toward the back of the gallery, however, there are a sizable inventory of two-dimensional art and some plausible choices for collectors of Keith Haring, Andy Warhol, and other pop artists. The originals, limited-edition graphics, and sculptures also include works by Marc Chagall, Pablo Picasso, Joan Miró, Roy Lichtenstein, and other noted artists. The focus is pop art and national and international artists. In Lahaina Market Place, 126 Lahainaluna Rd. ℂ 808/661-1788.

Na Mea Hawaii Arts, crafts, gifts, and clothing, all made by Hawaiian artists, fill this cozy niche of Lahaina in the historic Baldwin House on Front Street. Striking Tutuvi silk-screened dresses and shirts, and delicately patterned shawls and scarves by Maile Andrade depicting Hawaiian scenes, are highlights. You might find a beautifully made lauhala bag, a colorful muumuu, a Hawaii-themed book, or a pheasant hat lei made by master feather lei makers Mary Lou Kekuewa and Paulette Kahalepuna. The shop is tiny, filled with the colors, fibers, and spirit of Hawaii. Lahaina Cannery Mall, 1221 Honoapiilani Hwy. ℂ 808/667-5345.

The Old Lahaina Book Emporium This bookstore is a browser's dream. More than 25,000 quality used books are lovingly housed in this shop, where owner JoAnn Carroll treats books and customers well. Specialties include Hawaiiana, fiction, mystery, sci-fi, and military history, with substantial selections in cookbooks, children's books, and philosophy/religion. You could pay as little as $2 for a quality read or a whole lot more for that rare first edition. Books on tape, videos, and old guitar magazines are among the treasures here. 834 Front St. ℂ 808/661-1399.

Totally Hawaiian Gift Gallery This gallery makes a good browse for its selection of Niihau shell jewelry, excellent Hawaiian CDs, Norfolk pine bowls, and Hawaiian quilt kits. Hawaiian quilt patterns sewn in Asia (at least they're honest about it) are less expensive and attractive, although not totally Hawaiian. Hawaiian-quilt-patterned gift-wraps and tiles, perfumes and soaps, handcrafted dolls, and koa accessories are of good quality, and the artists, such as Kelly Dunn (Norfolk wood bowls), Jerry Kermode (wood), and Pat Coito (wood), are among the tops in their fields. In the Lahaina Cannery Mall, 1221 Honoapiilani Hwy. ℭ **808/667-2558.**

Village Galleries in Lahaina   Art collectors know the nearly 30-year-old Village Galleries as a respectable showcase for regional artists; the selection of mostly original two- and three-dimensional art offers a good look at the quality of work originating on the island. The newer contemporary gallery offers colorful gift items and jewelry. 120 and 180 Dickenson St. ℭ **808/661-4402** or 808/661-5559. Also at the Ritz-Carlton Kapalua, 1 Ritz-Carlton Dr. ℭ **808/669-1800.**

KAANAPALI

On a recent trip I was somewhat disappointed with upscale **Whalers Village,** 2435 Kaanapali Pkwy. (ℭ **808/661-4567**). Although it offers everything from whale blubber to Prada and Ferragamo, it is short on local shops, and parking at the nearby lot is expensive. The complex is also home to the Whalers Village Museum, with interactive exhibits and a 40-foot sperm-whale skeleton. You can find most of the items here in the shops in Lahaina and can avoid the parking hassle and the high prices by skipping Whalers Village.

If you do decide to check it out, don't miss my favorite shoe store, **Sandal Tree** (with two other locations—one at Hyatt Regency Maui and the other at Grand Wailea Resort in Wailea). **Martin & MacArthur,** a mainstay of the village, offers a dizzying array of Hawaii crafts. The always wonderful **Lahaina Printsellers** has a selection of antique prints, maps, paintings, and engravings, including 18th- to 20th-century cartography. You can find award-winning **Kimo Bean** coffee at a kiosk; an expanded **Reyn's** for aloha wear; and **Cinnamon Girl,** a hit in Honolulu for its matching mother–daughter clothing. The return of **Waldenbooks** makes it that much easier to pick up the latest bestseller on the way to the beach. Once you've stood under the authentic whale skeleton at the **Whale Center of the Pacific** (see chapter 6), you can blow a bundle at **Tiffany, Prada, Chanel, Ferragamo, Vuitton, Coach, Dolphin Galleries, The Body Shop,** or any of the more than 60 shops and restaurants that have sprouted up in this open-air shopping center.

Other mainstays: The **Eyecatcher** has an extensive selection of sunglasses; it's located just across from the busiest **ABC** store in the state. **Pizza Paradiso** has taken over the former **Maui Yogurt Company** and sells ice cream and smoothies in the food court. Whalers Village is open daily from 9:30am to 10pm.

Ki'i Gallery Those who love glass in all forms, from handblown vessels to jewelry, will love a browse through Ki'i. I found Pat Kazi's work in porcelain and found objects—such as the mermaid in a teacup, inspired by fairy tales and mythology—both fantastic and compelling. The gallery is devoted to glass and to original paintings and drawings; roughly half of the artists are from Hawaii. In the Hyatt Regency Maui, 200 Nohea Kai Dr. ℂ 808/661-4456. Also at the Grand Wailea Resort, ℂ 808/874-3059, and the Shops at Wailea, ℂ 808/874-1181.

Sandal Tree The Sandal Tree attracts a flock of footwear fanatics who come here from throughout the islands for rubber thongs and Top-Siders, sandals and dressy pumps, athletic shoes and hats, designer footwear, and much more. Sandal Tree also carries a generous selection of Mephisto and Arche comfort sandals, Donald Pliner, Anne Klein, Charles Jourdan, and beachwear and casual footwear. Accessories range from fashionable knapsacks to avant-garde geometrical handbags. Prices are realistic, too. In Whalers Village, 2435 Kaanapali Pkwy. ℂ 808/667-5330. Also in Grand Wailea Resort, 3850 Wailea Alanui Dr., Wailea (ℂ 808/874-9006); and in the Hyatt Regency Maui, 200 Nohea Kai Dr. (ℂ 808/661-3495).

KAHANA/NAPILI/HONOKOWAI

Those driving north of Kaanapali toward Kapalua will notice the **Honokowai Marketplace** on Lower Honoapiilani Road, only minutes before the Kapalua Airport. There are restaurants and coffee shops, a dry cleaner, the flagship **Star Market, Hula Scoops** for ice cream, a gas station, a copy shop, a few clothing stores, and the sprawling **Hawaiian Interiorz.**

Nearby **Kahana Gateway** is an unimpressive mall built to serve the condominium community that has sprawled along the coastline between Honokowai and Kapalua. If you need women's swimsuits, however, **Rainbow Beach Swimwear** is a find. It carries a selection of suits for all shapes, at lower-than-resort prices. **Hutton's Fine Jewelry** offers high-end jewelry from designers around the country (lots of platinum and diamonds). Tahitian black pearls and jade are among Hutton's specialties.

KAPALUA

Honolua Store Walk on the old wood floors peppered with holes from golf shoes and find your everyday essentials: bottled water, stationery, mailing tape, jackets, chips, wine, soft drinks, paper products, fresh fruit and produce, and aisles of notions and necessities. With picnic tables on the veranda and a takeout counter offering deli items—more than a dozen types of sandwiches, salads, and budget-friendly breakfasts—there are always long lines of customers. Golfers and surfers love to come here for the morning paper and coffee. 502 Office Rd. (next to the Ritz-Carlton Kapalua). © 808/669-6128.

Kapalua Shops   Shops have come and gone in this small, exclusive, and once-chic shopping center, now much quieter than in days past. The closing of elegant Mandalay is a big loss. The **Elizabeth Dole Gallery** has loads of Dale Chihuly studio glass, fabulous and expensive, a dramatic counterpoint to **South Seas Trading Post** and its exotic artifacts, such as New Guinea masks, Balinese beads, tribal jewelry, lizard-skin drums, and coconut-shell carvings with mother-of-pearl inlay. Otherwise, it's slim pickings for shoppers in Kapalua. In the Kapalua Bay Hotel and Villas. © 808/669-1029.

Village Galleries   Maui's finest exhibit their works here and in the other two Village Galleries in Lahaina. Take heart, art lovers: There's no clichéd marine art here. Translucent, delicately turned bowls of Norfolk pine gleam in the light, and George Allan, Betty Hay Freeland, Fred KenKnight, and Pamela Andelin are included in the pantheon of respected artists represented in the tiny gallery. Watercolors, oils, sculptures, handblown glass, Niihau shell leis, jewelry, and other media are represented. The Ritz-Carlton's monthly Artist-in-Residence program features gallery artists in demonstrations and special hands-on workshops—free, including materials. In the Ritz-Carlton Kapalua, 1 Ritz-Carlton Dr. © 808/669-1800.

3 South Maui

KIHEI

Kihei is one long stretch of strip malls. Most of the shopping here is concentrated in the **Azeka Place Shopping Center** on South Kihei Road, where you'll find fast food and tourist-oriented clothing shops like **Crazy Shirts.** Across the street **Azeka Place II** houses the **Coffee Store** and a cluster of specialty shops with everything from children's clothes to shoes, sunglasses, and swimwear. Also on South Kihei Road is the **Kukui Mall,** with movie theaters, **Waldenbooks,** and **Whaler's General Store.**

Hawaiian Moons Natural Foods   Hawaiian Moons is an exceptional health-food store, as well as a mini supermarket with one of the best selections of Maui products on the island. Much of the produce here, such as organic vine-ripened tomatoes and organic onions, is grown in the fertile upcountry soil of Kula. There are also locally grown organic coffee, gourmet salsas, Maui shiitake mushrooms, organic lemon grass and okra, Maui Crunch bread, free-range Big Island turkeys and chickens, and fresh Maui juices. Cosmetics are top-of-the-line: a staggering selection of sunblocks; oils; and Island Essence made-on-Maui mango–coconut and vanilla–papaya lotions, the ultimate in body pampering. The salad bar is very popular. 2411 S. Kihei Rd. ✆ 808/875-4356. Also on the west side at 3636 Lower Honoapiilani Rd. ✆ 808/665-1339.

Tuna Luna There are treasures to be found in this small cluster of tables and booths where Maui artists display their work. Ceramics, raku, sculpture, glass, koa-wood books and photo albums, jewelry, soaps, handmade paper, and fiber-art accessories make great gifts to go. Something to watch for: Maui Metal handcrafted journals, aluminum books with designs of hula girls, palms, fish, and seahorses. Tuna Luna also has a new booth in the back pavilion. In Kihei Kalama Village, 1941 S. Kihei Rd. ✆ 808/874-9482.

WAILEA

CY Maui Women who like washable, flowing clothing in silks, rayons, and natural fibers will love this shop. If you don't find what you want on the racks of simple bias-cut designs, you can have it made from the bolts of stupendous fabrics lining the shop. Except for a few hand-painted silks, everything in the shop is washable. In The Shops at Wailea, 3750 Wailea Alanui Dr, A-30. ✆ 808/891-0782.

Grand Wailea Shops The sprawling Grand Wailea Resort is known for its long arcade of shops and galleries tailored to hefty pocketbooks. However, gift items in all price ranges can be found at Lahaina Printsellers (for old maps and prints); Dolphin Galleries; H. F. Wichman; and Napua Gallery, which houses the private collection of the resort owner. Ki'i Gallery is luminous with studio glass and exquisitely turned woods, and **Sandal Tree** (p. 164) raises the footwear bar. At Grand Wailea Resort, 3850 Wailea Alanui Dr. ✆ 808/875-1234.

The Shops at Wailea This is the big shopping boost that resort-goers have been awaiting for years. Chains still rule (**Gap, Louis Vuitton, Banana Republic, Tiffany, Crazy Shirts, Honolua Surf Co.),** but there is still fertile ground for the inveterate shopper in the nearly 60 shops in the complex. **Martin & MacArthur** (furniture and gift gallery) has landed in Wailea as part of a retail mix that is similar to Whalers Village. The high-end resort shops sell expensive souvenirs, gifts, clothing, and accessories for a life of perpetual vacations. 3750 Wailea Alanui. © **808/891-6770.**

4 Upcountry Maui

MAKAWAO

Besides being a shopper's paradise, Makawao is the home of the island's most prominent arts organization, the **Hui No'eau Visual Arts Center,** 2841 Baldwin Ave. (© **808/572-6560;** www.hui noeau.com). Visiting artists offer lectures, classes, and demonstrations, all at reasonable prices, in basketry, jewelry making, ceramics, painting, and other media. Classes on Hawaiian art, culture, and history are also available. Call ahead for schedules and details. The exhibits here are drawn from a wide range of disciplines and multicultural sources, and include both contemporary and traditional art from established and emerging artists. The gift shop, featuring many one-of-a-kind works by local artists and artisans, is worth a stop. Hours are Monday through Saturday from 10am to 4pm.

Altitude   This tiny shop, run by Jeannine de Roode, is a treasure trove of interesting fashions found nowhere else on Maui, like custom jewelry by Monies (abalone shells, mother-of-pearl, and bone used to create big, big earrings, bracelets, and necklaces) and Hobo bags (Italian leather lined with contrasting fabric). She carries a range of clothing labels like Juicy Couture, James Perse, David Dart, Mica, and Sazah Arizona. 3660 Baldwin Ave. © **808/573-4733.**

Collections   This longtime Makawao attraction is one of my favorite Makawao stops, full of gift items and spirited clothing reflecting the ease and color of island living. Its selection of sportswear; soaps; jewelry; candles; and tasteful, marvelous miscellany reflects good sense and style. Dresses (including up-to-the-moment Citron in cross-cultural and vintage-looking prints), separates, home and bath accessories, sweaters, and more make this a Makawao must. 3677 Baldwin Ave. © **808/572-0781.**

Cuckoo for Coconuts   The owner's quirky sense of humor pervades every inch of this tiny shop, which is brimming with vintage collectibles, gag gifts, 1960s and 1970s aloha wear, tutus, sequined dresses, vintage wedding gowns, and all sorts of oddities. Things I've seen there: an Elvira wig, very convincing; a raffia hat looking suspiciously like a nest, with blue eggs on top; and some vintage aloha shirts that would make a collector drool (these get grabbed up fast). New items include crazy sunglasses, colored wigs, tie-dyes, and party hats. Services like singing telegrams, balloon deliveries, costumes, makeup, and gag gifts keep the laughs coming. 1158 Makawao Ave. ✆ 808/573-6887.

Gallery Maui Most of the works here are by Maui artists, and the quality is outstanding. About 30 artists are represented: Wayne Omura and his Norfolk pine bowls, Pamela Hayes's watercolors, Martha Vockrodt and her wonderful paintings, stunning Steve Hynson furniture. The two- and three-dimensional original works reflect the high standards of gallery owners Deborah and Robert Zaleski (a painter), who have just added to their roster the talented ceramic artist David Stabley, a two-time American Craft Council juror. 3643-A Baldwin Ave. ✆ 808/572-8092.

Gecko Trading Co. Boutique The selection in this tiny, homey boutique is eclectic and always changing: One day it's St. John's Wort body lotion and mesh T-shirts in a dragon motif; the next, it's Provence soaps and antique lapis jewelry. I've seen everything from hair scrunchies to handmade crocheted bags from New York, clothing from Spain and France, collectible bottles, toys, shawls, and Mexican hammered-tin candleholders. The prices are reasonable; the service is friendly; and it's not as self-conscious as some of the other local boutiques. 3621 Baldwin Ave. ✆ 808/572-0249.

Hot Island Glassblowing Studio & Gallery You can watch the artist transform molten glass into works of art and utility in this studio in Makawao's Courtyard, where an award-winning family of glassblowers built its own furnaces. It's fascinating to watch the shapes emerge from glass melted at 2,300°F (1,260°C). The colorful works range from small paperweights to large vessels. Four to five artists participate in the demonstrations, which begin when the furnace is heated, about half an hour before the studio opens at 9am. 3620 Baldwin Ave. ✆ 808/572-4527.

Hurricane This boutique carries clothing, gifts, accessories, and books that are two steps ahead of the competition. Tommy Bahama aloha shirts and aloha print dresses; Sigrid Olsen's knitted shells, cardigans, and extraordinary silk tank dresses; hats; art by local artists; a notable selection of fragrances for men and women; and hard-to-find, eccentric books and home accessories are part of the Hurricane appeal. 3639 Baldwin Ave. ✆ 808/572-5076.

Maui Hands Maui hands have made 90% of the items in this shop/gallery. Because it's a consignment shop, you'll find Hawaii-made handicrafts and prices that aren't inflated. The selection includes paintings, prints, jewelry, glass marbles, native-wood bowls, and tchotchkes for every budget. This is an ideal stop for made-on-Maui products and crafts of good quality. The original Maui Hands is in Makawao at the Courtyard, 3620 Baldwin Ave. © 808/572-5194. Another Maui Hands can be found in Paia at 84 Hana Hwy. © 808/579-9245.

The Mercantile   The jewelry, home accessories, dinnerware, Italian linens, plantation-style furniture, and clothing here are a salute to the good life. The exquisite bedding, rugs, and furniture include hand-carved armoires, down-filled furniture and slipcovers, and a large selection of Kiehl's products. The clothing—comfortable cottons and upscale European linens—is for men and women, as are the soaps, which include Maui Herbal Soap products and some finds from France. Maui-made jams, honey, soaps, and ceramics round out the selection. 3673 Baldwin Ave. © 808/572-1407.

Viewpoints Gallery   Maui's only fine-arts cooperative showcases the work of 20 established artists in an airy, attractive gallery located in a restored theater with a courtyard, glassblowing studio, and restaurants. The gallery features two-dimensional art, jewelry, fiber art, stained glass, paper, sculpture, and other media. This is a fine example of what can happen in a collectively supportive artistic environment. 3620 Baldwin Ave. © 808/572-5979.

EDIBLES

Working folks in Makawao pick up spaghetti, lasagna, sandwiches, salads, and wide-ranging specials from the **Rodeo General Store,** 3661 Baldwin Ave. (© **808/572-7841**). At the far end of the store is a superior wine selection housed in a temperature-controlled cave.

Down to Earth Natural Foods, 1169 Makawao Ave. (© **808/ 572-1488**), always has fresh salads and sandwiches, a full section of organic produce (Kula onions, strawberry papayas, mangos, and litchis in season), bulk grains, beauty aids, herbs, juices, snacks, tofu, seaweed, soy products, and aisles of vegetarian and health foods. Whether it's a smoothie or a salad, Down to Earth has fresh, healthy, vegetarian offerings.

In the more than 6 decades that the **T. Komoda Store and Bakery,** 3674 Baldwin Ave. (© **808/572-7261**), has spent in this spot, untold numbers have creaked over the wooden floors to pick up Komoda's famous cream puffs. Old-timers know to come early, before they're sold out. Then the cinnamon rolls, doughnuts, pies, and chocolate cake take over. Pastries are just the beginning: Poi, macadamia-nut candies and cookies, and small bunches of local fruit keep the customers coming.

FRESH FLOWERS IN KULA

Like anthuriums on the Big Island, proteas are a Maui trademark and an abundant crop on Haleakala's rich volcanic slopes. They also travel well, dry beautifully, and can be shipped with ease worldwide. Among Maui's most prominent sources is **Sunrise Protea** (℡ **808/876-0200;** www.sunriseprotea.com), in Kula. It offers a walk-through garden and gift shops, friendly service, and a larger-than-usual selection. Freshly cut flowers arrive from the fields on Tuesday and Friday afternoons. You can order individual blooms, baskets, arrangements, or wreaths. (Next door, the Sunrise Country Market offers fresh local fruits, snacks, and sandwiches.)

5 East Maui

ON THE ROAD TO HANA: PAIA

Biasa Rose Boutique   You'll find unusual gift items and clothing with a tropical flair: capri pants in bark cloth, floating plumeria candles, retro fabrics, dinnerware, handbags and accessories, and stylish vintage-inspired clothes for kids. If the aloha shirts don't get you, the candles and handbags will. You can also custom-order clothing from a selection of washable rayons. 104 Hana Hwy. ℡ 808/579-8602.

Hemp House   Clothing and accessories made of hemp, a sturdy, ecofriendly, and sensible fiber, are finally making their way into the mainstream. The Hemp House has as complete a selection as you can expect to see in Hawaii, with "denim" hemp jeans, lightweight linenlike trousers, dresses, shirts, and a full range of sensible, easy-care wear. 16 Baldwin Ave. ℡ 808/579-8880.

Maui Crafts Guild   The old wooden storefront at the gateway to Paia houses crafts of high quality and in all price ranges, from pit-fired raku to wood bowls. Artist-owned and -operated, the guild claims 25 members who live and work on Maui. Basketry, hand-painted fabrics, jewelry, beadwork, traditional Hawaiian stone work, pressed flowers, fused glass, stained glass, copper sculpture, banana bark paintings, pottery, and hundreds of items are displayed in the two-story gallery. Upstairs, sculptor Arthur Dennis Williams displays his breathtaking work in wood, bronze, and stone. **Aloha Bead Co.** (℡ **808/579-9709**), in the back of the gallery, is a treasure trove for beadworkers. 43 Hana Hwy. ℡ 808/579-9697.

Moonbow Tropics   If you're looking for a tasteful aloha shirt, go to Moonbow. The selection consists of a few carefully culled racks of the top labels in aloha wear, in fabrics ranging from the finest silks and linens to Egyptian cotton and spun rayons. Some of the finds: aloha shirts by Tori Richard, Reyn Spooner, Kamehameha, Paradise Found, Kahala, Tommy Bahama, and other top brands. Silk pants, silk shorts, vintage-print neckwear, and an upgraded women's selection hang on neat, colorful racks. The jewelry pieces, ranging from tanzanite to topaz, rubies, and moonstones, are mounted in unique settings made on-site. 36 Baldwin Ave. ℂ 808/579-8592.

HANA

Hana Coast Gallery   This gallery is a good reason to go to Hana. Tucked away in the posh hideaway hotel, the gallery is known for its high level of curatorship and commitment to the cultural art of Hawaii. Except for a section of European and Asian masters (Renoir, Japanese woodblock prints), the 3,000-square-foot gallery is devoted entirely to Hawaiian artists. Dozens of well-established local artists display their sculptures, paintings, prints, feather work, stonework, carvings, and koa-wood furniture.

Connoisseurs of hand-turned bowls will find the crème de la crème of the genre here. You won't find a better selection anywhere under one roof. The award-winning gallery has won accolades from the top travel and arts magazines in the country. In the Hotel Hana-Maui. ℂ 808/248-8636.

Hasegawa General Store   Established in 1910, immortalized in song since 1961, burned to the ground in 1990, and back in business in 1991, this legendary store is indefatigable and more colorful than ever in its fourth generation in business. The aisles are choked with merchandise: coffee specially roasted and blended for the store, Ono Farms organic dried fruit, fishing equipment, every tape and CD that mentions Hana, the best books on Hana to be found, T-shirts, beach and garden essentials, baseball caps, film, baby food, napkins, and other necessities. Hana Hwy., in Hana. ℂ 808/248-8231.

8

Maui After Dark

Centered in the $32 million **Maui Arts and Cultural Center** in Kahului (© **808/242-7469;** www.mauiarts.org), the performing arts are alive and well on this island. The MACC remains the island's most prestigious entertainment venue, a first-class center for the visual and performing arts. Bonnie Raitt has performed here, as have Hiroshima, Pearl Jam, Ziggy Marley, Tony Bennett, the American Indian Dance Theatre, the Maui Symphony Orchestra, and Jonny Lang, not to mention the finest in local and Hawaiian talent. The center is as precious to Maui as the Met is to New York, with a visual-arts gallery, an outdoor amphitheater, offices, rehearsal space, a 300-seat theater for experimental performances, and a 1,200-seat main theater. The center's activities are well publicized locally, so check the *Maui News* for what's going on during your visit.

People are still agog over **'Ulalena,** an extraordinary production that tells the story of Hawaii in chant, song, original music, acrobatics, and dance, using state-of-the-art technology and some of the most creative staging to be seen in Hawaii. There's nothing else like it in the state. A local and international cast performs this $9.5 million production at the comfy **Maui Myth and Magic Theatre** in Lahaina (see section 1 below). Recently opened at the **Kaanapali Beach Hotel** is a wonderful show called *Kupanaha* that is perfect for the entire family.

IN SEARCH OF HAWAIIAN, JAWAIIAN & MORE

Nightlife options on this island are limited. Revelers generally head for **Casanova** in Makawao and **Maui Brews** in Lahaina. The hotels generally have lobby lounges offering Hawaiian music, soft jazz, or hula shows beginning at sunset.

If **Hapa, Willie K., Amy Gilliom,** or the soloist **Keali'i Reichel** are playing anywhere on their native island, don't miss them; they're among the finest Hawaiian musicians around today. Most clubs with dance floors play a combination of Hawaiian and reggae, called Jawaiian, with a heated-up rhythm that young dancers love.

HAWAIIAN MUSIC   The best of Hawaiian music can be heard every Tuesday night at the indoor amphitheater at the Ritz-Carlton Kapalua with the **Masters of Hawaiian Slack Key Guitar Series** (✆ **808/669-3858;** www.slackkey.com). Tickets are $40.

1 West Maui: Lahaina, Kaanapali & Kapalua

Maui Brews, 900 Front St. (✆ **808/667-7794**), draws the late-night crowd with swing, salsa, reggae, and jams—either live or with a DJ every night. The nightclub opens at 9pm and closes at 2am. Depending on the entertainment, sometimes there's a cover charge after 9pm. For recorded information on entertainment (which changes, so it's a good idea to check), call ✆ **808/669-2739.**

At **Longhi's** (✆ **808/667-2288**) live music spills out into the streets from 9:30pm on weekends (with a cover charge of $5). It's usually salsa or jazz, but call ahead to confirm.

Loud, live tropical rock blasts into the streets and out to sea nightly at **Cheeseburger in Paradise** (✆ **808/661-4855**) from 4:30 to 11pm (no cover charge).

In addition, try the following venues for live music.

- **B.J.'s Chicago Pizzeria,** 730 Front St. (✆ **808/661-0700**), offers live music from 7:30 to 10pm every night.
- **Compadres Bar & Grill,** Lahaina Cannery Mall (✆ **808/661-7189**), features Salsa Night on Saturday starting at 10pm and local jam sessions on Wednesday (call for times).
- **Fish & Game Brewing Co.,** Kahana Gateway Center (✆ **808/669-3474**), has live music every night from 6:30 to 9:30pm (6–9pm in summer).
- **Hula Grill,** Whalers Village (✆ **808/667-6636**), has live music (usually Hawaiian) from 3 to 5pm and again from 6:30 to 9pm nightly.
- **Leilani's on the Beach,** Whalers Village (✆ **808/661-4495**), has live music from 4 to 6pm Wednesday through Sunday. The style ranges from contemporary Hawaiian to rock.
- **Pacific'O,** 505 Front St. (✆ **808/667-4341**), offers live jazz Friday and Saturday from 9pm to midnight.
- **Pancho & Lefty's,** Wharf Cinema Center (✆ **808/661-4666**), features live music from 9pm to midnight on Friday and from 6 to 9pm on Saturday and Sunday.
- **Paradise Bluz,** 744 Front St. (✆ **808/667-5299**), has live blues, live jazz, and other live music from 9pm to 2am; call for details.

- **Pioneer Inn,** 658 Wharf St. (© **808/661-3636**), offers a variety of live music every night starting at 6pm.
- **Sea Horse Restaurant,** Napili Kai Beach Resort (© **808/669-1500**), has live music from 7 to 9pm Wednesday through Monday and a Polynesian dinner show on Tuesday.
- **Tropica,** Westin Maui (© **808/667-2525**), offers nightly music (call for times).

A NIGHT TO REMEMBER: LUAU, MAUI STYLE

Most of the larger hotels in Maui's major resorts offer luaus on a regular basis. You'll pay about $75 to attend one. Don't expect it to be a homegrown affair prepared in the traditional Hawaiian way. There are, however, commercial luaus that capture the romance and spirit of the luau with quality food and entertainment in outdoor settings.

Maui's best luau is indisputably the nightly **Old Lahaina Luau** (© **800/248-5828** or 808/667-1998; www.oldlahainaluau.com). On its 1-acre site just oceanside of the Lahaina Cannery at 1251 Front St., the Old Lahaina Luau maintains its high standards in food and entertainment in a peerless setting. There's no fire dancing in the program, but you won't miss it (for that, go to **The Feast at Lele;** p. 81). This luau offers a healthy balance of entertainment, showmanship, authentic high-quality food, educational value, and sheer romantic beauty. The cost is $85 for adults and $55 for children 12 and under.

'ULALENA: HULA, MYTH & MODERN DANCE

The highly polished **'Ulalena,** staged in the Maui Myth and Magic Theatre, 878 Front St. (© **877/688-4800** or 808/661-9913; www.ulalena.com), is a riveting production that weaves Hawaiian mythology with drama, dance, and state-of-the-art multimedia capabilities in a brand-new, multimillion-dollar theater.

A local and international cast performs Polynesian dance, original music, acrobatics, and chant. It's interactive, with dancers coming down the aisles, drummers and musicians in surprising corners, and mind-boggling stage and lighting effects. The effects of the modern choreography and traditional hula, a fusion of genres, are surprisingly evocative and emotional. Performances are Tuesday through Saturday at 6:30pm. Tickets are $48 to $68 for adults and $28 to $48 for children ages 12 and under.

HAWAIIAN CULTURE

Not many visitors get to experience the art of Hawaiian storytelling, but the Ritz-Carlton Kapalua has a play called *The Legend of Kaulula'au,* every Sunday at 4 and 6:30pm, that is not to be missed. In the one-man play *The Legend of Kaulula'au,* Hawaiian actor Moses Goods gives a spellbinding performance as he acts out the legend of Kaulula'au, a mischievous child who was banished to the island of Lanai. Tickets for this hour-long performance are $30 and are available by calling © **888/808-1055.**

2 Kihei-Wailea

The Kihei area in South Maui features music in a variety of locations:

- **Bocalino,** 1279 S. Kihei Rd. (© **808/874-9299**), has live music Monday through Saturday starting at 10pm.
- **Hapa's Night Club,** 41 E. Lipoa St. (© **808/879-9001**), has nightly music, generally Hawaiian; call for details.
- **Henry's Bar and Grill,** 41 E. Lipoa (© **808/87-2949**), offers live music Thursday through Saturday from 9pm to midnight.
- **Kahale's Beach Club,** 36 Keala Place (© **808/875-7711**), offers a potpourri of live music nightly; call for details.
- **Life's a Beach,** 1913 S. Kihei Rd. (© **808/891-8010**), has nightly live music; call for times.
- **Lobby Lounge,** Four Seasons Wailea (© **808/874-8000**), features nightly live music from 8:30 to 11:30pm.
- **Lulu's,** 1945 S. Kihei Rd. (© **808/879-9944**), offers entertainment starting at 8pm; karaoke on Wednesday, live music Thursday through Sunday.
- **Mulligan's on the Blue,** 100 Kaukahi St., Wailea (© **808/874-1131**), has live music starting at 9pm Friday and Saturday.
- **Sansei,** Kihei Town Center (© **808/879-0004**), features karaoke Thursday through Saturday from 10pm to 1am.
- **Sports Page Bar,** 2411 S. Kihei Rd. (© **808/879-0602**), has live music Monday through Saturday starting at 9pm.
- **Tsunami Nightclub,** Grand Wailea Beach Hotel (© **808/875-1234**), offers dancing to a DJ's selection on Friday and Saturday from 9:30pm to 2am.
- **Yorman's by the Sea,** 760 S. Kihei Rd. (© **808/874-8385**), has live jazz from 6:30pm Wednesday through Sunday. Call for details.

3 Upcountry Maui

Upcountry in Makawao, the party never ends at **Casanova,** 1188 Makawao Ave. (© **808/572-0220**), the popular Italian ristorante where the good times roll. DJs take over on Wednesday (ladies' night), and on Thursday, Friday, and Saturday, live entertainment draws fun-lovers from all over the island. Entertainment starts at 9:45pm and continues to 1:30am. The cover is usually $5. Come Sunday afternoons from 3 to 6pm for excellent live jazz.

Another place for live music in the upcountry area is the **Stop-watch Sports Bar,** 1127 Makawao Ave. (© **808/572-1380**), which has live music from 9pm on Friday and Saturday.

4 Paia & Central Maui

In the unlikely location of Paia, **Moanai Bakery & Café,** at 71 Baldwin Ave. (© **808/579-9999**), not only has some of the best and most innovative cuisine around, but also recently added live music: vintage Hawaiian from 6:30 to 9pm on Wednesday, smooth jazz and hot blues from 6:30 to 9pm on Friday, and flamingo guitar and gypsy violin from 6 to 9pm on Sunday. Also in Paia, **Charley's Restaurant,** 142 Hana Hwy. (© **808/579-9453**), features an eclectic selection of music, from country and western to fusion/reggae to rip-roaring rock 'n' roll; call for details. Other venues for live music in Paia include **Jacque's,** 120 Hana Hwy. (© **808/579-8844**), and **Sand Bar and Grill,** 89 Hana Hwy. (© **808/579-8742**).

In central Maui the **Kahului Ale House,** 355 E. Kamehameha Ave. (© **808/877-9001**), features karaoke on Sunday, Monday, and Wednesday from 10pm to 2am, live music on Thursday and Friday (call for times), and a DJ on Saturday from 10pm.

Other locations for live music include: **Mañana Garage,** 33 Lono Ave., in Kahului (© **808/873-0220**), which has live music Wednesday through Saturday nights from 6:30pm on, and **Sushi Go,** in the Queen Kaahumanu Shopping Center, 275 Kaahumanu Ave., in Kahului (© **808/877-8744**), which also features live music on Friday and Saturday nights from 6:30 to 8:30pm.

Index

See also Accommodations, Restaurants, and Afternoon Tea indexes below.

THE NEW TRAVELOCITY GUARANTEE

EVERYTHING YOU BOOK WILL BE RIGHT, OR WE'LL WORK WITH OUR TRAVEL PARTNERS TO MAKE IT RIGHT, RIGHT AWAY.

*To drive home the point,
we're going to use the word "right" in every single sentence.*

Let's get right to it. Right to the meat! Only Travelocity guarantees everything about your booking will be right, or we'll work with our travel partners to make it right, right away. Right on!

Here's a picture taken smack dab right in the middle of Antigua, where the guarantee also covers you.

The guarantee covers all but one of the items pictured to the right.

Now, you may be thinking, "Yeah, right, I'm so sure." That's OK; you have the right to remain skeptical. That is until we mention help is always right around the corner. Call us right off the bat, knowing that our customer service reps are there for you 24/7. Righting wrongs. Left and right.

For example, what if the ocean view you booked actually looks out at a downright ugly parking lot? You'd be right to call – we're there for you. And no one in their right mind would be pleased to learn the rental car place has closed and left them stranded. Call Travelocity and we'll help get you back on the right track.

Now if you're guessing there are some things we can't control, like the weather, well you're right. But we can help you with most things – to get all the details in righting,* visit **travelocity.com/guarantee**.

*Sorry, spelling things right is one of the few things not covered under the guarantee.

I'd give my right arm for a guarantee like this, although I'm glad I don't have to.

travelocity
You'll never roam alone.

IF YOU BOOK IT, IT SHOULD BE THERE.

Only Travelocity guarantees it will be, or we'll work
with our travel partners to make it right, right away.
So if you're missing a balcony or anything else
you booked, just call us 24/7. **1-888-TRAVELOCITY.**

travelocity
You'll never roam alone.